First World War

and Army of Occupation

War Diary

France, Belgium and Germany

66 DIVISION
South African Brigade
1, 2 and 4 Battalion South African Infantry
1 September 1918 - 28 February 1919

WO95/3147

The Naval & Military Press Ltd
www.nmarchive.com
Published in association with The National Archives

Published by

The Naval & Military Press Ltd

Unit 10 Ridgewood Industrial Park,
Uckfield, East Sussex,
TN22 5QE England
Tel: +44 (0) 1825 749494

www.naval-military-press.com
www.nmarchive.com

This diary has been reprinted in facsimile from the original. Any imperfections are inevitably reproduced and the quality may fall short of modern type and cartographic standards.

Contents

Document type	Place/Title	Date From	Date To
Heading	66th Division 8th African Infy Bde 1st Sth African Infy Regt 1918 Sep-1919 From 9 Div		
War Diary	Bayenghem	02/09/1918	22/09/1918
War Diary	Wizernes	22/09/1918	22/09/1918
War Diary	Tincques Gouy-En-Ternois	23/09/1918	23/09/1918
War Diary	Gouy-En-Ternois	24/09/1918	28/09/1918
War Diary	Villers Bretonneux	29/09/1918	29/09/1918
War Diary	Chuignolles	30/09/1918	01/10/1918
War Diary	Mametz Wood	02/10/1918	04/10/1918
War Diary	Nurlu	04/10/1918	05/10/1918
War Diary	Ronssoy	06/10/1918	07/10/1918
War Diary	Baurevoir	08/10/1918	08/10/1918
War Diary	Serrin	09/10/1918	09/10/1918
War Diary	Reumont	10/10/1918	11/10/1918
War Diary	Le Cateau	12/10/1918	20/10/1918
War Diary	Serain	21/10/1918	02/11/1918
War Diary	Reumont	03/11/1918	04/11/1918
War Diary	Le Cateau	05/11/1918	05/11/1918
War Diary	Pommereuil	06/11/1918	06/11/1918
War Diary	Landrecies	07/11/1918	07/11/1918
War Diary	Basse Noyelle	08/11/1918	08/11/1918
War Diary	Dompierre	09/11/1918	09/11/1918
War Diary	Solre-Le-Chateau	10/11/1918	10/11/1918
War Diary	Hestrud	11/11/1918	18/11/1918
War Diary	Sivry	17/11/1918	19/11/1918
War Diary	Soumoy	20/11/1918	24/11/1918
War Diary	Bac du Prince	25/11/1918	14/12/1918
War Diary	Ferage	15/12/1918	15/12/1918
War Diary	Rochefort	16/12/1918	16/12/1918
War Diary	Marche	17/12/1918	22/01/1919
War Diary	Maffe	23/01/1919	23/01/1919
War Diary	Ohey	24/01/1919	24/01/1919
War Diary	Seilles	25/01/1919	30/01/1919
War Diary	Haillot	31/01/1919	31/01/1919
War Diary	Marche	01/01/1919	22/01/1919
War Diary	Maffe	23/01/1919	23/01/1919
War Diary	Ohey	24/01/1919	24/01/1919
War Diary	Seilles	25/01/1919	26/01/1919
War Diary	Marche	11/01/1919	21/01/1919
War Diary	Seille	26/01/1919	30/01/1919
War Diary	Haillot	31/01/1919	31/01/1919
War Diary	Ciney	01/02/1919	11/02/1919
War Diary	Huy	12/02/1919	28/02/1919
War Diary	Ciney	01/02/1919	11/02/1919
War Diary	Huy	12/02/1919	28/02/1919
War Diary	Ciney	03/02/1919	06/02/1919
War Diary	Serain	01/11/1918	02/11/1918
War Diary	Reumont	02/11/1918	04/11/1918
War Diary	Le Cateau	05/11/1918	05/11/1918
War Diary	Pommeruil	05/11/1918	06/11/1918

War Diary	Landrecies	06/11/1918	07/11/1918
Miscellaneous	Communication		
War Diary	Landrecies	07/11/1918	07/11/1918
War Diary	Basse Noyelles	07/11/1918	08/11/1918
War Diary	Dompierre	09/11/1918	09/11/1918
War Diary	Beugnies	09/11/1918	09/11/1918
War Diary	Solre Chateau	09/11/1918	10/11/1918
War Diary	Positions West Of Hestrude	10/11/1918	11/11/1918
War Diary	Hestrude	11/11/1918	12/11/1918
War Diary	Grandieu	12/11/1918	16/11/1918
War Diary	Sivry	16/11/1918	19/11/1918
War Diary	Villers Deux Eglises	20/11/1918	24/11/1918
War Diary	Agimont	24/11/1918	29/11/1918
Miscellaneous	Public Record Office		
War Diary	Agimont	30/11/1918	30/11/1918
Operation(al) Order(s)	2nd Regiment South African Infantry Order No. 20	01/11/1918	01/11/1918
Operation(al) Order(s)	2nd Regiment South African Infantry Order No. 21	04/11/1918	04/11/1918
Operation(al) Order(s)	2nd Regiment South African Infantry Order No. 22	05/11/1918	05/11/1918
Operation(al) Order(s)	2nd Regiment South African Infantry Order No. 23	06/11/1918	06/11/1918
Operation(al) Order(s)	2nd Regiment South African Infantry Order No. 24	07/11/1918	07/11/1918
Operation(al) Order(s)	2nd Regiment South African Infantry Order No. 25	08/11/1918	08/11/1918
Operation(al) Order(s)	2nd Regiment South African Infantry Order No. 26	09/11/1918	09/11/1918
Operation(al) Order(s)	2nd Regiment South African Infantry Order No. 27	10/11/1918	10/11/1918
Operation(al) Order(s)	2nd Regiment South African Infantry Order No. 28	10/11/1918	10/11/1918
Miscellaneous	Public Record Office		
Operation(al) Order(s)	2nd Regiment South African Infantry Order No. 29	11/11/1918	11/11/1918
Operation(al) Order(s)	2nd Regiment South African Infantry Order No. 30	12/11/1918	12/11/1918
Operation(al) Order(s)	2nd Regiment South African Infantry Order No. 31	16/11/1918	16/11/1918
Operation(al) Order(s)	2nd Regiment South African Infantry Order No. 32	18/11/1918	18/11/1918
Operation(al) Order(s)	2nd Regiment South African Infantry Order No. 33	23/11/1918	23/11/1918
War Diary	Marche	26/12/1918	31/12/1918
Operation(al) Order(s)	2nd Regiment South African Infantry Order No. 34	13/12/1918	13/12/1918
Operation(al) Order(s)	2nd Regiment South African Infantry Order No. 35	14/12/1918	14/12/1918
Operation(al) Order(s)	2nd Regiment South African Infantry Order No. 36	15/12/1918	15/12/1918
War Diary	Marche	17/12/1918	26/12/1918
War Diary	Rochefort	16/12/1918	17/12/1918
War Diary	Agimont	14/12/1918	14/12/1918
War Diary	Mesnil Eglise	14/12/1918	15/12/1918
War Diary	Agimont	12/12/1918	14/12/1918
War Diary	Agimont	09/12/1918	12/12/1918
War Diary	Agimont	07/12/1918	08/12/1918
War Diary	Agimont	04/12/1918	07/12/1918
War Diary	Agimont	01/12/1918	03/12/1918
Heading	66th Division South African Infy Brigade 2nd Sth African Infy Regt 1918 Sep-1919 Feb From 9 Div		
War Diary	Lumbres	01/09/1918	01/09/1918
War Diary	Line Of No. Arch	02/09/1918	02/09/1918
War Diary	Bouvelinghem	02/09/1918	11/09/1918
War Diary	Line Of March	12/09/1918	12/09/1918
War Diary	Seninghem	12/09/1918	22/09/1918
War Diary	Line Of March	22/09/1918	22/09/1918
War Diary	Magnicourt-Sur-Canche	23/09/1918	28/09/1918
War Diary	Line Of March	28/09/1918	29/09/1918
War Diary	Villers Bretonneux	29/09/1918	29/09/1918
War Diary	Framerville	29/09/1918	30/09/1918
Miscellaneous	2nd. Regiment-South African Infantry. Appendix I	01/09/1918	01/09/1918

Operation(al) Order(s)	2nd South African Infantry. Operation Order No. 1	02/09/1918	02/09/1918
Operation(al) Order(s)	2nd South African Infantry Order No. 2	11/09/1918	11/09/1918
Operation(al) Order(s)	2nd South African Infantry Order No. 3	21/09/1918	21/09/1918
Miscellaneous	2nd Regiment South African Infantry	21/09/1918	21/09/1918
Operation(al) Order(s)	2nd South African Infantry Order No. 4	27/09/1918	27/09/1918
Operation(al) Order(s)	2nd South African Infantry Order No. 5	29/09/1918	29/09/1918
War Diary	Lumbres	01/09/1918	03/09/1918
War Diary	Alquines	04/09/1918	12/09/1918
War Diary	Coulomby	13/09/1918	22/09/1918
War Diary	Ambrines	23/09/1918	28/09/1918
War Diary	Villers Bretonneux	29/09/1918	29/09/1918
War Diary	Foucaucourt Area	30/09/1918	30/09/1918
Miscellaneous	4th Regt. S.A. Infantry	30/09/1918	30/09/1918
Operation(al) Order(s)	South African Scottish Order No. 1	02/09/1918	02/09/1918
Operation(al) Order(s)	South African Scottish Order No. 2	12/09/1918	12/09/1918
Operation(al) Order(s)	South African Scottish Order No. 3	21/09/1918	21/09/1918
Miscellaneous	South African Scottish Warning Order	26/09/1918	26/09/1918
Operation(al) Order(s)	South African Scottish Order No. 4	27/09/1918	27/09/1918
Operation(al) Order(s)	South African Scottish Order No. 5	29/09/1918	29/09/1918
Miscellaneous	4th Regt. South African Infantry (South African Scottish)	30/09/1918	30/09/1918
Operation(al) Order(s)	South African Scottish Order No. 27	23/11/1918	23/11/1918
War Diary	Framerville	01/10/1918	01/10/1918
War Diary	Line Of March	01/10/1918	01/10/1918
War Diary	Camp Near Mametz Wood	02/10/1918	03/10/1918
War Diary	Mametz Wood Line Of March	04/10/1918	04/10/1918
War Diary	Nurlu	04/10/1918	05/10/1918
War Diary	Line Of March	05/10/1918	05/10/1918
War Diary	Ronssy Camp	06/10/1918	07/10/1918
War Diary	Line Of March	07/10/1918	07/10/1918
War Diary	Beaurevoir	08/10/1918	08/10/1918
War Diary	Serain Maretz Maurois	09/10/1918	09/10/1918
War Diary	Maurois Honnechy	09/10/1918	09/10/1918
War Diary	Le Cateau	10/10/1918	19/10/1918
War Diary	Reumont	20/10/1918	20/10/1918
War Diary	Line Of March	20/10/1918	20/10/1918
War Diary	Serain	20/10/1918	31/10/1918
Operation(al) Order(s)	2nd South African Infantry Order No. 6	01/10/1918	01/10/1918
Operation(al) Order(s)	2nd South African Infantry Order No. 7	03/10/1918	03/10/1918
Operation(al) Order(s)	2nd South African Infantry Order No. 8	04/10/1918	04/10/1918
Operation(al) Order(s)	2nd South African Infantry Order No. 9	05/10/1918	05/10/1918
Operation(al) Order(s)	2nd Regiment South African Infantry Order No. 10	07/10/1918	07/10/1918
Miscellaneous	2nd Regiment South African Infantry	07/10/1918	07/10/1918
Operation(al) Order(s)	2nd. South African Infantry Order No. 11	07/10/1918	07/10/1918
Operation(al) Order(s)	2nd Regiment South African Infantry Order No. 12	09/10/1918	09/10/1918
Operation(al) Order(s)	2nd Regiment South African Infantry Order No. 13	14/10/1918	14/10/1918
Operation(al) Order(s)	2nd Regiment South African Infantry Order No. 14	15/10/1918	15/10/1918
Operation(al) Order(s)	2nd Regiment South African Infantry Order No. 15	16/10/1918	16/10/1918
Operation(al) Order(s)	2nd Regiment South African Infantry Order No. 16	16/10/1918	16/10/1918
Operation(al) Order(s)	2nd Regiment South African Infantry Order No. 17	18/10/1918	18/10/1918
Operation(al) Order(s)	2nd Regiment South African Infantry Order No. 18	19/10/1918	19/10/1918
Operation(al) Order(s)	2nd Regiment South African Infantry Order No. 19	20/10/1918	20/10/1918
Miscellaneous	2nd Regiment South African Infantry	31/10/1918	31/10/1918
Heading	War Diary For Month Of January 1919 2nd Regt.-S.A. Infantry Vol 41		
War Diary	Marche	01/01/1919	28/02/1919

Miscellaneous	66th Division South African Infy Brigade 4th Sth African Infy Regt 1918 Sep-1919 Feb From 9 Div		
War Diary	Foucaucourt Area	01/10/1918	02/10/1918
War Diary	Montauban Area	02/10/1918	04/10/1918
War Diary	Nurlu	05/10/1918	05/10/1918
War Diary	Ronssoy Area	06/10/1918	07/10/1918
War Diary	Beaurevoir	08/10/1918	20/10/1918
War Diary	Serain	21/10/1918	31/10/1918
Operation(al) Order(s)	South African Scottish Order No. 7	03/10/1918	03/10/1918
Operation(al) Order(s)	South African Scottish Order No. 6	01/10/1918	01/10/1918
Operation(al) Order(s)	South African Scottish Order No. 8	04/10/1918	04/10/1918
Miscellaneous	South African Scottish	07/10/1918	07/10/1918
War Diary	Ref Map 54 B 1/40000 Serain	01/11/1918	01/11/1918
War Diary	Reumont	02/11/1918	02/11/1918
War Diary	Reumont	03/11/1918	03/11/1918
War Diary	Le Cateau	04/11/1918	04/11/1918
War Diary	Pommereuil	05/11/1918	06/11/1918
War Diary	Landrecies (Ref Map57A 1.40000)	06/11/1918	06/11/1918
War Diary	Basse Noyelles	07/11/1918	07/11/1918
War Diary	Dompierre	08/11/1918	09/11/1918
War Diary	Solre Le Chateau (Ref Map Namur 1,100,000)	09/11/1918	11/11/1918
War Diary	Beaurieux	12/11/1918	12/11/1918
War Diary	Grandrieu	13/11/1918	15/11/1918
War Diary	Beaurieux	16/11/1918	17/11/1918
War Diary	Sivry	18/11/1918	19/11/1918
War Diary	Senzeille	19/10/1918	22/11/1918
War Diary	Rosee	23/11/1918	23/11/1918
War Diary	Hermeton	24/11/1918	30/11/1918
Operation(al) Order(s)	South African Scottish Order No. 12	04/11/1918	04/11/1918
Operation(al) Order(s)	South African Scottish Order No. 13	05/11/1918	05/11/1918
Operation(al) Order(s)	South African Scottish Order No. 14	06/11/1918	06/11/1918
Operation(al) Order(s)	South African Scottish Order No. 15	07/11/1918	07/11/1918
Operation(al) Order(s)	South African Scottish Order No. 14	06/11/1918	06/11/1918
Operation(al) Order(s)	South African Scottish Order No. 19	12/11/1918	12/11/1918
Miscellaneous	South African Scottish Order No. 19	12/11/1918	12/11/1918
Operation(al) Order(s)	South African Scottish Order No. 22	17/11/1918	17/11/1918
Operation(al) Order(s)	South African Scottish Order No. 23	17/11/1918	17/11/1918
Operation(al) Order(s)	South African Scottish Order No. 24	18/11/1918	18/11/1918
Operation(al) Order(s)	South African Scottish Order No. 25	18/11/1918	18/11/1918
War Diary	Hermeton	01/12/1918	13/12/1918
War Diary	Houyet	14/12/1918	14/12/1918
War Diary	Jemelle	15/12/1918	15/12/1918
War Diary	Aye	16/12/1918	31/12/1918
Operation(al) Order(s)	South African Scottish Order No. 30	12/12/1918	12/12/1918
Operation(al) Order(s)	South African Scottish Order No. 28	12/12/1918	12/12/1918
Operation(al) Order(s)	South African Scottish Order No. 29	14/12/1918	14/12/1918
War Diary	Aye	01/01/1919	31/01/1919
Miscellaneous	Statement By Capt. G. Peirson. Who Was Captured By The Enemy in March 1918 While Holding The Appointment of Brigade Major in The 16th (Irish) Divn.		
Miscellaneous	Appendix B		
War Diary	Aye	01/02/1919	16/02/1919
War Diary	Huy	17/02/1919	25/02/1919
War Diary	Aye	07/02/1919	15/02/1919
War Diary	Huy	26/02/1919	28/02/1919
Operation(al) Order(s)	South African Scottish Order No. 36	15/02/1919	15/02/1919

Operation(al) Order(s)	South African Scottish Order No. 37	15/02/1919	15/02/1919
Operation(al) Order(s)	South African Scottish Order No. 35	14/02/1919	14/02/1919
Operation(al) Order(s)	South African Scottish Order No. 38	15/02/1919	15/02/1919
Miscellaneous	Routine Order No. 45 By Lieut. Colonel. E.F. Thackeray. C.M.G. D.S.O. Commanding South African Scottish	14/02/1919	14/02/1919

(5)

66TH DIVISION

STH AFRICAN INFY BDE

1ST STH AFRICAN INFY REGT

~~JAN - FEB 1919~~

1918 SEP - 1919 FEB

FROM 9 DIV

Army Form C. 2118.

Instructions regarding War Diaries and Intelligence Summaries are contained in F. S. Regs., Part II. and the Staff Manual respectively. Title pages will be prepared in manuscript. 1st Regiment South African Infantry

WAR DIARY
or
~~INTELLIGENCE SUMMARY.~~

(Erase heading not required.)

Place	Date	Hour	Summary of Events and Information	Remarks and references to Appendices
Bayenghem	2/9/18	8 AM to 1 PM	Training	
		2 PM to 3 PM	Recreation	
	3/9/18	8 AM to 1 PM	Training	
		2 PM to 3 PM	Recreation	
		5.30 pm	The Regimental Team met the 9th Batt R.S.F. in a friendly soccer match & lost by 5 goals to 2 goals.	
	4/9/18		Training as usual. Recreation as usual. Bathing parade took place during the day. Lieut J. W. Riley joined the Battalion last night and assumed the duties of Acting Adjutant 2nd Lt B. A. Logie being posted to "C" Company.	
	5/9/18		Traing & Recreation as usual. Lieut L. G. Mackay rejoined the Battalion & is posted to "C" Coy	

D. D. & L., London, E.C. (A8004) Wt. W1771/M2-31 750,000 5/17 Sch. 52 Forms/C2118/14

204

Army Form C. 2118.

Instructions regarding War Diaries and Intelligence Summaries are contained in F. S. Regs., Part II. and the Staff Manual respectively. Title pages will be prepared in manuscript.

WAR DIARY
or
~~INTELLIGENCE SUMMARY.~~
(Erase heading not required.)

1st REGIMENT SOUTH AFRICAN INFANTRY

Vol 30

Place	Date	Hour	Summary of Events and Information	Remarks and references to Appendices
BAYENGHEM	30/8/16		The 1st Regiment under MAJOR H. H. JENKINS arrived in Billets from LUMBRES at 5.30 p.m. & were addressed by the Commanding Officer. Reorganization of the Battalion is started. Officers are posted as shewn on attached annexures marked "A" & "B"	
	31/8/16	9 AM	Company Inspection.	
		2 PM to 3 PM	Recreation	
			Remainder of the day was devoted to organization	
	1/9/16	9 AM	Church Parade C of E.	
		9.50 AM	" " R. C's	
		11 AM	" " Other denominations	
			The following C of E services were conducted during the day. 7.30 AM Holy Communion, 4 PM Even Song	
		5.30 PM	The Regimental Team met the SAMC in a friendly soccer match resulting in a win for the latter, the score being 3 - nil	

205

D. D. & L., London, E.C. (A8004) Wt. W1771/M2-31 750,000 5/17 Sch. 52 Forms/C2118/14

Instructions regarding War Diaries and Intelligence Summaries are contained in F. S. Regs., Part II. and the Staff Manual respectively. Title pages will be prepared in manuscript.

WAR DIARY
or
~~INTELLIGENCE SUMMARY.~~
(Erase heading not required.)

Army Form C. 2118.

1st Regiment South African Infty

Place	Date	Hour	Summary of Events and Information	Remarks and references to Appendices
Boyenghem	6/9/18		The men were paid. Lieut B A Logie assumes the duties of O.C. "Hqrs" Coy and acting assistant Adjutant	
	7/9/18		Usual training + recreation	
		9am to 1pm	Commanding Officer's Parade.	
		7pm	Voluntary Confession for Roman Catholics	
	8/9/18		Owing to the unfavourable weather elements it was impossible to hold a C of E Church Parade. Voluntary Holy Communion was held a 7 a.m.	
		2pm to 3pm	Recreation	
	9/9/18		Training + recreation as usual.	
	10/9/18	9am to 1pm	Training	
			During afternoon the following Rugby + Association Football Matches were played, both games were won by the Battalion (1) Soccer. 1st SAI versus. SA Brigade (2) Rugby 1st SAI " 9th R.S.F. The men generally are taking a keen interest in the Regimental Sports	

D. D. & L., London, E.C.
(A8004) Wt. W1771/M2831 750,000 5/17 Sch. 52 Forms/C2118/14

202

Instructions regarding War Diaries and Intelligence Summaries are contained in F. S. Regs., Part II. and the Staff Manual respectively. Title pages will be prepared in manuscript.

Army Form C. 2118.

WAR DIARY
or
~~INTELLIGENCE SUMMARY.~~
(Erase heading not required.)

1st Regiment South African Infantry

Place	Date	Hour	Summary of Events and Information	Remarks and references to Appendices
BAYENGHEM	11/9/18		Training & Recreation as usual. The S.A. Bde came again into force on this date. The Brigade was withdrawn from the 9th (Scottish) Division	
	12/9/18		The S.A. Brigade upon being withdrawn from the 9th Division is composed as follows, under the Command of Brigadier-General W. C. Tanner. CMG DSO:- S. Afn. Bde HQ. S. Afn Bde HQ signal section 1st S.A.I. 2nd S.A.I. S.A.L.T.M. Battery The S. Afn Field Ambulance remained with the Brigade The 2nd Roy. Sc. Fus. & 9th Sc. Rifles passed to the Command of G.O.C. 28th Brigade Training & recreation as usual. The 2nd & 4th Regiments move from the ALQUINES AREA to the LUMBRES AREA their dispositions being:- 2nd S.A.I. - SENNINGHEM. 4th S.A.I. COLOMBY & SENNINGHEM. The S.A.L.T.M.B. moved to BAYENGHEM	
	13/9/18		Training & recreation as usual. The G.O.C. will inspect the Battalion tomorrow	

D. D. & L., London, E.C. (A5024) Wt. W1771/M2031 750,000 5/17 Sch. 52 Forms/C2118/14

203

Army Form C. 2118.

Instructions regarding War Diaries and Intelligence Summaries are contained in F. S. Regs., Part II. and the Staff Manual respectively. Title pages will be prepared in manuscript.

WAR DIARY
or
~~INTELLIGENCE SUMMARY.~~
(Erase heading not required.)

1st Regiment S. A. Infantry

Place	Date	Hour	Summary of Events and Information	Remarks and references to Appendices
BAYENGHEM	14/9/18		Owing to the very bad weather the G.O. Comdg's parade was cancelled. An inter-platoon competition for cleanliness & smartness was held. JUDGE - Lt Col BAMFORD OBE MC 2nd SAI No 8. Platoon B COMPANY was selected.	
	15/9/18		Church parades for all denominations were held during the morning; in addition, the following voluntary services were conducted during the day. 7.30 a.m Holy Communion C of E 7.30 P.M Evening Service C of E	
	16/9/18		Training & Recreation as usual. A Concert was given in the Evening, organized by Lieut A.M. Thomson, several men of the S.A.M.C assisted with the programme	
	17/9/18		The G.O.C inspected the Unit at 10 AM, after which the Battalion "Marched past" in platoons.	

D. D. & L., London, E.C. (A8004) Wt. W1771/M2231 750,000 5/17 Sch. 52 Forms/C2118/14

201

Instructions regarding War Diaries and Intelligence Summaries are contained in F. S. Regs., Part II. and the Staff Manual respectively. Title pages will be prepared in manuscript.

1st REGIMENT

~~INTELLIGENCE SUMMARY.~~

(Erase heading not required.)

1st S.A. Infy

Place	Date	Hour	Summary of Events and Information	Remarks and references to Appendices
BAYENGHEM	18/9/18		Training as usual. The Regimental Rugby & Association teams met the 2nd Regiment in friendly matches, both games concluding in our favour RESULTS RUGBY. 1st Regiment 3 Goals — 2nd REGIMENT Nil SOCCER 13 Points — Nil	
	19/9/18		The Battalion less "B" Coy marched to the "Y" Musketry Range LUMBRES to practice Range Firing. "B" Company proceeded for training at 2nd Army Gas School QUEQUES	
	20/9/18	8 Am to 9 am	Inspection by Company Commanders	
		9 am.	Foot & Boot Inspection by Medical Officer & Quarter-Master	
		11 Am.	Companies were at the disposal of Company Commanders until dinner hour	
		2 pm to 3 pm.	Recreation.	

D. D. & L., London, E.C. (A8004) Wt. W1771/M2031 750,000 5/17 Sch. 52 Forms/C2118/14

Instructions regarding War Diaries and Intelligence Summaries are contained in F. S. Regs., Part II. and the Staff Manual respectively. Title pages will be prepared in manuscript.

Army Form C. 2118.

WAR DIARY
or
~~INTELLIGENCE SUMMARY.~~
(Erase heading not required.)

1st REGIMENT 1st S A Infy

Place	Date	Hour	Summary of Events and Information	Remarks and references to Appendices
BAYENGHEM.	21/9/18.		Owing to bad weather no Church parades were held. Holy Communion (C of E) was conducted in the school-room	
BAYENGHEM + WIZERNES	22/9/18		The Battalion moved by march route to WIZERNES (approximately 10 Kilos) for entrainment for TINCQUES to join the 66th Division concentrating in the LE CAUROY area. Entraining at WIZERNES was completed by 8 pm. Warning Order for this operation was received from Brigade on the 18th Inst	
TINCQUES + GOUY-EN-TERNOIS	23/9/18		The Battalion detrained at TINCQUES at 12'30 am + moved by march route to GOUY-EN-TERNOIS via AVERDOINGT and MAIZIERES. and arrived at Billets at 3 am	
GOUY-EN-TERNOIS	24/9/18		8'15 am to 9 am. physical training and Bayonet fighting 9 am to 10 am Platoon in attack 10 am to 11 am Company in attack 11 am to 12 noon Anti-gas Drill (masks worn for 30 minutes) 12 noon to 1 pm Close-Order + Arms Drill. One hours recreational training was carried during the afternoon.	

D. D. & L., London, E.C. (A8004) Wt. W1771/M2-31 750,000 5/17 Sch. 52 Forms/C2118/14

199

Instructions regarding War Diaries and Intelligence Summaries are contained in F. S. Regs., Part II. and the Staff Manual respectively. Title pages will be prepared in manuscript.

WAR DIARY
or
~~INTELLIGENCE SUMMARY.~~
(Erase heading not required.)

Army Form C. 2118.

1st REGIMENT 1st S.A.Inf.Bde

Place	Date	Hour	Summary of Events and Information	Remarks and references to Appendices
Gouy-En-Ternois	25/9/18		The Battalion proceeded on a test Route March under Brigade Orders via MAGNICOURT, SARS-LEZ-BOIS, AMBRINES, MAIZEIRES, TERNAS, & MONTS-EN-TERNOIS. (approximately 16 kilos) about 2 kilos beyond MAGNICOURT Cancellation of the march was received by Runner & the Battalion returned to billets and carried on with the same training programme as for 24th Inst	Brigade Orders
"	26/9/18		The Battalion proceeded on the Route March as detailed for 25/9/18 parading at 8.30 a.m. and arriving back in Billets at 1 p.m.; only one man fell out on the line of March. The following letter was received from G.O.C. 9th Division "To G.O.C. S.A. Brigade" "I wish to express to you and to all Officers" "NCO's & men of the Brigade under your Command" "my great regret that the exigencies of the Service" "prevented my seeing you all personally, before you" "were transferred from the 9th Division, to say Good-bye." "For 2½ years your Brigade has shared the" "fortunes of the 9th Division, and at DELVILLE WOOD, at" ARRAS	Copy of Brigade letter [illegible]

(A8004) Wt. W1771/M2 31 750,000 5/17 Sch. 52 Forms/C2118/14
D. D. & L., London, E.C.

Instructions regarding War Diaries and Intelligence Summaries are contained in F. S. Regs., Part II. and the Staff Manual respectively. Title pages will be prepared in manuscript.

WAR DIARY
or
~~INTELLIGENCE SUMMARY.~~
(Erase heading not required.)

Army Form C. 2118.

1st REGIMENT 1st SA Infty

Place	Date	Hour	Summary of Events and Information	Remarks and references to Appendices
COUY-EN-TERNOIS	27/9/18		The Battalion paraded at 8.30 am under a Brigade order for a Route March via MAGNICOURT, SARS-lez-BOIS, BERLENCOURT, ETRÉE-WAMIN, LE-CAUROY, LIENCOURT, LIGNEREUIL AMBRINES and MAIZEIRES. The G.O.C. 66th Division inspected the Battalion as it marched through BLAVINCOURT.	
"	28/9/18		The Battalion moved by march route via MONTS-EN-TERNOIS, and BUNEVILLE to PETIT HOUVIN STATION entraining there at 2.30 p.m. for CORBIE, detraining at the latter station at 11 p.m. and moved by march route to VILLERS-BRETTNEUX arriving in Billets at about 1 am on 29/9/18.	
VILLERS BRETTEOUX	29/9/18		The Battalion moved by march route to CHUIGNOILLES ~~via~~ parading at 2.30 pm and arriving at the destination at 6 pm.	~~G.O.~~ ~~[illegible]~~
CHUIGNOILLES	30/9/18		Companies were at the disposal of Company Commanders throughout out the day for inspection Feet, boot, Arms, Gas masks, Iron rations & Identity Discs	

D. D. & L., London, E.C. (A8004) Wt. W1771/M2-31 750,000 5/17 Sch. 52 Forms/C2118/14

WAR DIARY

or

~~INTELLIGENCE~~ SUMMARY.

(Erase heading not required.)

Instructions regarding War Diaries and Intelligence Summaries are contained in F. S. Regs., Part II. and the Staff Manual respectively. Title pages will be prepared in manuscript.

Army Form C. 2118.

1st REGIMENT 1st S A Infty

197

Place	Date	Hour	Summary of Events and Information	Remarks and references to Appendices
			"ARRAS, YPRES, in the SOMME RETREAT, and finally at ~~MESSINES~~" "METEREN, has fully contributed in establishing & maintaining" "the glorious record of the 9th Division."	
			"The South African Brigade bore the brunt of" "the attack on the Divisional Front on March 21st," "18 and their final stand near BOUCHAVESNES on March" "24th, when they held out all day till their ammunition" "was exhausted, will live as one of the bravest feats of" "the arms of War."	
			"The Cheery keenness and Comradeship with which" "the South African Brigade has always worked and" "fought will be very much missed by me personally" "and by all the 9th Division. We wish you & your" "Brigade the best of fortune, and know that you" "will always fully maintain the splendid name" "you have earned."	
			(Signed) H. H. TUDOR Major-General Comdg 9th (Scottish) Division	

D. D. & L., London, E.C. (A8004) Wt. W1771/M2031 750,000 5/17 Sch. 52 Forms/C2118/14

1st S.S.A. [illegible]

Army Form C. 2118.

Instructions regarding War Diaries and Intelligence Summaries are contained in F. S. Regs., Part II. and the Staff Manual respectively. Title pages will be prepared in manuscript.

WAR DIARY
or
INTELLIGENCE SUMMARY.
(Erase heading not required.)

V R 31

Place	Date	Hour	Summary of Events and Information	Remarks and references to Appendices
CHUIGNOLLES	1/10/18		The Battalion paraded at 9 a.m. & marched via BRAY & MARICOURT to hutments on the east side of MAMETZ WOOD in the MONTAUBAN AREA	
MAMETZ WOOD	2/10/18	0009 9 am	Company Inspection	
		0015 3 PM	Company in Attack practice	
"	3/10/18	0009 9 am	Training. The men were paid in the afternoon	
MAMETZ WOOD COMBLES NURLU	4/10/18		The Battalion moved by march route via BERNAFAY WOOD & GUILLEMONT to COMBLES arriving in billets at about 11.30 a.m. In the afternoon Orders were received to be prepared to move at a moments notice. A few hours later this was confirmed by an order to move to NURLU AREA at ~~[illegible]~~ 0830 p.m. The Battalion paraded at ~~[illegible]~~ 0830 & moved by march route to the NURLU AREA arriving at billets at 2.30 am	

D. D. & L., London, E.C.
(A) Wt. W2771/M2 31 750,000 5/17 Sch. 52 Forms/C2118/14

194

Instructions regarding War Diaries and Intelligence Summaries are contained in F. S. Regs., Part II. and the Staff Manual respectively. Title pages will be prepared in manuscript.

WAR DIARY
or
~~INTELLIGENCE SUMMARY.~~

(Erase heading not required.)

Army Form C. 2118.

Place	Date	Hour	Summary of Events and Information	Remarks and references to Appendices
NURLU	5/10/18		The Battalion paraded at 9 a.m. and marched via LERAMONT & VILLERS FAUCON to RONSSOY and encamped on the Villers Faucon - Ronssoy Road 1 kilometre S.E. of RONSSOY. Blankets & Great Coats were dumped at Q M Stores & the march was performed in battle order. 'B' Team proceeded to join BRIGADE 'B' Teams Concentrating at MOISLAINS Under Major Clarke of the 4th Regiment	
RONSSOY	6/10/18		Companies were at the disposal of Company Commanders. A Draft of 4 Officers & 42 O Ranks arrived ex Base.	
"	7/10/18		The Battalion moved at 11.59 hours in battle order to the HINDENBURG LINE, preparatory to carrying out major operations as per order No 10 of even date. The Transport & administrative staff remained behind until further Orders.	

D. D. & L., London, E.C. (A8094) Wt W1771/M2031 750,000 5/17 Sch. 52 Forms/C2118/14

193

WAR DIARY
or
INTELLIGENCE SUMMARY.

(Erase heading not required.)

Instructions regarding War Diaries and Intelligence Summaries are contained in F. S. Regs., Part II. and the Staff Manual respectively. Title pages will be prepared in manuscript.

Place	Date	Hour	Summary of Events and Information	Remarks and references to Appendices
BAUREVOIR	8/10/18		At 00.15 hours the Battalion arrived on the Railway Embankment North of BAUREVOIR, simultaneously the enemy opened a heavy barrage in reply to a light one by our artillery, put down to deaden the noise of Tanks moving into their assembly positions, this caused 23 casualties to the Battalion. When the barrage subsided the Battalion moved to its assembly position in front of BAUREVOIR and in support to the 2nd & 4th Regiments which Regiments were to attack and penetrate the enemy positions on a front of 2000 yards & capture the RED LINE, a distance of 3500 yards from the jumping off point. ZERO HOUR was at 05.30 hours. During the operation one platoon of "A" Company was called upon to reinforce the 2nd Regiment & gave them all assistance possible Assisted by a creeping barrage and tanks, the attacking troops moved forward 3 mins after ZERO HOUR & long before mid-day had captured the objective. Advancing 700 yards in rear of attacking Battalions the 1st Regiment had to pass through BAUREVOIR which was being subjected to a terrific bombardment by the enemy — the losses suffered by the Battalion in BAUREVOR were comparatively small.	

195

D. D. & L., London, E.C. (A8094) Wt W1771/M2031 750,000 5/17 Sch. 52 Forms/C2118/14

Instructions regarding War Diaries and Intelligence Summaries are contained in F. S. Regs., Part II. and the Staff Manual respectively. Title pages will be prepared in manuscript.

WAR DIARY
or
INTELLIGENCE SUMMARY.
(*Erase heading not required.*)

Army Form C. 2118.

Place	Date	Hour	Summary of Events and Information	Remarks and references to Appendices
			When the RED LINE had been captured the 199th Brigade leap-frogged the S.A. Brigade and attacked and captured SERAIN. The Battalion at this juncture was withdrawn & remained in reserve throughout the night Capt Riley, J.W, who was the only Officer Casualty during this operation, was wounded in the neck The Transport and Administrative staff of the Battalion moved to BAUREVOIR.	
SERAIN	01/10/18		In the morning the 2nd & 4th Regiments with this Battalion in support again attacked the enemy positions on a front of 2000 yds and advanced the line approximately 4000 yards and taking all objectives. The Battalion remained in Brigade Reserves at Aveli & at 1430 hours received orders to move up at once and support the attacking Battalions & took up a position 1500 yards S W of MAUROIS, along the Railway Line and at 1930 hours two Companies were sent up to MAUROIS to assist the 2nd Regiment. At 2300 hours the Battalion moved up and occupied ~~MAUROIS~~ REUMONT Outposts were immediately sent out	

D. D. & L., London, E.C. (A8094) Wt W1771/M2031 750,000 5/17 Sch. 52 Forms/C2118/14

Instructions regarding War Diaries and Intelligence Summaries are contained in F. S. Regs., Part II. and the Staff Manual respectively. Title pages will be prepared in manuscript.

WAR DIARY
or
INTELLIGENCE SUMMARY.
(Erase heading not required.)

Army Form C. 2118.

Place	Date	Hour	Summary of Events and Information	Remarks and references to Appendices
REUMONT	10/10/18		At 0530 hours the Battalion was withdrawn from the Outpost positions to REUMONT and rested there for the day. The enemy shelled the village with H.E. & Gas shells causing 20 Casualties in the Battalion among who ~~was~~ 2nd Lt J W HIGGINS was wounded. The Transport moved ~~to~~ & billeted in a field 1 kilometre N. E. of MARETZ	
	11/10/18		The 199th & 198th Brigade continuing the advance reached the village of LE CATEAU, where a fierce enemy resistance was met. The Battalion remained at rest during the day and at 2000 hours moved into the line & relieved the Liverpool and East Lancashire Regiment at LE CATEAU and MONTAY.	
LE CATEAU	12/10/18		Artillery on both sides very active. Enemy machine guns very active	
	13/10/18		Patrols sent out during the night reported a system of short enemy trenches existing from K22 b.45 and K22 a.79 and that the Bosche was preparing to wire ~~thus~~ his positions in K.22 b.37 – K22. b.27. Artillery instructed to give attention to these During the night bridges were to have been thrown over.	

191

D. D. & L., London, E.C. (A8004) Wt W1771/M2031 750,000 5/17 Sch. 52 Forms/C2118/14

Army Form C. 2118.

WAR DIARY
or
INTELLIGENCE SUMMARY.
(Erase heading not required.)

Instructions regarding War Diaries and Intelligence Summaries are contained in F. S. Regs., Part II. and the Staff Manual respectively. Title pages will be prepared in manuscript.

190

Place	Date	Hour	Summary of Events and Information	Remarks and references to Appendices
			over the LA SELLE River and the Battalion was to push forward at the same time, as the H.L.I. attacked on the left. The bridging was not undertaken and consequently the Battalion could not carry out the proposed operation. Other than vigorous patrolling during the night, there was nothing to report. 2nd Lt B.A. LOGIE was wounded ~~during~~ in the Morning	
LE CATEAU	14/10/18		Hostile Artillery fired intermittently & Machine Guns & Snipers very active particularly from K22.d.67, K22.a.99, K22.b.94. and along the ravine in K.27.21. Enemy Aeroplanes were flying very low over LE CATEAU and seemed to be directing artillery fire on our forward posts. At 1730 hours a patrol was sent out to examine our post and vicinity in K34.b.40.85, from whence shouts were heard during the day. The patrol found the post unoccupied & discovered the packs & rifles of the personnel sent to man the post. A patrol sent to reconnoitre a bridge at K34.b.46 reported it blown away ~~centre~~ in the centre & to be totally unpassable. A bridge at K34.b.02 reported blown down was examined by one of our patrols; the debris it was found, had formed a crossing over the ~~river~~ river	

D. D. & L., London, E.C. (A8004) Wt W1771/M2031 750,000 5/17 Sch. 52 Forms/C2118/14

Instructions regarding War Diaries and Intelligence Summaries are contained in F. S. Regs., Part II. and the Staff Manual respectively. Title pages will be prepared in manuscript.

WAR DIARY
or
INTELLIGENCE SUMMARY.

(*Erase heading not required.*)

Army Form C. 2118.

Place	Date	Hour	Summary of Events and Information	Remarks and references to Appendices
			river, but the passage was commanded by enemy Machine Guns. One of our patrols came in contact with an enemy outpost	
LE CATEAU	15/10/18		During the night 14th/15th A & B Companies were relieved in the left sector by the Gloucester Pioneers & were withdrawn to Brigade Reserve. C & D Companies remained in the right sector & carried out vigorous patrolling, reconnoitring and guarding bridges. a patrol sent to reconnoitre bridge at K34 b 0010 and to procure a civilian, reported the bridge to be destroyed & the river at this point, 24 ft wide. Hostile Artillery active on the whole sector. Between 0300 & 0400 hours a number of very violent bursts were put on the ravine in K27 & at 0430 hours the enemy used gas shells. High flying aircraft fairly active & one low flying plane crossed over our lines at 1015 hours. Capt J.R. LEISK & Capt W. ALLARMUTH with 42 O. Ranks reported as reinforcements from the BASE	

D. D. & L., London, E.C. (A8094) Wt. W1771/M2031 750,000 5/17 Sch. 52 Forms/C2118/14

788

Instructions regarding War Diaries and Intelligence Summaries are contained in F. S. Regs., Part II. and the Staff Manual respectively. Title pages will be prepared in manuscript.

WAR DIARY
or
INTELLIGENCE SUMMARY.
(Erase heading not required.)

Army Form C. 2118.

Place	Date	Hour	Summary of Events and Information	Remarks and references to Appendices
LeCateau	16/10/18		On the night of 15th/16th it was found that the enemy held posts west of the La Selle River and "C" Company was ordered to do a minor operation and clear the enemy out of the sector. In this connection "A" Company was moved from Brigade Reserve into close support. Owing to the predominence of enemy machine guns it was considered inadvisable to effect the attack; all orders for this operation were cancelled and "A" Company returned to Brigade Reserve.	
			A patrol of 1 officer & 12 O. Ranks was sent at 1800 hours to reconnoitre road from K33 b 32 to bridge at K34 a 91. They did not come in contact with the enemy. They reported a light in house K34 Central which remained on for forty minutes & then went out reappearing for a few minutes later. A machine gun was reported to be firing from K34 b 1505. A bridge was found at K34. b02 in good repair & capable of bearing field guns. A 2nd Regiment picquet was met at K34 a. 92. The whole party returned at 0200 hours on 17th.	
			Another patrol was sent to reconnoitre from K28 a. 34 to the La Selle River at K34 b. 46. They reached the wood at K. 28 a 86. when machine guns opened from houses at K. 28 a. 8045 & K28. 9. 76 and the patrol was obliged to	

D. D. & L., London, E.C. (A8004) Wt W1771/M2031 750,000 5/17 Sch. 52 Forms/C2118/14

Instructions regarding War Diaries and Intelligence Summaries are contained in F. S. Regs., Part II. and the Staff Manual respectively. Title pages will be prepared in manuscript.

or

INTELLIGENCE SUMMARY.

(Erase heading not required.)

186

Place	Date	Hour	Summary of Events and Information	Remarks and references to Appendices
			to return. A third patrol carried out reconnaissance work from K28. a. 45. to the river at K 28 a 66. They also got as far as the wood at K 28 a. 86 & had to return on account of M. G fire. 2 Lt Geach was reported missing during this operation. Artillery on both sides very active throughout the 24 hours. Considerable enemy movement over ridge in K 29. 35. reported	
LE CATEAU	17/10/18		During the evening & night of 16th/17th A & B Companies were moved forward & "A", with "B" in support, cleared the enemy from the vicinity of the LE CATEAU – MONTAY ROAD & established themselves on the East bank of the LA SELLE RIVER and immediately set to work, bridging the river & clearing the wire. In the meantime "C" Coy cleared a wood on their right flank, taking one prisoner. C & D Coys then crossed the river & established a post to protect the right flank. ~~Here 2nd Lt [illegible] was killed~~ At 05.30 hours the 4th Regiment on the right, the 2nd Regiment on the left & D Coy of the 1st Regiment on the extreme left, attacked the enemy position on the Railway	

D. D. & L., London, E.C. (A8004) Wt W1771/M2031 750,000 5/17 Sch. 52 Forms/C2118/14

Instructions regarding War Diaries and Intelligence Summaries are contained in F. S. Regs., Part II. and the Staff Manual respectively. Title pages will be prepared in manuscript.

WAR DIARY
or
INTELLIGENCE SUMMARY.
(Erase heading not required.)

Army Form C. 2118.

Place	Date	Hour	Summary of Events and Information	Remarks and references to Appendices
			Railway embankment from K29.a.1.8 to K35 C.83. During the operation "A" Company was sent to reinforce the 11th Regiment, "B" Company was called for by the 2nd Regiment & finally in the afternoon, "C" Company was sent to strengthen the Centre. The enemy resistance was stubborn in the extreme but the objective was eventually taken. In the operation, & while holding the line, "D" Company was subjected to infiladed M.G. fire & suffered very severely, among the casualties were A/Capt A.M. Thomson & 2nd Lt. C.P. Scully and H.M. Hosking all wounded. In the evening orders were received to push northward & establish a post on the Railway embankment at K23.C.23 and form a defensive flank to the junction of the RICHEMONT and LA SELLE RIVERS. "B" Coy was successfully employed for this operation	
LE CATEAU.	18/10/18		Capt W.A. Lamsmith, Lieuts G. Ross, A.C. Stanley & 2nd Lt Pickard with a small party of men were sent from Transport Lines to reinforce the Regiment. The Regiment held on throughout the ~~day~~ day.	

D. D. & L., London, E.C.
(A8604) Wt W1771/M2031 750,000 5/17 Sch. 52 Forms/C2118/14

187

Army Form C. 2118.

WAR DIARY
or
INTELLIGENCE SUMMARY.
(Erase heading not required.)

Instructions regarding War Diaries and Intelligence Summaries are contained in F. S. Regs., Part II. and the Staff Manual respectively. Title pages will be prepared in manuscript.

Place	Date	Hour	Summary of Events and Information	Remarks and references to Appendices
LE CATEAU	19/10/18		During the night 18th/19th a relief by the Liverpool Regiment had started & in respect of "B" Company had been completed. Orders cancelling the relief were received & "B" Company had to return to the Line & in so doing suffered 13 casualties killed. 2nd Lt R. McGregor was fatally wounded. 2nd Lt C.H. Powell was killed during the night & 2nd Lt C.H. Perrem was severely wounded.	
LE CATEAU	20/10/18		During the night 19th/20th the Regiment was relieved by the Liverpool Regiment & until 1100 hours remained in LE CATEAU & moved from thence by small parties to REUMONT. Where packs were dumped & the Band met the Regiment. From REUMONT the Battalion moved by march route to billets in SERAIN via MARETZ	#
SERAIN.	21/10/18		Routine Reveille 0700 hours. Roll Call. 0730 hours. Breakfast. 0800 hours. Sick parade. 1000 hours.	185

D. D. & L., London, E.C. (A8co4) Wt W1771/M2031 750,000 5/17 Sch. 52 Forms/C2118/14

Army Form C. 2118.

WAR DIARY
or
INTELLIGENCE SUMMARY.
(*Erase heading not required.*)

Instructions regarding War Diaries and Intelligence Summaries are contained in F. S. Regs., Part II. and the Staff Manual respectively. Title pages will be prepared in manuscript.

Place	Date	Hour	Summary of Events and Information	Remarks and references to Appendices
			The following Casualties were experienced during the period in the Line 7th to 20th inclusive:- 13 Officers 377 O. Ranks.	
SERAIN	22/10/18		Companies were at disposal of Coy Commanders. The XIII Corps Commander inspected the Battalion in billets & expressed to the Commanding Officer his high appreciation of the splendid services rendered in the line by all ranks.	
	23/10/18		Routine & training as ~~[illegible]~~ laid down for 21st & 22nd. Draft of 4 O/Rs arrived from Rouen	

184

D. D. & L. London, E.C.

Army Form C. 2118.

WAR DIARY
or
INTELLIGENCE SUMMARY.
(Erase heading not required.)

Instructions regarding War Diaries and Intelligence Summaries are contained in F. S. Regs., Part II. and the Staff Manual respectively. Title pages will be prepared in manuscript.

Place	Date	Hour	Summary of Events and Information	Remarks and references to Appendices
SERAIN	24/10/18		Routine of Training as for previous days. Coys at the disposal of Company Commanders after inspection by Battalion Commander ~~The Battalion went on a route march~~	
"	25/10/18		Coys at the disposal of Coy Commanders after an Inspection by &c. Special attention being paid to ~~Lewis Gun~~ Training. Battalion on route march.	
"	26/10/18		Church Parades for all Denominations	
"	27/10/18		Battalion Parade then Coys trained under Coy arrangements. Special attention being paid to Lewis Gun work	
"	28/10/18		Training under Coy arrangements. In the afternoon the Regt Rugby team played the 199th Bde team & won 24 to Nil. In the evening a concert was held for the Regiment organized by Padre Roberts & proved a great success. Great assistance being rendered by the American Tank Corps	
"	29/10/18		Battalion Parade followed by training. Men inoculated. Football match against 2nd Regt in the afternoon which was won by 1st Regt	183

D. D. & L., London, E.C. (A8094) Wt. W1771/M2031 750,000 5/17 Sch. 52 Forms/C2118/14

Army Form C. 2118.

Instructions regarding War Diaries and Intelligence Summaries are contained in F. S. Regs., Part II. and the Staff Manual respectively. Title pages will be prepared in manuscript.

WAR DIARY
or
INTELLIGENCE SUMMARY.
(Erase heading not required.)

Place	Date	Hour	Summary of Events and Information	Remarks and references to Appendices
SERAIN	30/10/18		The Battalion acted as the enemy in a Divisional Scheme two employed the whole day much useful information was gained from the attacking troops.	
"	31/10/18		Training under Coy arrangements	

3/11/18

H. Jenkins Lt Col
Comdg 1st S.A.I

182

D. D. & L., London, E.C.

Instructions regarding War Diaries and Intelligence Summaries are contained in F. S. Regs., Part II. and the Staff Manual respectively. Title pages will be prepared in manuscript.

WAR DIARY
or
INTELLIGENCE SUMMARY.
(Erase heading not required.)

101-5A1

Army Form C. 2118.

9832

Place	Date	Hour	Summary of Events and Information	Remarks and references to Appendices
SERAIN	1/11/18.		The regiment paraded at 10.00 hours in "Battle order" and carried on with training till mid-day. Capt Pyott S.A.M.C. relieved Capt Levisseur as M.O. to the regiment. Lt. H. V. Artz proceeded on leave.	
"	2/11/18.		The regiment marched from SERAIN to REUMONT via ELINCOURT, CLARY & BERTRY. Lt Baldie returned from leave.	
REUMONT	3/11/18.		Church parades.	
"	4/11/18.		The regiment marched to LE CATEAU. Officers kits, great coats and all spare kit were dumped here.	
LE CATEAU	5/11/18.		The regiment marched to POMMEREUIL.	
POMMEREUIL	6/11/18		Marched to LANDRECIES.	
LANDRECIES	7/11/18		Marched to BASSE NOYELLE. Capt Roffe proceeded on leave.	
BASSE NOYELLE	8/11/18		Marched to DOMPIERRE.	

D. D. & L., London, E.C.
A5033 Wt. W1771/M2031 750,000 5/17 Sch. 52 Forms C2118/14

Instructions regarding War Diaries and Intelligence Summaries are contained in F. S. Regs., Part II. and the Staff Manual respectively. Title pages will be prepared in manuscript.

WAR DIARY
or
INTELLIGENCE SUMMARY.
(Erase heading not required.)

Army Form C. 2118.

Place	Date	Hour	Summary of Events and Information	Remarks and references to Appendices
DOMPIERRE	9/11/18		Marched to BEUGNIES and after an hours halt for tea moved on to SOLRE-LE-CHATEAU.	
SOLRE-LE-CHATEAU	10/11/18		The Battalion was detailed to act as Advance Guard to the South African Brigade Mobile Column commanded by Brig. Gen. W. Tanner, C.M.G. D.S.O. Detail of Advance Guard:- 1st S.A.I. Section of 430th Coy R.E.'s. Section of guns "B" Battery 431st F.A.B. Two sections of "C" Coy 100th M.G.C. The column moved out from SOLRE LE CHATEAU at 0700 hours with BEAUMONT as its objective as the enemy had been reported as retiring rapidly towards the MEUSE. Two kilos from SOLRE LE CHATEAU it was found necessary to repair a bridge this was speedily done by the R.E's. The Advance Guard and the column proceeded towards Hestrud on reaching the western outskirts of HESTRUD the cavalry (12th Lancers) reported that the enemy were holding the high ground west of GRANDIEU and these patrols were unable to advance	

174

D. D. & L., London, E.C. (A8051) Wt. W1771/M2031 750,000 5/17 Sch. 52 Forms C2118/14

Army Form C. 2118.

WAR DIARY
or
~~INTELLIGENCE SUMMARY.~~
(Erase heading not required.)

Instructions regarding War Diaries and Intelligence Summaries are contained in F. S. Regs., Part II. and the Staff Manual respectively. Title pages will be prepared in manuscript.

Place	Date	Hour	Summary of Events and Information	Remarks and references to Appendices
SOLRE LE CHATEAU	10/11/18		Orders were received from the B.G.C. to at once deploy three Companies and capture this high ground. Patrols were at once sent out to locate crossings over the river as the Lancers were unable to furnish this information, these were soon withdrawn as it was found that although the enemy had destroyed the bridge on the HESTRUD ROAD the river was fordable. A.B. + D Coys were sent across the river disposed as follows – "D" on the right, "A" on the left, "B" in the centre, with "C" in reserve in HESTRUD with Batt H.Q.s. The battalion immediately came under heavy M.G. fire + progress was very slow, it was found that the enemy was holding the whole front of GRANDIEU (approx 3K) with M.G.s in very strong positions. The enemy opened some sluice gates south of HESTRUD which caused the river to rise and become unfordable which	

(10540) Wt W5300/P713 750,000 3/18 E 1688 Forms/C2118/16. D. D. & L., London, E.C.

173

Instructions regarding War Diaries and Intelligence Summaries are contained in F. S. Regs., Part II. and the Staff Manual respectively. Title pages will be prepared in manuscript.

WAR DIARY
or
~~INTELLIGENCE SUMMARY.~~
(Erase heading not required.)

Army Form C. 2118.

172

Place	Date	Hour	Summary of Events and Information	Remarks and references to Appendices
SOLRE LE CHATEAU	10/11/18		caused great difficulty for our wounded to reach our Aid Post. The Companies pushed on and captured the high ground as they set out to do but were unable to make further progress. Shortly after this the enemy shelled HESTRUD heavily with HE and gas and heavily machine gunned the village, and then switched off the village to the main body of the mobile column on the road near SOLRE-LE-CHATEAU which they shelled very heavily. Targets were given to our section of guns but immediately they opened fire the enemy silenced them. Without proper artillery support the position was hopeless and although good work was done by a platoon of A Coy on the left commanded by 2/Lt Cawood progress could not be made & our casualties were mounting up. During the afternoon the village & main body were again heavily shelled and the Coy on the left were shelled with light	

D. D. & L., London, E.C.
(10340) Wt W5300/P713 750,000 3/18 E 2688 Forms/C2118/16.

WAR DIARY
or
INTELLIGENCE SUMMARY.
(Erase heading not required.)

Army Form C. 2118.

Instructions regarding War Diaries and Intelligence Summaries are contained in F. S. Regs., Part II. and the Staff Manual respectively. Title pages will be prepared in manuscript.

Place	Date	Hour	Summary of Events and Information	Remarks and references to Appendices
SOLRE LE CHATEAU	10/11/18		Trench Mortars. During the afternoon information was received that 199th Brigade were advancing towards SIVRY and orders were given to get in touch with them which was done. One section of M.G.s were brought East of the river and put in position to engage and keep down the hostile M.G. fire which was causing us considerable casualties. The other section was employed to look after the left flank as no troops were operating there our flank being in the air. It was decided to dig in and hold on to our present line which was practically 200 yds East of the Franco Belgian border which was done one platoon of "C" Coy being used to strengthen the left flank. Vigorous patrolling was carried out during the night as it was thought that the enemy might retire. During the night the village was again heavily shelled. 2/Lt Bentley returned from leave.	171

D. D. & L., London, E.C. (10340) Wt W5300/P713 750,000 3/18 E 2688 Forms/C2118/16.

Instructions regarding War Diaries and Intelligence Summaries are contained in F. S. Regs., Part II. and the Staff Manual respectively. Title pages will be prepared in manuscript.

WAR DIARY
or
INTELLIGENCE SUMMARY.
(Erase heading not required.)

Army Form C. 2118.

Place	Date	Hour	Summary of Events and Information	Remarks and references to Appendices
HESTRUD.	11/11/18		Orders were received to try and push on again at daybreak which was done, but no progress could be made. A patrol under 2/Lt Cawood pushed forward and did excellent work. Between 0700 and 0800 the village and locality were again shelled. At 1015 when the B.G.C was at Batt H.Q. the G.S.O. 2 arrived with orders that hostilities were to cease at 1100 as an armistice had been signed. Orders were at once sent to the troops to cease fire at 1100 and remain on the ground they were holding. At 1030 orders were received to push on right up to 1100 this was done but very little progress was made & the fighting continued right up to 1100 when the enemy stood up in his trenches and then came towards our line & wanted to fraternize but our troops ordered them back to their lines. Shortly after this two officers of the 443rd Rgt Prussian Guard came to our lines to discuss	170

D. D. & L., London, E.C.
(10340) Wt W5300/P713 750,000 3/18 E 1188 Forms/C2118/16.

Army Form C. 2118.

Instructions regarding War Diaries and Intelligence Summaries are contained in F. S. Regs., Part II. and the Staff Manual respectively. Title pages will be prepared in manuscript.

WAR DIARY
or
~~INTELLIGENCE~~ SUMMARY.
(Erase heading not required.)

Place	Date	Hour	Summary of Events and Information	Remarks and references to Appendices
HESTRUD	11/11/18		the line we would hold. They were blindfolded & taken to the B.G.C. who discussed the matter with them. The battalion remained in the line during the night and a platoon was sent towards SIVRY to link up with 199th brigade. Our losses were 5 killed. 1 Died of wounds. 26 wounded. The following O/R were wounded a few hours prior to the armistice:-	
			No 222 Pte Johnstone (since D.o.W.) 10866 Pte Miles. 4216 Sgt Miller. 17034 Pte Cherry. 4166 Pte Tenant.	
			The following officers brought a draft from England:- 2/Lt H.V. Mackay. Lt. D Good. 2/Lt D Hogg	
HESTRUD	11/12/18		As it was found that the enemy had retired from GRANDIEU the regiment moved forward and took up a line E. of the village linking up with 199 brigade. At 1630 the batt. was relieved & returned to billets in HESTROD.	

169

D. D. & L., London, E.C.
(10340) Wt W5300/P713 750,000 3/18 E 2688 Forms/C2118/10.

Instructions regarding War Diaries and Intelligence Summaries are contained in F. S. Regs., Part II. and the Staff Manual respectively. Title pages will be prepared in manuscript.

WAR DIARY
or
~~INTELLIGENCE SUMMARY.~~
(Erase heading not required.)

Army Form C. 2118.

Place	Date	Hour	Summary of Events and Information	Remarks and references to Appendices
HESTRUD	13/11/18		Regiment cleaning up. 2/Lts Hawke and England join from Woking. Lt Mackay returned from course at XIII Corps school.	
"	14/11/18		Inspection by C.O. at 1000 hours. Battle order.	
"	15/11/18		The regiment provided a guard of honor to the Corps Commander when he presented medals to the Division at SOLRE-LE-CHATEAU. 2/Lt Sampson and Holmes join from England.	
"	16/11/18		Marched to SIVRY	
SIVRY	17/11/18		Church parades. General Tanner inspected the regiment and addressed them on the recent operations.	
"	18/11/18		Training under Company arrangements. Lt Ingasfield attached to Brigade H.Q.	

D. D. & L., London, E.C. (A8051) Wt. W1771/M2031 750,000 5/17 Sch. 52 Forms C2118/14

Army Form C. 2118.

WAR DIARY
or
~~INTELLIGENCE SUMMARY.~~
(Erase heading not required.)

Instructions regarding War Diaries and Intelligence Summaries are contained in F. S. Regs., Part II. and the Staff Manual respectively. Title pages will be prepared in manuscript.

Place	Date	Hour	Summary of Events and Information	Remarks and references to Appendices
SIVRY	19/11/18		Marched to SOUMOY via RANCE and CERFONTAINE.	
SOUMOY	20/11/18.		Training under Company arrangements.	
"	21/11/18.		Training under Company arrangements. Lt Artz returned from leave in England.	
"	22/11/18		Training under Company arrangements.	
"	23/11/18		Marched to Philippeville. Capt Gray proceeded on leave.	
"	24/11/18		Marched to Bac du Prince on the Meuse	
Bac du Prince	25/11/18		Battalion parade.	
"	26/11/18		Company training. Capt. Roffe returned from leave.	
"	27/11/18		Battalion parade at 0900 hours, followed by training. Major [illegible] arrived from England.	167

D. D. & L., London, E.C. (A5984) Wt. W1771/M2031 750,000 5/17 Sch. 52 Forms C2118/14

Instructions regarding War Diaries and Intelligence Summaries are contained in F. S. Regs., Part II. and the Staff Manual respectively. Title pages will be prepared in manuscript.

WAR DIARY
or
INTELLIGENCE SUMMARY.
(Erase heading not required.)

Army Form C. 2118.

Place	Date	Hour	Summary of Events and Information	Remarks and references to Appendices
Baclu Prince	28/11/18		Training during morning. Rugger match with S.A.M.C. in afternoon, won 8 – 6.	
"	29/11/18		Training during morning. Football in afternoon. Capt C. A. Lewseur S.A.M.C. is attached vice Capt C. G. Pyott, as M.O. to the regiment.	
"	30/11/18		Regiment paraded in fighting order at 0915 hours for training. Rugby:– A & D v B & C at 1430 hours.	

166

D. D. & L., London, E.C. (A600) Wt. W1-71/M2031 750,000 5/17 Sch. 52 Forms C2118/14

24

Army Form C. 2118.

Instructions regarding War Diaries and Intelligence Summaries are contained in F. S. Regs., Part II. and the Staff Manual respectively. Title pages will be prepared in manuscript.

WAR DIARY - 1st. S.A.I.

or

~~INTELLIGENCE SUMMARY.~~ DEC., 1918.

(Erase heading not required.)

VR 3

Place	Date	Hour	Summary of Events and Information	Remarks and references to Appendices
Bac Du Prince	1/12/18		Battalion Church Parade at 0945 hours. A & D Coy vs B & C at rugger in the afternoon.	
"	2/12/18		Regiment paraded at 0915 hours for training. B & C Coys vs H.Q.s at Soccer at 1430 hours.	
"	3/12/18		Regiment paraded at 0915 for training. Lt Ingerfield appointed Brigade T.O. and struck off strength of regiment.	
"	4/12/18		Regiment paraded at 0915 and marched to training ground but returned & trained in billets owing to rain. Capt McMillan proceeded on leave.	

180

Instructions regarding War Diaries and Intelligence Summaries are contained in F. S. Regs., Part II. and the Staff Manual respectively. Title pages will be prepared in manuscript.

WAR DIARY
or
~~INTELLIGENCE SUMMARY.~~
(Erase heading not required.)

Army Form C. 2118.

Place	Date	Hour	Summary of Events and Information	Remarks and references to Appendices
Bac du Prince	5/12/18		Regiment paraded at 0915 hours & marched through GIVET & returned. 2/Lt Whiteross to D.A.H.	
			Capt Van der Spuy relieves Capt Levasseur as M.O. to the unit.	
	6/12/18		Regiment paraded for training at 0915 hours. Concert at 1800.	
	7/12/18		Regiment paraded for training at 0915 hours. Rugger match Possibles vs Probables. N.C. O's & Mens dance at 1800.	
	8/12/18		Church Parades for all denominations.	
	9/12/18		Companies paraded at 0900 hours for the selection of a model platoon from each Coy after which the balance of the regiment carried out L.G. & rifle firing.	

Army Form C. 2118.

WAR DIARY
or
~~INTELLIGENCE SUMMARY.~~
(Erase heading not required.)

Instructions regarding War Diaries and Intelligence Summaries are contained in F. S. Regs., Part II. and the Staff Manual respectively. Title pages will be prepared in manuscript.

Place	Date	Hour	Summary of Events and Information	Remarks and references to Appendices
BAC du PRINCE	10/12/18		Range practice carried out under Adjutant from 0930 hours to 1200 hours.	
"	11/12/18		Range practice 0930 to 1200 hours.	
"	12/12/18		The Battalion bathed and carried out fatigues on the captured trains.	
"	13/12/18		Companies carried out training from 0930 to 1100 hours.	
"	14/12/18		The regiment marched from BAC DU PRINCE to FERAGE where it was billetted for the night.	
FERAGE	15/12/18		Marched to ROCHEFORT and billetted there.	
ROCHEFORT	16/12/18		Marched to MARCHE. Inspected by divisional General on route. Major McEwen and Lt. Stanley proceeded to HAVESIN to meet draft from BOHAIN.	178

D. D. & L., London, E.C.
(A7093) Wt. W1771/M2031 750,000 5/17 Sch. 52 Forms C2118/14

Army Form C. 2118.

WAR DIARY
or
INTELLIGENCE SUMMARY.
(Erase heading not required.)

Instructions regarding War Diaries and Intelligence Summaries are contained in F. S. Regs., Part II. and the Staff Manual respectively. Title pages will be prepared in manuscript.

Place	Date	Hour	Summary of Events and Information	Remarks and references to Appendices
MARCHE	17/12/18		Companies at disposal of Coy Com. Draft arrived under Lt Tyers, 2/Lt Burton, & 2/Lt Montgomery; was inspected by C.O. and sent to billets in WAILLET under the command of Capt. Larmuth. Draft officers remained with battalion.	177
"	18/12/18		Coys. at disposal of Coy Com. Commanding Officer proceeded to WAILLET and inspected draft.	
"	19/12/18		Training under company arrangements.	
"	20/12/18		Coy arrangements. Coy. Com. inspected draft at WAILLET	
"	21/12/18		Coy training arrangements. Capt Gray returned from leave.	
"	22/12/18		Church parades. Draft returned from WAILLET after being inspected by C.O. Lt Featherstone reported from hospital.	

D. D. & L., London, E.C.
(A8004) Wt W1771/M2031 750,000 5/17 Sch. 52 Forms/C2118/14

Instructions regarding War Diaries and Intelligence Summaries are contained in F. S. Regs., Part II. and the Staff Manual respectively. Title pages will be prepared in manuscript.

WAR DIARY
or
INTELLIGENCE SUMMARY.
(Erase heading not required.)

Army Form C. 2118.

Place	Date	Hour	Summary of Events and Information	Remarks and references to Appendices
MARCHE	23/12/18		Battalion paraded at 09-30 hours and after inspection training was carried out under Company arrangements.	
"	24/12/18		Inspection at 0915 hours remainder of day spent in decorating for Christmas.	
"	25/12/18		Church parades.	
"	26/12/18		Inspection by H.R.H. The Prince of Wales. Capt Mackay and 2/Lt Garrett on leave to U.K.	
"	27/12/18		Battalion route march 0930 to 1130 hours. Col Jenkins on leave to U.K. Major McEwen assumes command.	
"	28/12/18		Battalion parade at 0930. Capt McMillan returns from leave.	
"	29/12/18		Church parades. Lt Ingarfield reported from Brigade	176

D. D. & L., London, E.C. (A8004) Wt W1771/M2031 750,000 5/17 Sch. 52 Forms/C2118/14

Instructions regarding War Diaries and Intelligence Summaries are contained in F. S. Regs., Part II. and the Staff Manual respectively. Title pages will be prepared in manuscript.

WAR DIARY
or
INTELLIGENCE SUMMARY.
(Erase heading not required.)

Army Form C. 2118.

Place	Date	Hour	Summary of Events and Information	Remarks and references to Appendices
MARCHE	30/12/18		Training under Company arrangements on battalion parade ground.	
"	31/12/18		Training in billets owing to wet weather.	

D. D. & L., London, E.C.
(10340) Wt W5300/P713 750,000 3/18 E 2688 Forms/C2118/16.

5/1

Army Form C. 2118.

WR 34

Instructions regarding War Diaries and Intelligence Summaries are contained in F. S. Regs., Part II. and the Staff Manual respectively. Title pages will be prepared in manuscript.

WAR DIARY
or
INTELLIGENCE SUMMARY.

(Erase heading not required.)

1st S.A. Infantry

Place	1919 Date Jan	Hour	Summary of Events and Information	Remarks and references to Appendices
MARCHE	1st		Company Inspection at 0930 hours, the men were then free for rest of the day.	
"	2nd		Route march at 0930 hours returning to billets for dinner	
"	3rd		Training under Company arrangements at 0930 hours.	
"	4th		Company arrangements.	
"	5th		Church parades. Rugby team training under Capt Sales.	
"	6th		Company arrangements.	
"	7th		Company arrangements Lt Stanley proceeded on leave to U.K.	
"	8th		Company inspection. Battalion marches to see match vs Australians. score Bat. won 15 to Nil. 2/Lts Pickard and Pillow on leave to U.K. Officers give a successful dance	
"	9th		Company parades at 0930 hours Lt Col. Jenkins awarded D.S.O. 1/1/19	
"	10th		Parades under Company arrangements from 0930 hours.	206

• D. D. & L., London, E.C.
(10340) Wt W5300/P713 750,000 3/18 E 2688 Forms/C2118/16.

Army Form C. 2118.

5/2

Instructions regarding War Diaries and Intelligence Summaries are contained in F. S. Regs., Part II. and the Staff Manual respectively. Title pages will be prepared in manuscript.

WAR DIARY
or
~~INTELLIGENCE SUMMARY.~~
(Erase heading not required.)

Place	1919 Date JAN	Hour	Summary of Events and Information	Remarks and references to Appendices
MARCHE	11th		Parades under Company arrangements from 0930 hours	
"	12th		Church parades for all denominations.	
"	13th		Battalion parade at 0900 hours	
"	14th		Short route march under Company arrangements	
"	15th		Training under Company arrangements	
"	16th		Training under Company arrangements	
"	17th		Company route march. Capt Forbes D.S.O. returned from U.K.	
"	18th		Company route march. Rugger match vs A.S.C.	
"	19th		Church parades 2/Lt Cawood on leave to U.K.	
"	20th		Company parades. Capt Hoppe M.C. to 66th Division	
"	21st		Company route march. Col Jenkins from leave in U.K. resumes command of Battalion. Transport competition Winners of 1st prize Ptes Porter, Crowe and Pattinson	

D. D. & L., London, E.C.
(10340) Wt W5300/P713 750,000 3/18 E 2688 Forms/C2118/16.

5/3

Army Form C. 2118.

WAR DIARY
or
~~INTELLIGENCE SUMMARY~~.
(*Erase heading not required.*)

Instructions regarding War Diaries and Intelligence Summaries are contained in F. S. Regs., Part II. and the Staff Manual respectively. Title pages will be prepared in manuscript.

Place	Date 1919 JAN	Hour	Summary of Events and Information	Remarks and references to Appendices
MARCHE	22nd		The Regiment marched to MAFFE via LIEGE ROAD and SOMMELEUZE	
MAFFE	23rd		The Regiment marched to OHEY via HAYLANCE and EVELETTE	
			A and B Companies billeted in OHEY and C. D + H.Q.s at HAILLOT	
OHEY	24th		The Regiment marched to SEILLES via ANDENNE arriving at 1400 hours. "D" Coy billeted at ANDENNE and piqueted all billets occupied by X Corps until taken over by Canadian Corps. X Corps demobilisation camp taken over by Battalion and placed under charge of Capt Featherstone, with staff of 2/Lts Falkiner and Hoff and 40 other ranks.	
SEILLES	25th		Training under Company arrangements. Coys lectured on venereal. "D" Coy arrived at SEILLE having handed over billets to Canadian Corps.	
"	26th		Church parades for all denominations. Capt Mackay and 2/Lt Garrett from leave in U.K. Football team to Cologne to play the New Zealanders. Team consisted of Capt Forbes Lts Ryal + Artz Sgt Bruckman Ptes Schwartz, Rosow + Windell	

208

D. D. & L., London, E.C.
(10340) Wt W5300/P713 750,000 3/18 E 2688 Forms/C2118/16.

5/41

Instructions regarding War Diaries and Intelligence Summaries are contained in F. S. Regs., Part II. and the Staff Manual respectively. Title pages will be prepared in manuscript.

WAR DIARY
or
~~INTELLIGENCE SUMMARY.~~
(Erase heading not required.)

Army Form C. 2118.

Place	Date 1919 JAN	Hour	Summary of Events and Information	Remarks and references to Appendices
SEILLE	26th		A guard under Sgt Flannagan "C" Coy was supplied to R.T.O. ANDENNE & a guard under Sgt Butler "A" Coy to SCLAIGNEAUX.	
"	27th		Company arrangements. Lt Stanley from leave in U.K.	
"	28th		Lecture by M.O. on venereal to all ranks. Two officers of Gloucesters arrived to take over our billets and Lts Stanley and England proceeded to CINEY to take over the Gloucesters billets	
"	29th		Company arrangements. Coys lectured on venereal	
"	30th		Regiment marched to HAILLOT and billeted in HAILLOT & OHEY. Regiment inspected by Divisional General on line of march	
HAILLOT	31st		Regiment marched to CINEY via main road arriving at CINEY at 1430 hours.	

[signature]
LIEUT. COLONEL,
COMMANDING 1ST S.A. INFANTRY.

D. D. & L., London, E.C.
(10340) Wt W5300/P713 750,000 3/18 E 2688 Forms/C2118/16.

209

Instructions regarding War Diaries and Intelligence Summaries are contained in F. S. Regs., Part II. and the Staff Manual respectively. Title pages will be prepared in manuscript.

WAR DIARY
or
~~INTELLIGENCE SUMMARY.~~
(Erase heading not required.)

Army Form C. 2118.

34

1st S. A. Infantry

Place	1919 Date Jan	Hour	Summary of Events and Information	Remarks and references to Appendices
MARCHE	1st		Company Inspection at 0930 hours, the men were then free for rest of the day	
"	2nd		Route march at 0930 hours returning to billets for dinner	
"	3rd		Training under Company arrangements at 0930 hours.	
"	4th		Company arrangements.	
"	5th		Church parades. Rugby team training under Capt Forbes	
"	6th		Company arrangements.	
"	7th		Company arrangements. Lt Stanley proceeded on leave to U.K.	
"	8th		Company inspection. Battalion marches to see match vs Australians. score S.A. win 15 to Nil. 2/Lts Pickard and Pillow on leave to U.K. Officers give a successful dance	
"	9th		Company parades at 0930 hours. Lt Col. Jenkins awarded D.S.O. 1/1/19	
"	10th		Parades under Company arrangements from 0930 hours	

D. D. & L., London, E.C. (00540) Wt W3300/P713 750,000 3/18 E 2588 Forms/C2118/10.

213

5/3

Instructions regarding War Diaries and Intelligence Summaries are contained in F. S. Regs., Part II. and the Staff Manual respectively. Title pages will be prepared in manuscript.

WAR DIARY
or
~~INTELLIGENCE SUMMARY.~~
(Erase heading not required.)

Army Form C. 2118.

Place	1919 Date JAN	Hour	Summary of Events and Information	Remarks and references to Appendices
MARCHE	22nd		The Regiment marched to MAFFE via LIEGE ROAD and SOMME LEUZE	
MAFFE	23rd		The Regiment marched to OHEY via HAYLANCE and EVELETTE. A and B Companies billeted in OHEY and C, D & H.Q.s at HAILLOT	
OHEY	24th		The Regiment marched to SEILLES via ANDENNE arriving at 1400 hours. "D" Coy billeted at ANDENNE and piqueted all billets occupied by X Corps until taken over by Canadian Corps. X Corps demobilisation camp taken over by Battalion and placed under charge of Capt Featherstone, with staff of 2/Lts Falkner and Hoff and 40 other ranks.	
SEILLES	25th		Training under Company arrangements. Coys lectured on venereal. "D" Coy arrived at SEILLE having handed over billets to Canadian Corps.	
"	26th		Church parades for all denominations. Capt Mackay and 2/Lt Garrett from leave in U.K. Football team to Cologne to play the New Zealanders. Team consisted of Capt Forbes Lts Ryal & Artz Sgt Bruckman Ptes Schwartz, Rosom & Windell	

211

D. D. & L., London, E.C.
(20540) Wt W5300/P713 750,000 3/18 E 1868 Forms/C2118/16.

5/2

Army Form C. 2118.

WAR DIARY
or
~~INTELLIGENCE SUMMARY.~~
(Erase heading not required.)

Instructions regarding War Diaries and Intelligence Summaries are contained in F. S. Regs., Part II. and the Staff Manual respectively. Title pages will be prepared in manuscript.

Place	1919 Date JAN	Hour	Summary of Events and Information	Remarks and references to Appendices
MARCHE	11th		Parades under Company arrangements from 0930 hours	
"	12th		Church parades for all denominations.	
"	13th		Battalion parade at 0900 hours.	
"	14th		Short route march under Company arrangements	
"	15th		Training under Company arrangements.	
"	16th		Training under Company arrangements	
"	17th		Company route march. Capt Forbes D.S.O. returned from U.K.	
"	18th		Company route march. Rugger match vs A.S.C.	
"	19th		Church parades 2/Lt Cawood on leave to U.K.	
"	20th		Company parades. Capt Roffe M.C. to 66th Division	
"	21st		Company route march. Col Jenkins from leave in U.K. resumes command of Battalion. Transport competition. Winners of 1st prizes Ptes Nortier, Crowe and Pattinson.	

D. D. & L., London, E.C. (10540) Wt W5300/P713 750,000 3/18 E 1886 Forms/C2118/16.

212

5/4

Army Form C. 2118.

WAR DIARY
or
~~INTELLIGENCE SUMMARY.~~
(Erase heading not required.)

Instructions regarding War Diaries and Intelligence Summaries are contained in F. S. Regs., Part II. and the Staff Manual respectively. Title pages will be prepared in manuscript.

Place	Date 1919 JAN	Hour	Summary of Events and Information	Remarks and references to Appendices
SEILLE	26th		A guard under Sgt Flannagan "C" Coy was supplied to R.T.O. ANDENNE & a guard under Sgt Butler "A" Coy to SCLAIGNEAUX.	
"	27th		Company arrangements. Lt Stanley from leave in U.K.	
"	28th		Lecture by M.O. on venereal to all ranks. Two officers of Gloucesters arrived to take over our billets and Lts Stanley and England proceeded to CINEY to take over the Gloucesters billets	
	29th		Company arrangements. Coys lectured on venereal.	
"	30th		Regiment marched to HAILLOT and billeted in HAILLOT & OHEY. Regiment inspected by Divisional General on line of march.	
HAILLOT	31st		Regiment marched to CINEY via main road arriving at CINEY at 1430 hours.	

[signature]
LIEUT. COLONEL,
COMMANDING 1st S.A. INFANTRY.

210

D. D. & L., London, E.C.
(10340) Wt W5300/P713 750,000 3/18 E 1888 Forms/C2118/16.

5/6

Instructions regarding War Diaries and Intelligence Summaries are contained in F. S. Regs., Part II. and the Staff Manual respectively. Title pages will be prepared in manuscript.

WAR DIARY
or
INTELLIGENCE SUMMARY.
(Erase heading not required.)

Army Form C. 2118.

1 S A Infy Bn
VOL 35

Place	Date 1919 FEB	Hour	Summary of Events and Information	Remarks and references to Appendices
CINEY	1st		Companies at the disposal of Company Commanders. The following Gloucester guards were relieved. – ASSESSE L/C Stickell "A" Coy and 3 men. SORINNE LA LONGUE Corp Mundy "D" and 3 men. 10 K stone NAMUR – MARCHE road L/C Holliday "C" Coy and 3 men. Commanding Officer inspected the billets of "C" & "A" companies. Capt Forbes and football team returned from Cologne. Weather – Dull and cold.	
"	2nd		Church parades cancelled owing to weather and a voluntary service held. Commanding Officer inspected billets of "B" and "D" Companies. 2/Lt Pickard returned from leave in U.K. The following daily duties commenced 1 NCO & 7 men to D.A.D.O.S. 9 am. 1 Sgt & 15 men to Town Major 9 am. Weather Dull, some snow fell during night.	

D. D. & L., London, E.C. (10340) Wt W5300/P713 750,000 3/18 E 2683 Forms/C2118/16.

5/7

Army Form C. 2118.

Instructions regarding War Diaries and Intelligence Summaries are contained in F. S. Regs., Part II. and the Staff Manual respectively. Title pages will be prepared in manuscript.

WAR DIARY
or
INTELLIGENCE SUMMARY.
(Erase heading not required.)

Place	1919 Date Feby	Hour	Summary of Events and Information	Remarks and references to Appendices
CINEY	3rd		All Companies bathed and were issued with clean clothes. Guard consisting of Sgt Kernan and 28 men reported to R.S.O. Ciney station. Capt Featherstone, Lts Falkner and Hogg with 40 O/R reported back from SEILLE demobilisation camp. Weather. Bright and very cold.	
"	4th		Company Inspection at 0930 hours followed by short route march. Weather:- Dull, some snow.	
"	5th		Commanding Officers parade ordered but cancelled owing to the cold weather, Company Inspections carried out. 2/Lt Cawood returned from leave in U.K. Weather Dull & cold	
"	6th		Companies at disposal of Company Commanders. From leave in U.K. 2/Lt Pillow. L/C Edwards & 3 men of "B" Coy to 53rd C.C.S. i/c of prisoner under close arrest. A platoon of "A" Coy under 2/Lt Hogg & a platoon of "B" Coy under 2/Lt Bentley sent to 68th Battery R.F.A. for duty. 18 O/R returned from 68th Battery R.F.A. One platoon of "B" Coy under 2/Lt Pickard reported to Camp Commandant NAMUR for guard duties. Weather:- Dull & a little snow. Very cold	

D. D. & L., London, E.C.
(10340) Wt W5300/P713 750,000 3/18 E 2688 Forms/C2118/16.

215

5/8

Army Form C. 2118.

WAR DIARY
or
~~INTELLIGENCE SUMMARY.~~
(Erase heading not required.)

Instructions regarding War Diaries and Intelligence Summaries are contained in F. S. Regs., Part II. and the Staff Manual respectively. Title pages will be prepared in manuscript.

Place	1919 Date Feb	Hour	Summary of Events and Information	Remarks and references to Appendices
CINEY	7th		Company inspection. Gen Tanner addressed a few men in the Regimental recreation room on demobilisation. Weather Bright + cold	
"	8th		Lorries take about 200 all ranks to MARCHE to see Rugby match against the New Zealanders. Eight officers and 200 O/R went to hear a lecture by Rev. Kennedy M.C. who however did not arrive to lecture. Lts Ryat & Falkner on leave to U.K. Weather bright + extremely cold.	
"	9th		Btn Church parade at 0945 hours. Col Jenkins D.S.O addressed the regiment informing them they were moving to HUY the following day. Weather bright + cold	
"	10th		The Battalion was ordered to march to HUY but these orders were cancelled and later orders were given to move at 0800 hours the following morning.	
"	11th		At 0800 hours the battalion moved to HUY by lorry and took over billets from the Kings Liverpools. Weather Very bright sunshine, snow on ground	

216

5/9

Army Form C. 2118.

Instructions regarding War Diaries and Intelligence Summaries are contained in F. S. Regs., Part II. and the Staff Manual respectively. Title pages will be prepared in manuscript.

WAR DIARY
or
~~INTELLIGENCE SUMMARY.~~
(Erase heading not required.)

Place	Date 1919 Feb	Hour	Summary of Events and Information	Remarks and references to Appendices
HUY	12th		Company Inspection and cleaning of equipment. The following officers reported from U.K. Lt Vincent, 2/Lts Jeffrey, Alderson, Smith D.C.M., M.M. Winch, & Nuttall. Dull.	
"	13th		The C.O inspected billets and addressed Companies on their behaviour at CINEY. The regiment stood by for inspection by Gen Botha. Weather dull, little rain.	
"	14th		The regiment inspected by Gen the Right Hon L. Botha in grounds of Chateau near river. Cheers & the war-cry were given for the General who addressed the regiment. Weather Dull.	
"	15th		A & C Coys Company Inspections. B & D Coys moved billets. Four guards on barges & a bomb dumps taken over from Manchesters & Connaughts. Weather. little rain & sleet.	

D. D. & L., London, E.C. Wt W5300/P713 750,000 3/18 E 2688 Forms/C2118/16.

5/10

Army Form C. 2118.

WAR DIARY
or
~~INTELLIGENCE SUMMARY.~~
(Erase heading not required.)

Instructions regarding War Diaries and Intelligence Summaries are contained in F. S. Regs., Part II. and the Staff Manual respectively. Title pages will be prepared in manuscript.

Place	Date 1919 Feb	Hour	Summary of Events and Information	Remarks and references to Appendices
HUY	16th		Church Parades for all denominations. S. A. Brigade H.Q.'s arrived in HUY. Weather – Fine.	
"	17th		Company Inspection & short route march. A court of enquiry assembled under Major McEwen to enquire into complaints re rations and comforts. Weather – Dull.	
"	18th		The B.G.C. inspected billets of the regiment at 10.00 hours. Platoon & Coy inspections at 09.30 hours followed by short route march. Weather:- dull.	
"	19th		Coy & Platoon inspections followed by arms drill. The Commanding Officer saw all officers & N.C.O.'s and addressed them in connection with the disturbances at CINEY. A circular was received from the Bdge H.Q.'s to be read to the men on three successive parades in conjunction with that portion of the Army Act dealing with mutiny. Weather – Wet.	

(10340) Wt W5300/P713 750,000 3/18 E 2688 Forms/C2118/16. D. D. & L., London, E.C.

218

5/11

Army Form C. 2118.

Instructions regarding War Diaries and Intelligence Summaries are contained in F. S. Regs., Part II. and the Staff Manual respectively. Title pages will be prepared in manuscript.

WAR DIARY
or
~~INTELLIGENCE SUMMARY.~~

(Erase heading not required.)

Place	Date 1919 Feb	Hour	Summary of Events and Information	Remarks and references to Appendices
HUY	20th		Coy inspection followed by one hours route march. Weather:- Dull a little rain.	
"	21st		Coy inspection and arms drill. Pt C Macdonald - Dunlop reported from base. 2/Lt England to U.K. on leave Capt Gray MC transfers to H.Q.s & Capt Tyers assumes command of "A" Coy from this date. Fine.	
"	22nd		Coy inspection followed by short route march. Capt Gray proceeded to Bonn to arrange a rest house for parties of men on leave to Germany. A party of 2 off & 20 O/R to Liege on short leave. This party leave every alternate day. Weather Wet	
"	23rd		Church parades for all denominations. Weather dull	
"	24th		Coy inspections at 0930 hours & baths. A party of 2 off & 20 O/R proceeded on short leave to Bonn. This party leaves every three days. To U.K. Lt Dunlop, draft conducting. Concert party at Y.M.C.A. Weather Wet.	

D.D. & L., London, E.C. (10340) Wt W5300/P713 750,000 3/18 E 2688 Forms/C2118/16.

5/12

Army Form C. 2118.

WAR DIARY
or
~~INTELLIGENCE SUMMARY.~~
(Erase heading not required.)

Instructions regarding War Diaries and Intelligence Summaries are contained in F. S. Regs., Part II. and the Staff Manual respectively. Title pages will be prepared in manuscript.

Place	1919 Date Feb	Hour	Summary of Events and Information	Remarks and references to Appendices
HUY	25th		0900 hours platoon & Coy inspection. Weather - wet.	
"	26th		0900 hours platoon & Coy inspection followed by short route march. Weather - Wet.	
"	27th		Companies will bathe & carry out Coy inspection. The band proceeded on short leave to BRUSSELLS Weather. Fine	
"	28th		Coy & Platoon inspection followed by arms drill & P.T. The first party of men under the quota scheme proceeded to England, 33 O/R. Weather - Wet.	

D. D. & L., London, E.C.
(10340) Wt W5300/P713 750,000 3/18 E 2688 Forms/C2118/16.

Instructions regarding War Diaries and Intelligence Summaries are contained in F. S. Regs., Part II. and the Staff Manual respectively. Title pages will be prepared in manuscript.

WAR DIARY
or
~~INTELLIGENCE SUMMARY.~~
(Erase heading not required.)

1 S A Infy Bn
VOL 35

Army Form C. 2118.

Place	Date 1919 FEB	Hour	Summary of Events and Information	Remarks and references to Appendices
CINEY	1st		Companies at the disposal of Company Commanders. The following Gloucester guards were relieved:- ASSESSE L/C Stickell "A" Coy and 3 men. SORINNE LA LONGUE Corp Mundy "D" and 3 men. 10 K stone NAMUR – MARCHE road L/C Holliday "C" Coy and 3 men. Commanding Officer inspected the billets of "C" & "A" companies. Capt Forbes and football team returned from Cologne. Weather:- Dull and cold.	
	2nd		Church parades cancelled owing to weather and a voluntary service held. Commanding Officer inspected billets of "B" and "D" Companies. 2/Lt Pickard returned from leave in U.K. The following daily duties commenced 1 N.C.O. & 7 men to D.A.D.O.S. 9 a.m. 1 Sgt & 15 men to Town Major 9 a.m. Weather. Dull, some snow fell during night.	

Army Form C. 2118.

Instructions regarding War Diaries and Intelligence Summaries are contained in F. S. Regs., Part II. and the Staff Manual respectively. Title pages will be prepared in manuscript.

WAR DIARY
or
~~INTELLIGENCE SUMMARY.~~
(Erase heading not required.)

Place	1919 Date Feb	Hour	Summary of Events and Information	Remarks and references to Appendices
CINEY	7th		Company inspection. Gen Tanner addressed a few men in the Regimental recreation room on demobilisation. Weather Bright & cold	
"	8th		Lorries take about 200 all ranks to MARCHE to see Rugby match against the New Zealanders. Eight officers and 200 O/R went to hear a lecture by Rev. Kennedy MC who however did not arrive to lecture. Lts Rigal & Falkiner on leave to U.K. Weather bright & extremely cold.	
"	9th		Btn Church parade at 0945 hours. Col Jenkins D.S.O. addressed the regiment informing them they were moving to HUY the following day. Weather bright & cold.	
"	10th		The Battalion was ordered to march to HUY but these orders were cancelled and later orders were given to move at 0800 hours the following morning.	
"	11th		At 0800 hours the battalion moved to HUY by lorry and took over billets from the Kings Liverpools. Weather Very bright sunshine, snow on ground	

D. D. & L., London, E.C. (10240) Wt W5300/P713 750,000 1/18 E 1688 Forms/C2118/16.

5/9

Army Form C. 2118.

WAR DIARY
or
~~INTELLIGENCE SUMMARY.~~
(Erase heading not required.)

Instructions regarding War Diaries and Intelligence Summaries are contained in F. S. Regs., Part II. and the Staff Manual respectively. Title pages will be prepared in manuscript.

Place	Date 1919 Feb	Hour	Summary of Events and Information	Remarks and references to Appendices
HUY	12th		Company Inspection and cleaning of equipment. The following officers reported from U.K. Lt Vincent, 2/Lts Jeffreys, Alderson, Smith D.C.M. M.M. Winch, & Nuttall. Dull.	
"	13th		The C.O inspected billets and addressed Companies on their behaviour at CINEY. The regiment stood by for inspection by Gen Botha. Weather dull, little rain.	
"	14th		The regiment inspected by Gen the Right Hon L. Botha in grounds of Chateau near river. Cheers & the war-cry were given for the General who addressed the regiment. Weather Dull.	
"	15th		A & C Coys Company Inspections. B & D Coys moved billets. Four guards on barges & a bomb dumps taken over from Manchesters & Connaughts. Weather. little rain & sleet.	

D. D. & L., London, E.C.
(10340) Wt W5300/P713 750,000 3/18 E 2688 Forms/C2118/16.

Army Form C. 2118.

Instructions regarding War Diaries and Intelligence Summaries are contained in F. S. Regs., Part II. and the Staff Manual respectively. Title pages will be prepared in manuscript.

WAR DIARY
or
~~INTELLIGENCE SUMMARY.~~
(Erase heading not required.)

Place	Date 1919 Feb	Hour	Summary of Events and Information	Remarks and references to Appendices
HUY	16th		Church Parades for all denominations. S. A. Brigade H.Q.'s arrived in HUY. Weather:- Fine.	
"	17th		Company Inspection & short route march. A court of enquiry assembled under Major McEwen to enquire into complaints re rations and comforts. Weather:- Dull.	
"	18th		The B.G.C. inspected billets of the regiment at 10.00 hours. Platoon & Coy inspections at 0930 hours followed by short route march. Weather:- dull.	
"	19th		Coy & Platoon inspections followed by arms drill. The Commanding Officer saw all officers & N.C.O.'s and addressed them in connection with the disturbances at CINEY. A circular was received from the Bdge H.Q.'s to be read to the men on three successive parades in conjunction with that portion of the Army Act dealing with mutiny. Weather:- Wet.	

D. D. & L., London, E.C. (20340) Wt W5300/P713 750,000 3/18 Forms/C2118/16.

Instructions regarding War Diaries and Intelligence Summaries are contained in F. S. Regs., Part II. and the Staff Manual respectively. Title pages will be prepared in manuscript.

WAR DIARY
or
~~INTELLIGENCE SUMMARY.~~
(Erase heading not required.)

Army Form C. 2118.

Place	1919 Date Feb	Hour	Summary of Events and Information	Remarks and references to Appendices
HUY	20th		Coy inspection followed by one hours route march. Weather:- Dull a little rain.	
"	21st		Coy inspection and arms drill. Pt C Macdonald - Dunlop reported from base. 2/Lt England to U.K. on leave. Capt Gray M.C. transfers to H.Q. & Capt Tyers assumes command of "A" Coy from this date. Fine.	
"	22nd		Coy inspection followed by short route march. Capt Gray proceeded to Bonn to arrange a rest house for parties of men on leave to Germany. A party of 2 off & 20 O/R to Liege on short leave. This party leave every alternate day. Weather Wet.	
"	23rd		Church parades for all denominations. Weather dull	
"	24th		Coy inspections at 0930 hours & baths. A party of 2 off & 20 O/R proceeded on short leave to Bonn. This party leaves every three days. To U.K. Lt Dunlop, draft conducting. Concert party at Y.M.C.A. Weather Wet.	222

Army Form C. 2118.

Instructions regarding War Diaries and Intelligence Summaries are contained in F. S. Regs., Part II. and the Staff Manual respectively. Title pages will be prepared in manuscript.

WAR DIARY

or

~~INTELLIGENCE SUMMARY.~~

(*Erase heading not required.*)

Place	1919 Date Feb	Hour	Summary of Events and Information	Remarks and references to Appendices
HUY	25th		0900 hours platoon & Coy inspection. Weather:- wet.	
"	26th		0900 hours platoon & Coy inspection followed by short route march. Weather:- Wet.	
"	27th		Companies will bathe & carry out Coy inspection. The band proceeded on short leave to BRUSSELLS. Weather. Fine	
"	28th		Coy & Platoon inspection followed by arms drill & P.T. The first party of men under the quota scheme proceeded to England, 33 O/R. Weather:- Wet.	

221

D. D. & L., London, E.C.
(10540) Wt W5300/P713 750,000 3/18 E 1688 Forms/C2118/16.

Army Form C. 2118.

Instructions regarding War Diaries and Intelligence Summaries are contained in F. S. Regs., Part II. and the Staff Manual respectively. Title pages will be prepared in manuscript.

WAR DIARY
or
INTELLIGENCE SUMMARY.
(Erase heading not required.)

Place	1919 Date Feby	Hour	Summary of Events and Information	Remarks and references to Appendices
CINEY	3rd		All Companies bathed and were issued with clean clothes. Guard consisting of Sgt Karsen and 28 men reported to R.S.O. Ciney station. Capt Featherstone, Lts Falkner and Hogg with 40 O/R reported back from SEILLE demobilisation camp. Weather. Bright and very cold.	
"	4th		Company Inspection at 0930 hours followed by short route march. Weather:- Dull, some snow.	
"	5th		Commanding Officers parade ordered but cancelled owing to the cold weather, Company Inspections carried out. 2/Lt Cawood returned from leave in U.K. Weather. Dull & cold.	
"	6th		Companies at disposal of Company Commanders. From leave in U.K. 2/Lt Pillow. L/C Edwards & 3 men of "B" Coy to 53rd C.C.S. i/c of prisoner under close arrest. A platoon of "A" Coy under 2/Lt Hogg & a platoon of "B" Coy under 2/Lt Bentley sent to 68th Battery R.F.A. for duty. 18 O/R returned from 68th Battery R.F.A. One platoon of "B" Coy under 2/Lt Pickard reported to Camp Commandant NAMUR for guard duties. Weather:- Dull & a little snow. Very cold	

D. D. & L., London, E.C. (10340) Wt W5300/P713 750,000 3/18 E 1888 Forms/C2118/16.

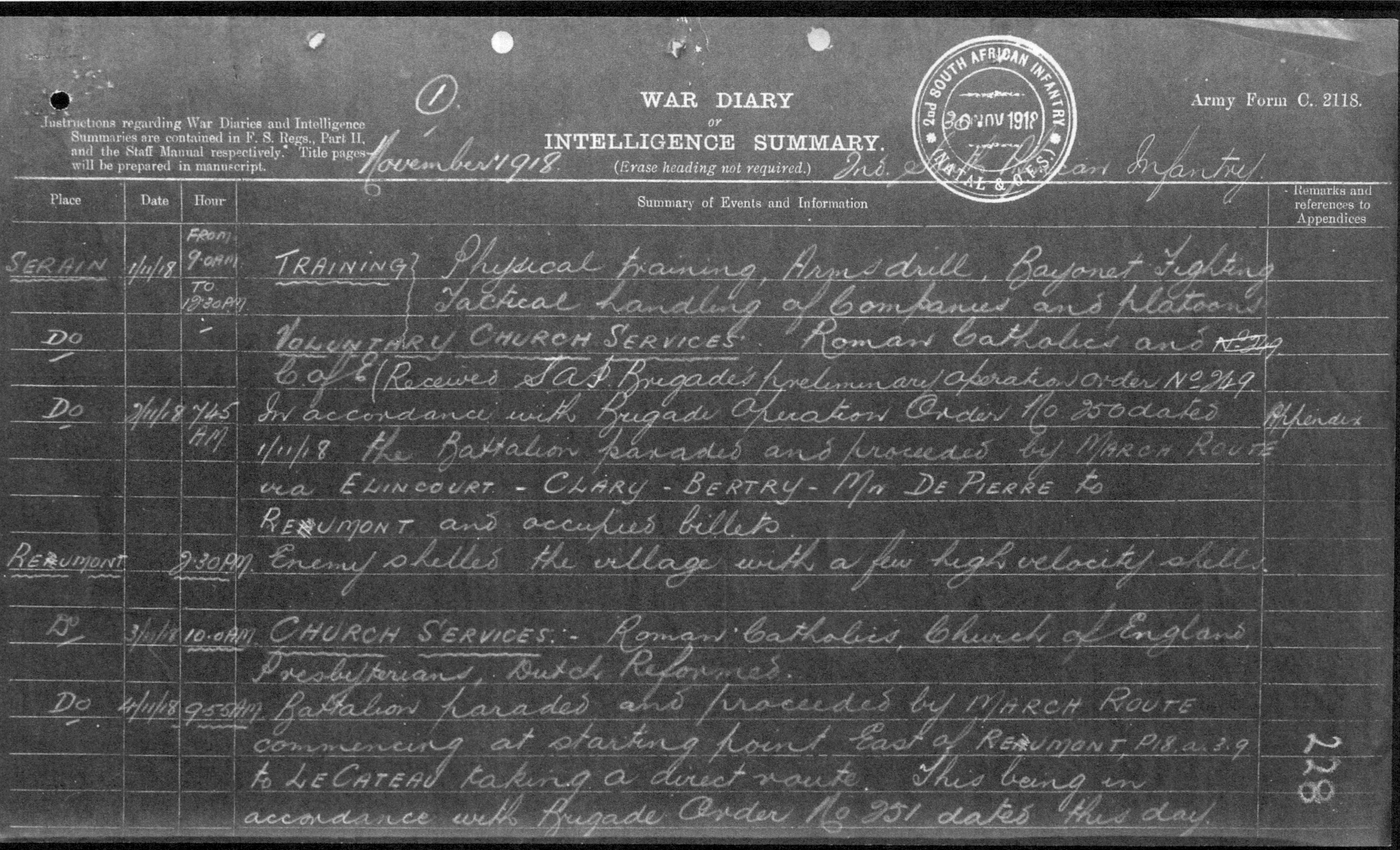

Instructions regarding War Diaries and Intelligence Summaries are contained in F. S. Regs., Part II, and the Staff Manual respectively. Title pages will be prepared in manuscript.

(1)

WAR DIARY
or
INTELLIGENCE SUMMARY.
(Erase heading not required.)

Army Form C. 2118.

November 1918 — 2nd South African Infantry

Place	Date	Hour	Summary of Events and Information	Remarks and references to Appendices
SERAIN	1/11/18	FROM 9-0AM TO 12-30PM	TRAINING } Physical training, Arms drill, Bayonet Fighting, Tactical handling of Companies and platoons	
DO		–	VOLUNTARY CHURCH SERVICES. Roman Catholics and ~~No 249~~ C of E (Received S A I Brigade's preliminary Operation Order No 249	
DO	2/11/18	7.45 AM	In accordance with Brigade Operation Order No 250 dated 1/11/18 the Battalion paraded and proceeded by MARCH ROUTE via ELINCOURT - CLARY - BERTRY - Mn DE PIERRE to REUMONT and occupied billets.	Appendix
REUMONT		2.30PM	Enemy shelled the village with a few high velocity shells.	
Do	3/11/18	10.0AM	CHURCH SERVICES. - Roman Catholics, Church of England, Presbyterians, Dutch Reformed.	
DO	4/11/18	9.55AM	Battalion paraded and proceeded by MARCH ROUTE commencing at starting point East of REUMONT, P18.a.3.9 to LE CATEAU taking a direct route. This being in accordance with Brigade Order No 251 dated this day.	

228

(9)

Instructions regarding War Diaries and Intelligence Summaries are contained in F. S. Regs., Part II. and the Staff Manual respectively. Title pages will be prepared in manuscript.

WAR DIARY
or
INTELLIGENCE SUMMARY.
(Erase heading not required.)

2nd Regiment S A Infantry

Army Form C. 2118.

Place	Date	Hour	Summary of Events and Information	Remarks and references to Appendices
LE CATEAU	5/11/18	9.0 AM	Billeting party consisting of one N.C.O. from each Coy and of one from Headquarters proceeded under 2nd Lieut R. Haskis to POMMERUIL to secure billets for the Battalion. Brigade Order No 955 received.	
Do	5/11/18	9.45 AM	The Battalion less "B" TEAMS proceeded by MARCH ROUTE to POMMERUIL in the following order. Headquarters C, D, A "B", Companies and transport. Route - "DIRECT."	
			"B" TEAMS remained at LE CATEAU under Captain Jacobs	
			WEATHER:- Very wet.	

STRENGTH OF BATTALION	OFFS	ORS
With Battalion	18	395
Field Ambulance	1	9
On Courses	1	9
On Leave	1	30
Detached Duties		22
TOTAL STRENGTH	21	465

229

Instructions regarding War Diaries and Intelligence Summaries are contained in F. S. Regs., Part II. and the Staff Manual respectively. Title pages will be prepared in manuscript.

3/

WAR DIARY
or
INTELLIGENCE SUMMARY.
(Erase heading not required.)

2nd Regiment S A Infantry

Army Form C. 2118.

Place	Date	Hour	Summary of Events and Information	Remarks and references to Appendices
POMMERUIL ~~[illegible]~~	5/11/18		The Brigade at this time was in Divisional Reserve and was constantly under an hours notice to move and take up a position in the forward area.	
POMMERUIL				
	DO	2.40PM	Wire from Brigade BS.162 informing that Battalion will not be required to move during the night, received.	
DO	6/11/18	7.0AM	Warning Order to be prepared to move issued through signals, received.	
			WEATHER - Raining - Battalion under notice to move.	
DO		2.53PM	Wire from Brigade, (BM/166) reading "The S A Brigade will prepare to move immediately," received	
DO		3.30PM	Brigade Operation Order No 256 detailing move to LANDRECIES, received.	
DO		4PM	In accordance with B.O.O. No 256 the Battalion proceeded by MARCH ROUTE direct to LANDRECIES.	
LANDRECIES		7PM	Arrived at LANDRECIES and occupied billets East of CANAL - SAMBRE.	
LANDRECIES				230

(A9175) Wt W2358/P560 600,000 12/7 D. D. & L. Sch 52a. Forms/C2118/15

Page Three.

X. COMMUNICATIONS.

(a). The Divisional line of communication will be the road [illegible] A.17.c.5.4 - [illegible] - [illegible] FARM - LA [illegible] - LA FOLIE FARM.

(b). Runners posts will be established at suitable intervals along this line.

(c). Companies will keep touch throughout by visual with Battalion Headquarters.

(d). No cable will be laid till objective (RED LINE) is gained.

XI. LIAISON.

Close Liason must be kept with troops on either flank by means of interlocked posts.

XII. AMMUNITION SUPPLY.

Small dumps of S.A.A. and No. 36 Grenades will be established at Battalion Headquarters by Zero.

XIII. RATIONS.

Each man will carry rations for 2 day in addition to iron rations.

XIV. WATER.

Each Company will arrange to carry four petrol tins of water forward during the assault.

Further tins will be at Battalion Headquarters by Zero.

XV. PRISONERS OF WAR.

All prisoners will be handed over to "D" Company to escort to Battalion Headquarters. The same escort will proceed on with the prisoners from Battalion Headquarters to Brigade Headquarters in MUSHROOM QUARRY where they will be handed over and receipt obtained. Escorts then return to their Companies via Battalion Headquarters.

XVI. INTELLIGENCE.

66th Division Instruction No. 1. "Intelligence Arrangements during Battle" have already been issued to Companies and will be adhered to.

XVII. AIRCRAFT.

Instruction No. 2. issued by 66th Division have already been distributed down to Platoon Commanders.

XVIII. HEADQUARTERS.

(a). Brigade Headquarters will be in MUSHROOM QUARRY.

(b). Battalion Headquarters will be notified later.

Each Company will leave a Runner at Battalion Headquarters at Zero. This runner will return to Company later and notify Company Commanders of position of Battalion Headquarters after Zero.

XIX. REPORTS.

It is of the utmost importance that information is passed back to Battalion Headquarters with the greatest speed.

The visual signal for "objective gained" will be [illegible] followed by "B" Company, "A" Company, etc, as the case may be.

4

Instructions regarding War Diaries and Intelligence Summaries are contained in F. S. Regs., Part II. and the Staff Manual respectively. Title pages will be prepared in manuscript.

WAR DIARY
or
INTELLIGENCE SUMMARY.
(Erase heading not required.) 2nd Regiment S.A. Infantry

Army Form C. 2118.

Place	Date	Hour	Summary of Events and Information	Remarks and references to Appendices
LANDRECIES	7/11/18	2-15 PM	Left Landrecies at short notice and proceeded by MARCH ROUTE to BASSE NOYELLES	
BASSE NOYELLES		5 PM	Battalion arrived at BASSE NOYELLES and occupied billets	
			Extracts from 66th Division Order No. 118 re situation, Intention, Objectives of the 66th and 25th Division shown as an appendix.	
BASSE NOYELLES	8/11/18	8-0 AM	Moved by MARCH ROUTE to DOMPIERRE and billeted for the remainder of the day and night	
DOMPIERRE	9/11/18		DIVISION takes over forward ~~area~~ Corps area with South African Infantry Brigade in support this day	
DO		12.55 PM	In accordance with 1st S.A.I. Brigade's Operation Order No. 257, the Battalion less TRANSPORT proceeded by MARCH ROUTE, commencing at Road Junction in J.7.a.5.9 to BEUGNIES. Route:- Road Junction in J.9.a.2.5 - LA TUILERIE thence 2nd Class Road J.6.c.4.5	

(A9175) Wt W2355/P360 600,000 11/7 D. D. & L. Sch 52a. Forms/C2118/15

Instructions regarding War Diaries and Intelligence Summaries are contained in F. S. Regs., Part II. and the Staff Manual respectively. Title pages will be prepared in manuscript.

5

WAR DIARY
or
INTELLIGENCE SUMMARY.
(Erase heading not required.) 2nd Regiment S A Infantry

Army Form C. 2118.

Place	Date	Hour	Summary of Events and Information	Remarks and references to Appendices
DOMPIERRE			thence from LA CENSE - POTELLE FARM - FARM LA JONQUIERRE to BEUGNIES	
BEUGNIES	9/11/18	6·30pm	Upon arrival at BEUGNIES verbal order was received from Staff Captain of S A I Brigade to the effect that British Cavalry were occupying Solre le Chateau and that the 2nd Regiment S A I was to continue its march and occupy this Town.	
SOLRE CHATEAU 9/11/18		8 0 pm	Battalion arrived at SOLRE LE CHATEAU and occupied billets. The march was a tiring one owing to round about route taken and halts made; caused by the enemys destruction of bridges and roads with the assistance of mines. In some areas the roads were almost impassable by the TRANSPORT and on two or three occasions on this route the transport got stuck, arriving at SOLRE LE CHATEAU at 3·0 AM. on the 10/11/18. The Enemy reported to be retiring rapidly and destroying	

233

Instructions regarding War Diaries and Intelligence Summaries are contained in F. S. Regs., Part II. and the Staff Manual respectively. Title pages will be prepared in manuscript.

6

Army Form C. 2118.

WAR DIARY
or
INTELLIGENCE SUMMARY. 2nd Regiment S.A.I.
(Erase heading not required.)

Place	Date	Hour	Summary of Events and Information	Remarks and references to Appendices
			communications as he withdraws	
SOLRE CHATEAU	10/11/18	6 AM	Orders received to the effect that the South African	
			Brigade will form part of the MOBILE COLUMN. The	
Do.		-	2nd Regiment to march with the main body.	
			Intention: The S. A. Brigade (less 4th S.A.I. which will	
"			remain at SOLRE LE CHATEAU under Divisional Orders will	
			move on BEAUMONT with the object of crossing the	
			river and securing itself in BEAUMONT for the night of	
			10/11th November. The advance of the column to be covered by	
			mounted troops comprising Scots Greys, XII Lancers, XXth	
			Hussars	
Do		7 AM	Battalion less transport proceeded by MARCH ROUTE	
		-	along main road in rear of the 1st S.A.I. who were	
			acting as advance guard	
		10.0 AM	The Enemy is reported to be resisting stubbornly and very	
		-	little progress being made by the Bde advance guard	

234

Instructions regarding War Diaries and Intelligence Summaries are contained in F. S. Regs., Part II, and the Staff Manual respectively. Title pages will be prepared in manuscript.

7/

WAR DIARY
or
INTELLIGENCE SUMMARY.
(Erase heading not required.) 2nd Regiment S A Infantry

Army Form C. 2118.

Place	Date	Hour	Summary of Events and Information	Remarks and references to Appendices
POSITIONS WEST OF HESTRUDE	10/11/18		Our troops hold line roughly high ground at point 140, immediately west of VIVIERIAUX. The centre	
	10/11/18		through village of GRANDIEU. On the left they were checked on the crest of the high ground immediately	
DO			North of A. on Grandieu.	
		DUSK	"C" Coy plus one platoon of "A" Coy moved forward to	
DO			strengthen the positions held by the 1st S.A.I. on the flanks of the village.	
DO			"B" "D" Headquarters and the remainder of "A" Coy dug in on the ground already occupied.	
	10/11th November 1918		Enemy shelled our positions pretty heavily throughout the night, particularly Battalion Headquarters which was situated in a house on the main road. A number of casualties occurred whilst in these positions.	
			WEATHER :- Cold and wet.	
DO	10/11/18	11-0AM	Hostilities cease at 11.0 AM.	

(39175) Wt W2358/P360 600,000 12/17 D. D. & L. Sch. 52a. Forms/C2118/15

8

Army Form C. 2118.

Instructions regarding War Diaries and Intelligence Summaries are contained in F. S. Regs., Part II, and the Staff Manual respectively. Title pages will be prepared in manuscript.

WAR DIARY
or
INTELLIGENCE SUMMARY.
(Erase heading not required.) 2nd Regt. S.A. Infantry.

Place	Date	Hour	Summary of Events and Information	Remarks and references to Appendices
POSITIONS WEST OF HESTRUDE	11/11/18	4.0 pm	The Battalion moved off in accordance with Operation Order No. 99 of to-days date and occupied billets in HESTRUDE	
HESTRUDE		6.0 PM	DRAFT :- Major C R Heenan DSO, Lieutenant Macfarlane MC 2nd Lieut. Willard, 2nd Lieut. Mills and 279 Other Ranks joined Unit from England.	
DO		8.30pm	South African Brigade MOBILE ORDER No. 3 detailing relief of the 1st S.A.I. in OUT POST positions received.	
DO	12/11/18	3.15pm	In accordance with Mobile Order No. 3 dated 11/11/18, the Battalion proceeded by MARCH ROUTE and occupied OUT POST positions East of GRANDIEU and accordingly relieved the 1st S.A.I. (S.A.I. Brigades Mobile Order No. 4 received.	
GRANDIEU				
DO	12/11/18		Major C R Heenan DSO having arrived from England assumes command of the Regiment as from to-day	
DO	13/11/18		Companies less those on duty occupying out post positions, undergoing training.	236

(A9175) Wt W2358/P360 600,000 11/7 D. D. & L. Sch. 52a. Forms/C2118/13

Instructions regarding War Diaries and Intelligence Summaries are contained in F. S. Regs., Part II. and the Staff Manual respectively. Title pages will be prepared in manuscript.

9

WAR DIARY
or
INTELLIGENCE SUMMARY.
(Erase heading not required.) 2nd Regiment S.A. Infantry

Army Form C. 2118.

Place	Date	Hour	Summary of Events and Information	Remarks and references to Appendices
GRANDIEU	14/11/18	-	Companies less those occupying OUT POST positions undergoing training.	
DO			Guard of Honour comprising 3 Officers and 50 Other Ranks proceeded to Solre Chateau in honour of the 4th ARMY COMMANDER.	
			Major L. F. Sprenger DSO MC proceeded to England on leave	
DO	15/11/18		Same as for Routine of the 13th inst.	
			WEATHER Frosty. 2nd Lieut. S H H Lowe rejoined from Hospital	
DO	16/11/18		Relieved by the 1st Cameron Highlanders of the 1st	
	12 NOON		DIVISION the Battalion in accordance with Brigade Operation Order No 31 proceeded by MARCH ROUTE to SIVRY	
SIVRY			On arrival at SIVRY billets were occupied. (Transferred from XIII Corps to 9th Corps)	
			DRAFT. 2/Lieut F. G. Norris and 50 Other Ranks from England joined Unit. 2nd Lieut Mills proceeded to Hospital	
DO	17/11/18		Church Parades	
			2nd Lieut C. H. Fraser rejoined from Course and posted to "C" Coy	237

(A9175) W: W2358/P360 600,000 12/17 D. D. & L. Sch. 52a. Forms/C2118/15

Instructions regarding War Diaries and Intelligence Summaries are contained in F. S. Regs., Part II. and the Staff Manual respectively. Title pages will be prepared in manuscript.

10

WAR DIARY
or
INTELLIGENCE SUMMARY.
(Erase heading not required.)

2nd Regiment S.A. Infantry

Army Form C. 2118.

Place	Date	Hour	Summary of Events and Information	Remarks and references to Appendices
SIVRY	18/11/18	-	GENERAL Cleaning up in the morning. Commanding Officers parade in the afternoon.	
			WEATHER - Freezing	
SIVRY	18/19/11/18	MIDNIGHT	Battalion Operation Order No. 39 detailing move of the Battalion to Villers Deux Eglises on the 19th issued to companies.	
Do	19/11/18	9.35 AM -	In accordance with Operation Order No. 39 dated 18/11/18 the Battalion paraded on road immediately WEST of Cross Roads	
Do	Do	10.35 AM	Head of BATTALION COLUMN passed starting point (Cross roads due North of S in VIEUX SART and proceeded by MARCH ROUTE via SENZEILLE to VILLIERS.	
VILLERS DEUX EGLISES. Do		6.30 PM	Battalion arrived at VILLIERS DEUX EGLISES and billeted	
Do	20/11/18	-	Cleaning up in the morning for G.O.C. inspection	
		2.30 PM	The G.O.C. S.A. Brigade inspected the Battalion.	
Do			FATIGUES 1 Officer and 50 men on Road fatigue.	238

(A9175) Wt W2358/P760 600,000 11/17 D. D. & L. Sch 52a. Forms/C2118/15

Instructions regarding War Diaries and Intelligence Summaries are contained in F. S. Regs., Part II. and the Staff Manual respectively. Title pages will be prepared in manuscript.

11

WAR DIARY
or
INTELLIGENCE SUMMARY.
(Erase heading not required.) 2nd Regiment S. A. Infantry

Army Form C. 2118.

Place	Date	Hour	Summary of Events and Information	Remarks and references to Appendices
VILLERS DEUX EGLISES.	21/11/18	From 9.30 to 12.15	TRAINING { Cleaning up and inspection by Company Officers. Handling of arms, Company Drill. Physical training and bayonet fighting	
		14.00 to 16.00	Further training under Company arrangements.	
Do.	22/11/18		Training { Cleaning up and inspection by Company Officers. Handling of arms, Company Drill. Physical training & bayonet fighting	
		14.00 to 16.00	Recreational training	
Do.	22/11/18		STRENGTH - INCREASE - OFFICERS.	
			LIEUT. C. O. CONNOCK M.C. having joined Unit from Depot is posted to "B" Company.	
Do.	23/11/18	9.30	Commanding Officer inspects Battalion.	
"	"	10.00 to 12.30	TRAINING { Handling of Arms. Close order drill. Physical Training & Bayonet fighting	
		14.00 to 16.00	Recreational	
"	23/11/18.		SOUTH AFRICAN BRIGADE LESS 2nd REGt. moved to new area.	239

(A9175) Wt W2358/P562 600,000 12/17 D. D. & L. Sch. 87a. Forms/C2118/12.

Instructions regarding War Diaries and Intelligence Summaries are contained in F. S. Regs., Part II, and the Staff Manual respectively. Title pages will be prepared in manuscript.

12.

WAR DIARY
or
INTELLIGENCE SUMMARY.
(Erase heading not required.) 2nd Regiment S A Infantry

Army Form C. 2118.

Place	Date	Hour	Summary of Events and Information	Remarks and references to Appendices
VILLERS DEUX EGLISES	24/11/18	4 AM.	Billeting party consisting of one N.C.O from each Coy & one from Headquarters proceeded under 2/Lt. W. J. Bowes to AGIMONT to secure billets for the Battalion.	
"	"		BRIGADE moved forward to new area in accordance with Order No. 265.	
"	"	7.30.	In accordance with Brigade Operation Order No. 265 dated 22/11/18 the Battalion paraded and proceeded to starting point :- x Roads S of O in VODECEE.	
"	"	9.15.	The Battalion proceeded by MARCH ROUTE via VILLERS DE CAMBON - ROMEDENNE - VODELEE to AGIMONT and occupied billets 14.30 hrs.	
			WEATHER Bright & freezing.	
			TRANSPORT LESS (the four company cookers, mess cart & two water carts which accompanied Battalion) was brigaded and moved along the main PHILIPPEVILLE - GIVET road.	

240

(A9175) Wt W2358/P560 600,000 12/17 D. D. & L. Sch 52a. Forms/C2118/15

Instructions regarding War Diaries and Intelligence Summaries are contained in F. S. Regs., Part II. and the Staff Manual respectively. Title pages will be prepared in manuscript.

WAR DIARY or INTELLIGENCE SUMMARY.

(Erase heading not required.)

Army Form C. 2118.

13. 2nd Regiment S A Inf

Place	Date	Hour	Summary of Events and Information	Remarks and references to Appendices
AGIMONT.	24/11/18	15.00	On arrival at this village, which was gaily bedecked with flags, the Battalion was heartily welcomed by the inhabitants. The School Master, speaking in the name of the Mayor, read an address to the Battalion. At the conclusion of the address a boquet was presented to the Commanding Officer. The Padre, Capt P J Walshe MC, speaking for the C.O. gave a very suitable reply. In conclusion the C.O. called upon the Battalion to give – "Three Hearty Cheers"	
"	25/11/18		B.O/542. 1 Officer + 25 O R will work 4 hrs daily on road between Soulme + Agimont	
"	"	8-30	TRAINING. Cleaning up parade under supervision of Officers + inspection under Company arrangements.	
			Brigade Order BM/999 24/11/18. Ceremonial training will be carried out 4 hrs daily.	
	26/11/18	8-30 to 12-30	TRAINING Inspection under Coy arrangements. C.O's inspection Close order drill Physical training 1100-1600 hrs Recreational	241

Instructions regarding War Diaries and Intelligence Summaries are contained in F. S. Regs., Part II. and the Staff Manual respectively. Title pages will be prepared in manuscript.

Army Form C. 2118.

WAR DIARY
or
INTELLIGENCE SUMMARY.
(Erase heading not required.)

14 — 2nd Regiment S A Infantry

Place	Date	Hour	Summary of Events and Information	Remarks and references to Appendices
AGIMONT	27/11/18	0900 to 12.30	TRAINING { Inspection under Company arrangements. Ceremonial Drill. Close order drill. Physical training and bayonet fighting.	
Do	"	14.00 to 16.00	Recreational training.	
		14.00	NCO's parade for instruction under R.S.M	
Do:	"		Appointments - Commissions	
			No 5540 C.Q.M.S. M KING, to be Temporary 2/LIEUT (on probation) 20-11-1918. & to be Acting Quartermaster.	
"	"		Censorship Regulations are to be relaxed - "Men may state where they have been and where they are."	
Do.	"	9.00 to 12.30	TRAINING. Inspection under Company Arrangements, Ceremonial Drill. Close Order Drill Physical training and bayonet fighting. Saluting drill & handling of arms.	
		14.00	NCO's parade for instruction under R.S.M.	242

(A9173) Wt W2353/P360 600,000 11/7 D. D. & L. Sch. 52a. Forms/C2118/15.

Instructions regarding War Diaries and Intelligence Summaries are contained in F. S. Regs., Part II, and the Staff Manual respectively. Title pages will be prepared in manuscript.

Army Form C. 2118.

WAR DIARY
or
INTELLIGENCE SUMMARY.
(Erase heading not required.)

15. 2nd Regiment S. A. Infantry

Place	Date	Hour	Summary of Events and Information	Remarks and references to Appendices
AGIMONT.	28/11/18.		HONOURS AND AWARDS. Under authority granted by His Majesty the King, the Field Marshal, Commanding-in-Chief, has awarded the following decorations.	
			D. S. O. :- T/Capt. L. M. JACOBS.	
			BAR to M. C. :- T/Lieut W. L. KING M.C. D.C.M.	
			M. C. :- T/Lieut. H. N. HEELEY	
			T2/Lieut C. W. ROBERTS.	
			T2/Lieut R. D. HEWAT.	
			T2/Lieut H. A. MARTIN.	
			D. C. M. :- No. 2471. Sgt. C. G. ALEXANDER.	
Do.	29/11/18.	09.00 to 12.30	TRAINING. Inspection under Company Arrangements, Ceremonial Drill, Close order drill, Saluting Drill & Handling of Arms. Physical Training & Bayonet Fighting.	
		14.00 to 15.00	NCO's parade under R S M.	
		14.00 16.00	Recreational Training	243

PUBLIC RECORD OFFICE

Reference WO 95/3147

DUE TO A FAULTY DEXTER MACHINE.

FOLIOS 244 DO NOT EXIST

Army Form C. 2118.

Instructions regarding War Diaries and Intelligence Summaries are contained in F. S. Regs., Part II, and the Staff Manual respectively. Title pages will be prepared in manuscript.

WAR DIARY
or
INTELLIGENCE SUMMARY.
(Erase heading not required.)

16. 2nd Regiment South African Inf.

Place	Date	Hour	Summary of Events and Information	Remarks and references to Appendices
AGIMONT	30/11/18	09·00 to 12 30	TRAINING Inspection under Company arrangements.	
			Close order drill. Physical Training & Bayonet	
			Fighting. Saluting Drill & Handling of Arms.	
			Battalion & Ceremonial Drill.	
"	"	14·00 15·00	N.C.Os parade under R.S.M.	
		14·00 16·00	Recreational Training.	

245

SECRET. 246

2ND. REGIMENT. SOUTH AFRICAN INFANTRY.

Reference: ORDER NO. 20.

SHEET 57. B. 1ST NOVEMBER 1918.
Addition Ia. 1/40000.

---

1. South African Brigade will move by march route tomorrow, 2nd November, 1918, to REUMONT.

2. Battalion will parade in road running past Orderly Room ready to move off at 07.45. ~~xxx~~ in following order:-

Headquarters.
"D" Company.
"A" Company.
"B" Company.
"C" Company.
Transport.

3. (a). Starting point at MILL in U.14.b. central
(b). DRESS - Full marching Order.
Mounted Officers with Sam Brown Belts.
(c). Head of column will pass starting point at 08.05.
(d). Interval of 100 yards will be observed between Companies and Transport.
(e). Transport will move at intervals of 25 yards between every 6 vehicles.

4. Marching out states and certificates to the effect that Billets have been left clean will be handed to Adjutant at starting point.
Captain Jacobs, with the Medical Officer, will inspect all billets after departure of Battalion.

5. A Billeting party of 1 N.C.O. per Company and 1 from Headquarters under 2/Lieut. Haskis will report at Battalion Headquarters at 07.30.

6. (a). Officers kits, Mess kits, and Regimental Canteen kit to be at R.Q.M. Stores by 07.15.

(b). All blankets to be rolled in bundles of 10 and stacked outside Company Orderly Rooms by 07.00.

7. Men excused marching will report with Medical Officer's certificate to Battalion Headquarters at 07.30.

8. Transport Officer will ensure that Water Carts are filled prior to departure.

9. ROUTE : Via ELINCOURT - CLARY - BERTHY - - Mn. DE PIERRE.

F. Walsh
Captain.
Acting Adjutant.
2nd. Regt. South African Infantry.

247

2ND. REGIMENT. SOUTH AFRICAN INFANTRY.

Reference:

ORDER NO. 21.

Sheet 57B.
Edition a
1/40000.

4TH. NOVEMBER 1918.

1. The South African Brigade will move by march Route to LE CATEAU today, 4.11.18.

2. The Battalion will parade in field just West of Battalion Headquarters ready to move off at 09.55. Hrs. in following order:-

Headquarters.
"A" Company.
"B" Company.
"C" Company.
"D" Company.
Transport.

3. (a). Starting point East of REUMONT P.18.a.3.2.
(b). DRESS- Full marching Order.
Mounted Officers with Sam Brown Belts.
(c). Head of Column will pass starting point at 10.00. Hrs.
(d). The usual interval between Companies and Transport will be observed.

4. Marching out states and certificates to the effect that Billets have been left clean, will be handed to Adjutant on Parade.

Capt. Jacobs and Medical Officer, will inspect all Billets after departure of Battalion.

5. A Billeting Party of 1. N.C.O. per Company and 1 from Headquarters under 2/Lieut. Haskis will report at Battalion Headquarters at 07.30. Hrs.

6. (a). Officers Kits, Mess Kits, and Regimental Canteen Kit to be at R.Q.M. Stores by 09.00.Hrs.
(b). All Blankets to be rolled in bundles of 10 and stacked at R.Q.M. Stores by 09.00.Hrs.

7. Men Excused Marching will report with Medical Officer's Certificate to Battalion Headquarters at 09.30. Hrs.

8. Transport Officer will ensure that Water Carts are filled before departure.

9. ROUTE : - : DIRECT.

Captain.
Acting Adjutant.
2nd. Regt. South African Infantry.

SECRET. 2ND REGIMENT. SOUTH AFRICAN INFANTRY. 248

Reference: ORDER NO. 22. 5TH NOVEMBER, 1918.

Sheet 57B.
Edition Ia.
1/40,000

I. The South African Brigade will move by march route to POMMERUIL today, 5.II.18.

2. The Battalion will parade in road running past Regimental ~~xxxxxx xxxxx~~ Quartermaster Stores ready to move off at 09.50.Hrs. in following order:-

Headquarters.
"C" Company.
"D" Company.
"A" Company.
"B" Company.
Transport.

3. (a). Starting point K.35.c.2.5.
(b). DRESS - Full marching order.
Mounted Officers with sam brown belts.
(c). Head of column will pass starting point I0.I4 Hrs.
(d). The usual interval between Companies and Transport will be observed.

4. Marching out states will be handed to Adjutant on parade.

5. A Billeting party of I N.C.O. per Company and I from Headquarters, under 2/Lieut.Haskis, will report at Battalion Headquarters at 09.00.Hrs. and will meet Staff Captain at Area Commandant,POMMERUIL, by I0.00.Hrs.

6. (a). Officers kits, Mess kits, Regimental Canteen kit, etc, to be at R.Q.M.Stores by 08.45.Hrs.
(b). All blankets to be rolled in bundles of I0 and stacked at R.Q.M.Stores by 08.45.Hrs.

7. "B" Teams will remain at LE CATEAU under Capt.Jacobs and will report at Battalion Headquarters in full Marching Order by 09.00.Hrs.
Nominal rolls from Companies will accompany them.

8. Transport Officer will ensure that Water Carts are filled before departure.

9. ROUTE :-: DIRECT.

[signature]

Captain.
Acting Adjutant.
2nd.Regt.South African Infantry.

SECRET.

249

2ND. REGIMENT. SOUTH AFRICAN INFANTRY.

Reference: ORDER NO. 23

6TH. NOVEMBER 1918.

Sheet 57B
Edition 1a. 1/40,000.
Sheet 57A
Edition 1. 1/40,000.

I. The South African Brigade will move by march route to LANDRECIES today, 6th November, 1918.

2. The Battalion will parade on road running past Battalion Headquarters just West of cross roads in village, ready to move off at (Time will be notified later) in the following order:-

Headquarters.
"D" Company.
"A" Company.
"B" Company.
"C" Company.
Transport.

3. (a). Starting point will be notified later.
(b). DRESS - Battle order.
(c). The usual interval between Companies and Transport will be observed.

4. Officers Kits, mess kits, coats and blankets will be dumped in accordance with instructions issued yesterday, 5.11.18.

5. Transport Officer will ensure that water carts are filled before departure.

6. ROUTE :-: To be notified later.

[signature]
Captain.
Acting Adjutant.
2nd. Regt. South African Infantry.

250

2ND. REGIMENT. SOUTH AFRICAN INFANTRY.

Reference.

Sheet 57 A.
Addition I. I/40,000.

ORDER NO. 24.

7TH.NOVEMBER.1918.

I. The South African Brigade will move by march route to BASSE NOYELLES today,7.II.I8.

2. The Battalion will parade on road running past Battalion Headquarters, ready to move off by I4.I0.Hrs. in the following order:-

Headquarters,
"A" Company.
"B" Company.
"C" Company.
"D" Company.
Transport.

3. (a). Starting point at road junction C.23.d.I.8.
(b). DRESS - Battle order.
(c). Usual interval between Companies and transport to be observed.
(d). Head of column will pass starting point at I4.20.Hrs.

4. Officers kits,mess kits and blankets to be stacked as arranged.

5. Transport Officer will ensure that water carts are filled before departure.

6. Marching out states to be handed to Adjutant on parade.

7. ROUTE:-: Via MAROILLES.

[signature]

Captain.
Acting Adjutant.
2nd.Regt.South African Infantry.

SECRET.

2ND. REGIMENT. SOUTH AFRICAN INFANTRY.

Reference:
Sheet 57.A.
Edition I. 1/40,000.

ORDER NO.25.

8TH NOVEMBER.1918.

I. The South African Brigade will move by march route to DOMPIERRE today, 8.II.18.

2. The Battalion will parade on road running past Battalion Headquarters, ready to move off by 08.00.Hrs. in the following order:-

Headquarters.
"B" Company.
"C" Company.
"D" Company.
"A" Company.
Transport.

3. (a). Starting point at road junction C.25.d.27.
(b). DRESS - Battle order.
(c). Usual interval between Companies and Transport to be observed.
(d). Head of column will pass starting point at 08.24.Hrs.

4. Officers kits, mess kits, and blankets to be stacked at R.Q.M.Stores by 07.30.Hrs.

5. Transport Officer will ensure that water carts are filled before departure.

6. Marching out states to be handed to Adjutant on parade.

7. ROUTE:-: DIRECT.

[signature]
Captain.
Acting Adjutant.
2nd.Regt.South African Infty.

SECRET.

252

2ND. REGIMENT. SOUTH AFRICAN INFANTRY.

Reference.

ORDER NO. 26.

9TH NOVEMBER, 1918.

Sheets 57A
Edition Ia. 1/40,000.
NAMUR 8. I.100,000.

I. The South African Brigade will move by march route to BUIGNIES today.

2. The Battalion will parade at Road Junction I.12.a.20.75. ready to move off at 12.55 Hrs. in the following order:-

Headquarters.
"C" Company.
"D" Company.
"A" Company.
"B" Company.

3. (a). Starting point at Road Junction at J.7.a.5.9.
(b). DRESS - Battle Order.
(c). Usual interval will be observed between Companies.
(d). Head of column will pass starting point at 13.30.Hrs.

4. Officers kits, mess kits, and blankets ,etc, to be stacked as arranged.

5. Marching out states to be handed to Adjutant on parade.

6. Transport will be Brigaded under Lieut.Johnson of 4th South African Infantry.

7. ROUTE :-: Road Junction, J.2.a.25. - LA TUILIERE, then 2nd class J.6.c.4.5. , then if road finished by engineers from LA CENSE - POTTELLE FARM - FARM LA JONQUIERE.

Captain.
Acting Adjutant.
2nd.Regt.South African Infantry.

SECRET.

2ND. REGIMENT. SOUTH AFRICAN INFANTRY.

Reference.

Map NAMUR 8.
I/100,000.

ORDER NO.27.

10TH. NOVEMBER.1918.

1. (a). The enemy is reported to be retiring rapidly.
(b). Last night our mounted troops held frontier from point East of ESTRUDE to the F of CLAIR FAYTS.

2. The South African Brigade will form part of the Mobile Column.
2nd. Regiment will march with the main body.

3. (a). The Battalion, less I Platoon of "A" Company, will pass the starting point (Cross Roads North of E. of SORLE LE CHATEAU) at 07.02. Hrs. in the following order:-

"D" Company.
"A" Company.
"B" Company.
"C" Company.
Headquarters.

(b). One Platoon of "A" Company will march with baggage train and will report to Major Browne, 4th South African Infantry, on square at SORLE LE CHATEAU at 07.00.Hrs.

(c). DRESS - Battle Order.

(d). Usual interval between Companies to be observed.

4. Transport. ~~-~~ Pack Animals, Lewis Gun Limbers, Field Kitchens and Mess Cart will move in rear of Main Body.
Remainder of Transport will be Brigaded under Major Browne, 4th South African Infantry.

[signature]

Captain.
Acting Adjutant.
2nd.Regt; South African Infantry.

254

SECRET.

2ND. REGIMENT. SOUTH AFRICAN INFANTRY.

ORDER NO.28.

Reference. IOTH.NOVEMBER.1918.

Map. NAMUR. 8.
I/100,000.

I. The enemy is offering a stubborn resistance on the Right. Our troops hold line roughly, High Ground at point 240, immediately West of VIVIERIAUX. The centre through village of GRANDRIEU, on the Left they were checked on the crest on the High Ground immediately North of A in GRANDRIEU.

2. INTENTION. The Commanding Officer intends to support the Ist South African Infantry with "C" Company, plus I Platoon of "A" Company during the night and will report back to their Battalion Area at dawn, II.II.I8.

"A", "B" and "D" Companies will dig in on the ground they already occupy.

3. Detailed orders for the advance will be issued tomorrow, IIth instant.

Captain.
Acting Adjutant.
2nd.Regt.South African Infantry.

PUBLIC RECORD OFFICE

Reference WO 95/3147

DUE TO A FAULTY DEXTER MACHINE.

FOLIOS 255 DO NOT EXIST

SECRET. 256

2ND. REGIMENT. SOUTH AFRICAN INFANTRY.

ORDER NO.29.

Reference. IITH NOVEMBER.1918.

Map NAMUR. 8.
I/100,000

I. (a). INFORMATION. Hostilities ceased at II.00.Hours this morning.
(b). Our Line runs as per Operation Order No.28. issued yesterday

2. The Battalion will move forward into Billets, HESTRUDE, at 16.00.Hours today.

3. (a). A Billeting party of I N.C.O. per Company and I from Headquarters will report to 2/Lieut.R.Haskis at Brigade Headquarters in Village.
(b). Companies will move into Billets independantly .
(c). Transport will be billeted in Village.

4.

Captain.
Acting Adjutant.
2nd.Regt.South African Infantry.

SECRET. 257

2nD. REGIMENT. SOUTH AFRICAN INFANTRY.

ORDER NO.30.

Reference. 12TH.NOVEMBER.1918.

Map. NAMUR. 8.
1/100,000.

I. The Battalion will relieve the Ist South African Infantry today in the outpost lines East of GRANDRIEU.

2. The Battalion will parade on road running past Battalion Headquarters ready to move off at 15.00. hours, in the following order:-

Headquarters.
"A" Company.
"B" Company.
"D" Company.
"C" Company.
Transport.

3. (a). Starting point Bridge in Village.
(b). DRESS - Battle Order.
(c). Interval of 200 yards will be observed between Companies and Transport.
(d). Head of Column will pass starting point at I5.I0.Hours.

4. Marching out states to be handed to Adjutant on parade.

5. Completion of move will be notified to Battalion Headquarters by Code Word "ZERU".

6. ROUTE :-: DIRECT.

[signature]

Captain.
Acting Adjutant.
2nd.Regt.South African Infantry.

SECRET.

258

2ND. REGIMENT. SOUTH AFRICAN INFANTRY.

Reference: ORDER NO.31.

16TH. NOVEMBER.1918.

Map NAMUR 8.
1/100,000.

I. The Battalion will be relieved by the Ist Cameron Highlanders at II.00.Hrs. today, I6th instant.

"A" Coy. ,Ist Cameron Highlanders	will relieve	"A" Coy. 2nd. S.A.I.
"B" " " " "	" "	"B" " " "
"C" " " " "	" "	"D" " " "
"D" " " " "	" "	"C" " " "

Relief to be completed by I2.00.Hours.

2. The Battalion will move by march route to SIVRY, today, and will be paraded on open field immediately South of Cross Roads in village, ready to move off at I2.45.Hours, in the following order:-

Headquarters.
"A" Company.
"B" Company.
"C" Company.
"D" Company.
Transport.

3. (a). Starting point where track crosses 2nd Class road West of VIVERIAUX.

(b). DRESS - Full marching order.
Mounted Officers- Sam Brown Belts.

(c). Head of column will pass starting point at I3.I5. Hours.

4. Marching out states to be handed to the Adjutant on parade.

5. A Billeting party of I. N.C.O. per Company and I from Headquarters, under 2/Lieut. Bowes, will meet the Brigade I/O at SIVRY at II.00. Hours.

6; (a). Officers kits to be at R.Q.M.Stores by II.00.Hours.

(b). All Great Coats to be rolled in bundles of IO and stacked at R.Q.M.Stores by II.00.Hours.

(c). Company Officers Mess Kits will be carried on Kitchen.

(d). Lewis Guns to be loaded on transport by II.00.Hours

7. Transport Officer will reconnoitre the route before hand.

8. ROUTE - DIRECT.

[signature]

Captain.
Adjutant.
2nd.Regt.South African Infantry.

SECRET.

259

2ND. REGIMENT. SOUTH AFRICAN INFANTRY.

ORDER NO.32.

Reference: 18TH. NOVEMBER.1918.

Map NAMUR 8.
1/100,000.

1. The South African Brigade will move into a new area by march route tomorrow,19th instant.

The Battalion will be billeted in VILLERS deux EGLISES tomorrow night,19th instant.

2. The Battalion will parade , ready to move off at 09.35.Hours, on road immediately West of Cross Roads at Battalion Orderly Room, in the following order.:-

Headquarters.
"B" Company.
"C" Company.
"D" Company.
"A" Company.
Transport.

3. (a). Starting point cross roads due North of S. in VIEUX SART .

(b). DRESS - Full marching order.
Mounted Officers, Sam Brown Belts.

(c). Head of column will pass starting point at 10.25.Hours.

4. Marching out states will be handed to Adjutant on parade.

5. A Billeting party as already detailed will meet the Battalion on Western outskirts of VILLERS deux EGLISES.

6. (a). Officers kits; mess kits;etc. to be stacked at Company Orderly Rooms by 07.30.Hrs.

(b). All great coats to be rolled in bundles of 10 and stacked at Company Headquarters at 07.30.Hrs.

(c). In view of the non arrival of 2nd.Blanket, the blanket on hand will be carried on transport.
They will be rolled in bundles of 10 and stacked at Company Orderly Rooms by 07.30.Hrs.

(d). Baggage wagons willbe loaded at 08.00 Hrs. and will report to 548 Company A.S.C. at 08.45.Hrs.

7. The following distance will be observed during the march between units ... 50 Yards.
Between Companies ... 10 Yards.
Between Companies & Transport ... 20 Yards.

8. The Transport Officer will ensure that Water Carts are filled prior to departure.

9. ROUTE. :-: Via SENZEILLES.

10. The Midday halt will be from 11.30 to 13.00.Hours.

The SGT.Cook will have dinner cooked "en route" .

11. Certificates to the effect that billets have been left clean and that latrines have been filled in and marked, will be handed to Adjutant on parade.

Issued at 21.00 hours

[signature]

Captain. &
Adjutant

260

SECRET.

2nd. REGIMENT. SOUTH AFRICAN INFANTRY.

Reference.

ORDER NO.33.

23RD. NOVEMBER.1918.

NAMUR 8.
I/100,000.

I. The South African Brigade will move, into a new area, by march route tomorrow, 24th instant.
The Battalion will be billeted in AGIMONT tomorrow night, 24th instant.

2. The Battalion will be paraded ready to move off at 07.30.Hrs. on field immediately North of the Chateau, in the following order:-

Headquarters.
"C" Company.
"D" Company.
"A" Company.
"B" Company.

3. (a). One Marker per Company and one from Headquarters will report to R.S.M. on ground at 07.15.Hrs.
Companies will march on to their respective markers at 07.20.Hrs.
(b). Starting point Cross roads South of O in VODECEE.
(c). DRESS - Full marching order.
Mounted Officers, sam brown belts.
(d). Head of column will pass starting point at 09.15.Hrs.

4. A Billeting party of one N.C.O. per company and one from Headquarters, under 2/Lieut.W.V.Bowes, will report at Battalion Headquarters for instructions at 07.00.Hrs.

5. (a). Officers kits, mess kits, etc., to be stacked at Company Messes by 06.45.Hrs.
(b). All great coats, 2nd.Blanket, to be rolled in bundl--es of 10 and stacked at Chateau at 06.45.Hrs. ("D" Company and Headquarters will stack great coats and 2nd.Blanket at Company Headquarters.)
(c). First Blanket will be carried on men.
(d). One representative per Company and one from headquarters will be detailed to accompany baggage wagons.

6. TRANSPORT. Transport will be Brigaded. Regimental transport (Cookers kitchens and Officers mess cart) will report to 548 Coy. A.S.C. on main road just East of VILLERS le GAMBON by 10.00.Hrs.

7. Marching out states and certificates to the effect that Billets have been left clean and that the latrines have been filled in and marked, will be handed to the Adjutant on parade.

8. The Medical Officer will inspect all billets prior to departure.

9. The usual distance between Companies will be observed.

10. ROUTE :-: VILLERS le GAMBON - ROMEDENNE - VODELLE - AGIMONT.

11. Standing orders as issued for the march to the RHINE LAND will be strictly adhered to.

[signature]
Captain &
Adjutant.
2nd.Regt.South African Infty.

ISSUED AT 10.30. HOURS.

Instructions regarding War Diaries and Intelligence Summaries are contained in F. S. Regs., Part II. and the Staff Manual respectively. Title pages will be prepared in manuscript.

WAR DIARY
or
INTELLIGENCE SUMMARY.
(Erase heading not required.)

Army Form C. 2118.

11 — 2nd Regiment S. A. Infantry

Place	Date	Hour	Summary of Events and Information	Remarks and references to Appendices
MARCHE.	26/12/18.		Seven other ranks per Company + two from Headquarters acted as Road Police.	
Do.	27/12/18.		TRAINING. Cleaning up parade under the supervision of Officers & N.C.Os.	
Do.	28/12/18.		TRAINING As per programme issued.	
		09 30	COURT OF ENQUIRY.	
			A court of enquiry assembled at D Company Orderly Room to enquire into the explosion that occurred th[ere] on the night of the 26th inst.	
			President Capt. F L MARILLIER	
			Members. LIEUT D H ELIAS.	
			2/LIEUT P H HAVILAND.	
Do.	28/12/18.		LIEUT. C H FRASER proceeded on leave to the United Kingdom.	261
Do.	29/12/18.		CHURCH SERVICES. Church of England. Presbyterian. Dutch Reformed. Wesleyan, Baptists, Congregationalists	

D. D. & L., London, E.C. (A8001) Wt W1771/M2031 750000 5/17 Sch. 52 Forms/C2118/14

Army Form C. 2118.

WAR DIARY
or
INTELLIGENCE SUMMARY.
(*Erase heading not required.*)

Instructions regarding War Diaries and Intelligence Summaries are contained in F. S. Regs., Part II. and the Staff Manual respectively. Title pages will be prepared in manuscript.

12 — 2nd Regiment S.A.I.F.

262

Place	Date	Hour	Summary of Events and Information	Remarks and references to Appendices
MARCHE	27/12/18		APPOINTMENTS. Capt. F. G. WALSH M.C. assumes temporary command of Regiment from 27-12-18 during the absence of Major C. R. HEENAN D.S.O on short leave.	
Do.	30/12/18		TRAINING As per programme issued	
Do.	31/12/18		Do. Do.	
Do.	do.		STRENGTH OF BATTALION.	

	OFFs.	O.R's
With Battalion	30	1126
Field Ambulance	4	10
On Course		9
On Leave	4	27
Detached Duties	1	46
Total.	39	1218

S E C R E T.

2ND. REGIMENT. SOUTH AFRICAN INFANTRY.

263

Reference: ORDER NO.34.

13TH.DECEMBER.1918.

NAMUR 8.
1/100,000.
MARCHE 9.
1/100,000.

---

1. The South African Brigade will move into the HOUYET Area, by march route, tomorrow,14th instant.
The Battalion will be billeted in MESNIL EGLISE tomorrow night, 14th instant.

2. The Battalion will be paraded in column of Three's ready to move off at 08.30.Hours on road running past Regimental Orderly Room in the following order:-

Headquarters.
"D" Company.
"A" Company.
"B" Company.
"C" Company.
Transport.

3. (a). Companies will be on parade at 08.25.Hours.
(b). Starting point - River Bridge,GIVET.
(c). DRESS -Full marching order.
(d). Head of Column will pass starting point at 09.35.Hours.

4. (a). Officers kits,mess kits, etc, to be stacked at Regimental Quartermaster Stores by 07.00.Hours.
(b). All great coats, 2nd.Blanket, and palliasses,to be rolled in bundles of 10 and stacked at Regimental Quartermaster stores by 07.00.Hours.
(c). First Blanket will be carried on men.

5. Marching out states and certificates to the effect that Billets have been left clean and that the latrines have been filled in and marked, will be handed to the Adjutant on Parade.

6. The Medical Officer will inspect all Billets prior to Departure.

7. The Usual distance between Companies will be ;observed.

8. ROUTE :-: ~~East~~ West Side of River, Givet Bridge, PETIT CAPORAL , FESCHAUX, MESNIL ENGLISE.

9. Standing Orders as issued for the March to the RHINE LAND will be strictly adhered to.

[signature]
Captain &
Adjutant.
2nd.Regt.South African Infantry.

ISSUED AT 15.00. HOURS.

War Diary

2ND. REGIMENT. SOUTH AFRICAN INFANTRY. **SECRET.**

264.

REFERENCE:

ORDER NO.35.

NAMUR 8.
1/100,000
MARCHE 9.
1/100,000.

14TH. DECEMBER.1918.

1. The South African Brigade will move into the ROCHEFORT AREA by march route tomorrow,15th instant.
The Battalion will be billeted in ROCHEFORT,15th instant.

2. The Battalion will be paraded in column of three's ready to move off at 07.30.Hours on road running past Church, in the following order:-

Headquarters.
"A" Company.
"B" Company.
"C" Company.
"D" Company.
Transport.

3. (a). Companies will be on parade at 07.25.Hours.
(b). Starting point - River Bridge East of Level Crossing,HOUYET.
(c). DRESS - Full Marching order.
(d). Head of column will pass starting point at 09.30. Hours.

4. (a). Officers kits,mess kits,etc, to be stacked at R.Q.M.Stores by 06.00.Hours.
(b). All Great Coats,2nd Blanket, and Palliasses to be rolled in bundles of 10 and stacked at R.Q.M.Stores by 06.00.Hrs.
(c). First Blanket will be carried on man.
(d). Midday Halt will be observed between 11.50. and 13.00. Hours.

5. Marching out states and certificates to the effect that billets have been left clean and that the latrines have been filled in and marked, to be handed to the Adjutant on Parade.

6. The Medical Officer will inspect all billets prior to departure.

7. The usual distance between Companies will be observed.

8. ROUTE :-: HOUYET, and CIERGNON.

9. Standing orders as issued for the march to the RHINE LAND will be strictly adhered to.

[signature]

Captain &
Adjutant.
2nd.Regt.South African Infantry.

I

ISSUED AT 15.30. HOURS.

SECRET.

265

2ND. REGIMENT. SOUTH AFRICAN INFANTRY.

Reference:

ORDER NO. 36.

MARCHE 9.
1/100,000.

15TH. DECEMBER 1918.

1. The South African Brigade will move by march route into the MARCHE AREA tomorrow, 16th instant.
The Battalion will be billeted in MARCHE tomorrow night, 16th instant.

2. The Battalion will be paraded in column of three's ready to move off at 08.55 Hrs. on road running through ROCHEFORT, with Head of Column just South of Main Cross Roads in village, in the following order:-

Headquarters.
"B" Company.
"C" Company.
"D" Company.
"A" Company.
Transport.

3. (a). Companies will be on parade by 08.50 Hours.
(b). Starting point - Level Crossing South of First R in ROCHEFORT.
(c). DRESS - Full marching order.
(d). Head of Column will pass starting point at 09.10 Hrs.

4. (a). Officers kits, mess kits, etc, to be stacked at R.Q.M.Stores by 07.30 Hours.
(b). All Great Coats, 2nd Blanket, and Pallaisses to be rolled in bundles of 10 and stacked at R.Q.M.Stores by 07.30 Hours.
(c). First Blanket to be carried on man.
(d). There will be no midday Halt.

5. Marching out states, and certificates to the effect that billets have been left clean and that the latrines have been filled in and marked, will be handed to the Adjutant on parade.

6. The Medical Officer will inspect all billets prior to departure.

7. The usual distances between Companies will be observed.

8. ROUTE :-: HARGIMONT -

9. Standing orders as issued for the march to the RHINE LAND will be strictly adhered to.

[signature]

Captain &
Adjutant.
2nd.Regt. South African Infantry.

ISSUED AT 17.45. HOURS.

War Diary

Army Form C. 2118.

WAR DIARY
or
INTELLIGENCE SUMMARY.
(Erase heading not required.)

Instructions regarding War Diaries and Intelligence Summaries are contained in F. S. Regs., Part II. and the Staff Manual respectively. Title pages will be prepared in manuscript.

10

2nd Regiment South African Inf

Place	Date	Hour	Summary of Events and Information	Remarks and references to Appendices
MARCHE	23/12/18		TRAINING As per programme issued.	
			STRENGTH. - DECREASE.	
			The undermentioned Officer having reported for duty at Home Depot is struck of strength of Regiment as from 22-12-18.	
			MAJOR. L F. SPRENGER DSO MC	
Do	24/12/18		No training, the day being devoted to Xmas preparations	
"	25/12/18		CHURCH PARADES. Church of England, Roman Catholics, Wesleyans Baptists Congregationalists, Dutch Reformed, Presbyterians.	
Do	2?/12/18		Many Xmas greetings were received by the Battalion	
Do	26/12/18	11h	His Royal Highness, The Prince of Wales, inspected the Battalion at 11 hrs.	
			A Guard of Honour consisting of eight O.R's from each company and one from Headquarters was supplied: Capt H. G. Mossop in command.	

D. D. & L., London, E.C.
(A8001) Wt W1771/M2011 750,000 4/17 Sch. 52 Forms/C2118/14

266

Instructions regarding War Diaries and Intelligence Summaries are contained in F. S. Regs., Part II. and the Staff Manual respectively. Title pages will be prepared in manuscript.

WAR DIARY
or
INTELLIGENCE SUMMARY.
(*Erase heading not required.*)

Army Form C. 2118.

9 — 2nd Regiment South African Inf.

Place	Date	Hour	Summary of Events and Information	Remarks and references to Appendices
MARCHE.	20/12/18.		on strength of Regiment as from 17/12/18.	
"	Do		TRAINING As per programme issued.	
"	21/12/18.		TRAINING As per programme issued.	
Do.	Do.		STRENGTH OF BATTALION. OFFS. ORs.	
			With Battalion 32 1096	
			Field Ambulance 3 12	
			On Leave 5 37	
			Detached Duties 2 77	
			Total Strength 42 1222	
Do	21/12/18		2/Lt. W V Bowes proceeded on leave to the United Kingdom	
Do.	22/12/18.		CHURCH SERVICES. Roman Catholics, Church of England, Wesleyans, Congregationalists, Baptists Presbyterians & Dutch Reformed.	
Do	23/12/18		STRENGTH INCREASE. Five ORs having joined from BASE are taken on strength as from 20-12-18	267

D. D. & L., London, E.C.
(A8004) Wt. W1771/M2031 750,000 5/17 Sch. 52 Forms/C2118/14

Instructions regarding War Diaries and Intelligence Summaries are contained in F. S. Regs., Part II. and the Staff Manual respectively. Title pages will be prepared in manuscript.

Army Form C. 2118.

WAR DIARY
or
INTELLIGENCE SUMMARY.

(*Erase heading not required.*)

8

2nd Regiment South African Inf

Place	Date	Hour	Summary of Events and Information	Remarks and references to Appendices
MARCHE	17/12/18		STRENGTH INCREASE A draft of 7 Officers & 441 ORs having arrived from Reception Camp is taken on strength of Regiment.	
"	17/12/18	09.00	2/Lt A.H. HUNDLEY with his platoon proceeded to MELREUX to provide two guards on dumps at MELREUX STATION & MELREUX BRIDGE	
"	18/12/18		TRAINING (A) Cleaning up parades under the supervision of Officers & NCOs (B) Draft Company will organize & carry out cleaning parades.	
"	19/12/18	08.30	TRAINING. The Battalion, less the new draft, proceeded on a route march	
		09.30	The Commanding Officer inspected the new draft	
"	20/12/18		STRENGTH. INCREASE. 10 ORs having joined from base are taken	268

D. D. & L., London, E.C. (A8094) Wt W1771/M2031 750,000 5/17 Sch. 52 Forms/C2118/14

Instructions regarding War Diaries and Intelligence Summaries are contained in F. S. Regs., Part II. and the Staff Manual respectively. Title pages will be prepared in manuscript.

WAR DIARY
or
INTELLIGENCE SUMMARY.
(Erase heading not required.)

Army Form C. 2118.

2nd Regt. South African Inf.

Place	Date	Hour	Summary of Events and Information	Remarks and references to Appendices
ROCHEFORT			was billeted.	
Do		14/12/18	Operation Order No. 36 The Battalion paraded on road running through ROCHEFORT with HEAD of column just South of Main Cross Roads in village, in the following order – Headquarters. B C D A Coys Transport at 8.55 hrs. Head of column passed starting point – Level crossing SOUTH of first R in ROCHEFORT at 9.10 hours. ROUTE – HARGIMONT MARCHE. The march was carried out with no midday halt the Battalion arrived in MARCHE at 12.30 hrs and was billeted.	
Do		15/12/18	TRAINING Cleaning up parade will be carried out under the supervision of Officers & NCOs.	

269

D. D. & L., London, E.C. (A8004) Wt W1771/M2031 750,000 5/17 Sch. 52 Forms/C2118/14

Army Form C. 2118.

WAR DIARY
or
INTELLIGENCE SUMMARY.
(Erase heading not required.)

Instructions regarding War Diaries and Intelligence Summaries are contained in F. S. Regs., Part II. and the Staff Manual respectively. Title pages will be prepared in manuscript.

6 — 2nd Regiment S. A. Inf

Place	Date	Hour	Summary of Events and Information	Remarks and references to Appendices
AGIMONT	14/12/18		A halt of one hour, 12 noon to 13 hrs. for the midday meal, was observed.	270
MESNIL EGLISE	14/12/18		The Battalion arrived at MESNIL EGLISE at 14 hrs & occupied billets.	
	14/12/18	15 hrs	The same billeting party proceeded to procure billets in ROCHEFORT.	
Do.	15/12/18		Operation Order No 35. The Battalion paraded on road running past Church in the following order:- Headquarters, A B C D Coys. Transport.	
			In order to reach Starting Point at 9.30 hrs the Battalion moved off at 7.30 hrs.	
			STARTING POINT River bridge EAST of level crossing HOUYET.	
			The Route taken was as follows - HOUYET and CIERGNON.	
			The halt for a midday meal was observed.	
			The Battalion arrived at ROCHEFORT at 16.30 hrs and	

Army Form C. 2118.

WAR DIARY
or
INTELLIGENCE SUMMARY.
(Erase heading not required.)

Instructions regarding War Diaries and Intelligence Summaries are contained in F. S. Regs., Part II. and the Staff Manual respectively. Title pages will be prepared in manuscript.

5. 2nd Regiment S A I F

Place	Date	Hour	Summary of Events and Information	Remarks and references to Appendices
ACIMONT	12/12/18		WEATHER. Raining.	
Do	13/12/18	09.00 to 12.30	TRAINING. As per programme issued.	
Do:	"		Administrative Instruction No. 1 in connection with South African Brigade Order 266 received 08.00 hrs. One NCO from Headquarters and one from each Coy proceeded under 2/Lt F. G. Norres to secure billets at MESNIL EGLISE.	
"	14/12/18.		In accordance with Operation Order No. 34 the Battalion paraded in column of threes in front of the Regimental Orderly Room and moved off at 8.30 hrs in the following order Hqr. D. A B C Transport. Starting point – River Bridge GIVET 5J 92 65 NAMUR 8. Head of column passed starting point at 9.35 hours. ROUTE. West side of River. Givet Bridge. PETIT CAPOREL. FESCHAUX. The march was somewhat severe owing to the prolonged marches between halts.	271

D. D. & L., London, E.C.
(A8504) Wt W1771/M2031 750,000 5/17 Sch. 52 Forms/C2118/14

Instructions regarding War Diaries and Intelligence Summaries are contained in F. S. Regs., Part II. and the Staff Manual respectively. Title pages will be prepared in manuscript.

Army Form C. 2118.

4

WAR DIARY
or
INTELLIGENCE SUMMARY.

(*Erase heading not required.*)

2nd Regt S A I.

Place	Date	Hour	Summary of Events and Information	Remarks and references to Appendices
AGIMONT	9/12/18	09.15	Commanding Officer inspected the Battalion. After inspection the Battalion proceeded on Route March. ROUTE - AGIMONT, through village, by 3rd class road running past station to BON SECOURS, thence by 2nd class road through GIVET to Ft de Vignes, returning through GIVET along 1st class road to PETIT DOISCHE, then NORTH EAST to Junction of 1st & 2nd class roads, then by 2nd class road to AGIMONT	
Do.	10/12/18		TRAINING. As per programme issued. STRENGTH - INCREASE - OFFICERS. LIEUT C.J. SWEENEY having joined Unit from Reception Camp is posted to A Company	
Do.	11/12/18		TRAINING As per programme issued.	
Do	12/12/18	09.00 to 10.45	TRAINING. Under Company arrangements.	
Do	"	13.15	~~The Battalion will be paraded on road running past Orderly Room in column of threes at 13.15 hrs in the~~	

272

D. D. & L., London, E.C. (A8001) W1 W1771/M2031 750,000 5/17 Sch. 52 Forms/C2118/14

Instructions regarding War Diaries and Intelligence Summaries are contained in F. S. Regs., Part II. and the Staff Manual respectively. Title pages will be prepared in manuscript.

WAR DIARY
or
INTELLIGENCE SUMMARY.

3.

(*Erase heading not required.*) ~~2nd Regt South African Inf~~

Army Form C. 2118.

Place	Date	Hour	Summary of Events and Information	Remarks and references to Appendices
AGIMONT	7/12/18	10-45 to 12-30	C + D Companies (plus Lewis Gunners) will carry out firing practice on Range	
			A + B Companies. Close order drill + handling of arms.	
"	8/12/18		CHURCH SERVICES. Roman Catholics, Presbyterians, Church of England. Wesleyans, Congregationalists, Baptists, Dutch Reformed.	
"	9/12/18		STRENGTH OF BATTALION	

	OFFS.	ORs
With Battalion	21	638
Field Ambulance	3	4
On Course		1
On Leave	4	46
Detached Duties	8	221
Total Strength	36	910

D. D & L., London, E.C.
(A8204) Wt W1771/M2031 750,000 5/17 Sch. 52 Forms/C2118/14

273

Army Form C. 2118.

WAR DIARY
or
INTELLIGENCE SUMMARY.
(Erase heading not required.)

Instructions regarding War Diaries and Intelligence Summaries are contained in F. S. Regs., Part II. and the Staff Manual respectively. Title pages will be prepared in manuscript.

2 December 1918. 2nd Regiment South African Inf.

Place	Date	Hour	Summary of Events and Information	Remarks and references to Appendices
AGIMONT	4/12/18		TRAINING - As on previous day	
	5/12/18		" Do	
"			Working Party - One NCO and five men per Company will be detailed daily to report at Battalion Headquarters at 09.00 hours.	
"	6/12/18		TRAINING - As per programme.	
			STRENGTH INCREASE A draft of 21 other ranks having arrived at Divisional Reception Camp is taken on strength of Regiment 5-12-18	
"	6/12/18.		On instructions received from Brigade (66th Div Order 128) an advanced party of six NCOs (1 per Coy + 2 Hdqs) under 2/Lt W. V. Bowes proceeded to new area.	
"	7/12/18.	09.00 to 10.45	TRAINING. "A" + "B" Companies (plus Lewis Gunners) will carry out firing practice on Range "C" + "D" Close order drill + handling of arms.	

D. D. & L., London, E.C. (A8094) Wt W1771/M2031 750,000 5/17 Sch. 52 Forms/C2118/14

274

Army Form C. 2118.

Instructions regarding War Diaries and Intelligence Summaries are contained in F. S. Regs., Part II. and the Staff Manual respectively. Title pages will be prepared in manuscript.

(1)

WAR DIARY
or
INTELLIGENCE SUMMARY.
(Erase heading not required.)

December 1918 — 2nd Regt. South African Inf.

Place	Date	Hour	Summary of Events and Information	Remarks and references to Appendices
AGIMONT	1/12/18		CHURCH SERVICES. Roman Catholics, Wesleyans, Congregationalists, Baptists, Presbyterians, Church of England, Dutch Reformed	
			APPOINTMENTS – Commissions	
			LIEUT. J T HUMPHREY to be acting Captain whilst commanding a Company.	
Do	2/12/18	09.00–12.30	TRAINING Inspection under Company Arrangements Close Order Drill. Physical Training Saluting Drill & Handling of Arms. Battalion & Ceremonial Drill	
		14.00–15.00	NCOs parade under R S M.	
		14.00–16.00	Recreational Training	
Do	2/12/18		CAPT E R BEGLEY & 2nd/LT H J ALLEN proceeded on leave to the United Kingdom	
Do	3/12/18		TRAINING – As on previous day	275 END

D. D. & L., London, E.C. (A8004) Wt. W2771/M2031 750,000 5/17 Sch. 52 Forms/C2118/14

66TH DIVISION
SOUTH AFRICAN INFY BRIGADE

44

2ND STH AFRICAN INFY REGT

~~JAN - FEB 1919~~

1918 SEP - 1919 FEB

~~To~~

FROM 9 DIV

Army Form C. 2118.

1.

WAR DIARY
or
~~INTELLIGENCE SUMMARY~~

(Erase heading not required.)

SEPTEMBER 1918 — 2nd South African Infantry.

Instructions regarding War Diaries and Intelligence Summaries are contained in F. S. Regs., Part II. and the Staff Manual respectively. Title Pages will be prepared in manuscript.

Place	Date	Hour	Summary of Events and Information	Remarks and references to Appendices
LUMBRES	1.9.18		The South Afr (Composite) Battalion is still definitely a Unit of the 9th Division but the process of amalgamation with the draft recently arrived in France and reorganisation into three Battalions to reform the South African Brigade, in anticipation of our leaving the 9th Division, gradually taking place. The four platoons of the 2nd Coy S.A. (Comp.) Battalion, forming the nucleus of the four Coys of the Battalion and together with the men of the 2nd Regt. of the draft the Battalion is being reorganised, about 700 men being in camp. Officers are posted to Companies (Appendix I).	APPENDIX I (Posting of Officers)
Line of March & BOUVELINGHEM.	2.9.18		The 2nd Regt. marches to the ALQUINES area and is distributed as follows: HQrs & B Coy BOUVELINGHEM. A Coy at LE BUISSANT. C Coy at HARLETTE. D Coy at FROMENTAL (Appendix II Operation Order No. 1). Coys from 1 to 2 miles apart & billets accommodation most unsuitable.	APPENDIX II (Operation Order No. 1)
BOUVELINGHEM.	3.9.18		Regimental Canteen formed. Visited by Prime Minister's Representative from S. Africa. Reorganisation [illegible]. Lieut E.J. BROOK rejoined for duty. Weather much colder.	
BOUVELINGHEM	4.9.18		Usual training. Decided that numeral 2 should no longer be worn on either shoulder straps or [illegible]. Capt. A.H. GIFFORD S.A.M.C. relieves CAPT. G.A. BEYERS S.A.M.C.	

2449 Wt. W14957/M90 750,000 1/16 J.B.C. & A. Forms/C.2118/12.

Army Form C. 2118.

WAR DIARY
or
INTELLIGENCE SUMMARY

(Erase heading not required.)

Instructions regarding War Diaries and Intelligence Summaries are contained in F. S. Regs., Part II. and the Staff Manual respectively. Title Pages will be prepared in manuscript.

2

SEPTEMBER 1918 — 2nd South African Infantry

Place	Date	Hour	Summary of Events and Information	Remarks and references to Appendices
BOUVELINGHEM	5.9.18 to 6.9.18		Usual training and reorganisation. Lieut & Q.M. [illegible] CARDING proceeds to England on 6 months tour of duty (5.9.18). R.Q.M.S. SMITH carries out duties of Q.M. Heavy rain showers.	
BOUVELINGHEM	7.9.18 to 11.9.18		Training and reorganisation of Coys. and Regt. gradually slowly but surely settling down on good basis. Weather persistently bad and rain more or less continuous.	
Line of march & SENINGHEM	12.9.18		Battalion marches to SENINGHEM in order H.Q., C, D, B, A Companies. Head of column moving at 10.30 am. Billets with good and civilians distinctly hostile. (Appendix III Operation Order No. 2) Brigade now definitely part of 9th Division dating from 11.9.18	APPENDIX III (Operation Order No. 2).
SENINGHEM	13.9.18 to 15.9.18		Rev. G.W.L. TOBIAS attached to Battalion 13.9.18. Reorganisation and training. Weather generally very bad. Unsettled and sudden and constant heavy showers of rain	
SENINGHEM	16.9.18		Inspection and march past of Regt. by Brigade Commander (General Tanner). No 10 Platoon in competition best platoon on parade	
SENINGHEM	17.9.18 to 21.9.18		Usual training including musketry on VAL-DE-LUMBRES Range gas demonstration etc. and lecture at Corps Gas School HARLETTE. South African Y.M.C.A. marquee opened by Rev. ALDRIDGE 19.9.18.	
SENINGHEM & Line of March	22.9.18		Battalion marches at 4.0 pm to entrain at WIZERNES to proceed South to LE CAUROY area to join 66th Division. (Appendix IV Operation Order No 3). (Cont'd)	APPENDIX IV (Operation Order No. 3)

16

2449 Wt. W14957/M90 750,000 1/16 J.B.C. & A. Forms/C.2118/12.

Army Form C. 2118.

WAR DIARY
~~or~~
~~INTELLIGENCE SUMMARY~~
(Erase heading not required.)

Instructions regarding War Diaries and Intelligence Summaries are contained in F. S. Regs., Part II. and the Staff Manual respectively. Title Pages will be prepared in manuscript.

SEPTEMBER 1918. 2nd South African Infantry

Place	Date	Hour	Summary of Events and Information	Remarks and references to Appendices
	22.9.18 (Cont'd)		Regt and Transport entrain and Train pulls out 9.30 pm proceeding via HAZEBROUCK - LILLERS - ST. POL - TINQUES. Weather much colder. No one have hot tea before entraining.	
MAGNICOURT-SUR-CANCHE	23.9.18		Battalion and Transport detrain at TINQUES 4.5 am and proceed via PENIN and MAZIERES to MAGNICOURT-SUR-CANCHE. Billets extremely bad and Transport lines impossible to use. No help from Civilians. Very cold.	
MAGNICOURT-SUR-CANCHE	24.9.18 to 25.9.18		Training by Coys. developing into tactical schemes by Platoon then Coys. A route march taken place on 25th & 26th by Battalion (as strong as possible). Length of march twelve miles starting at 8.30 am. Battalion inspected by Div. Commander (General Lukin CMG DSO) on latter date during march. 2/Lt. E.D. DIRREL reports for duty 26.9.18.	
	27.9.18		Battalion Transport moves by road South to VILLERS BRETONNEUX	
MAGNICOURT-SUR-CANCHE & line of march	28.9.18		Battalion moves at 7.55 am (less Transport) via MONT-en-TERNOIS - BUNEVILLE to entrain at PETIT HOUVIN 10.23 am. (Appendix V Operation Order No. 4). Train late and move off 3.15 pm. No one standing in open cars through train route via DOULLENS - AMIENS thence to CORBIE where Regt detrain and proceed by march route to VILLERS-BRETONNEUX arriving about 11.45 pm.	APPENDIX V (Operation Order No. 4)

15

2449 Wt. W14957/M90 750,000 1/16 J.B.C. & A. Forms/C.2118/12.

4.

Army Form C. 2118.

WAR DIARY
or
~~INTELLIGENCE SUMMARY~~

(Erase heading not required.)

Instructions regarding War Diaries and Intelligence Summaries are contained in F. S. Regs., Part II. and the Staff Manual respectively. Title Pages will be prepared in manuscript.

SEPTEMBER 1918. 2nd South African Infantry

Place	Date	Hour	Summary of Events and Information	Remarks and references to Appendices
VILLERS-BRETONNEUX on the march to FRAMERVILLE	29/9/18		Battalion moves 2.0 pm by road to FRAMERVILLE (Appendix VI Operation Order No. 5) arriving 6.20 pm. Whole of the country deserted by civilians and surroundings with the exception of villages which are badly knocked about, shows little sign of recent occupation by enemy. The Medical Officer, Capt. Gibbons S.A.M.C. proceeds on leave and is relieved by Capt. M M ADAMS S.A.M.C.	APPENDIX VI (Operation Order No. 5)
FRAMERVILLE	30/9/18		Usual training in Coys. Billets fairly good. [illegible] and cold	

Daily State as at 30.9.18.

	Officers	O.R.
[illegible]	2	7[illegible]
Hospital	—	[illegible]
[illegible]	[illegible]	[illegible]
[illegible]	[illegible]	3[illegible]
[illegible]	[illegible]	[illegible]
Total	32	805

[illegible] Bamford? [illegible]

Commanding 2nd S.A.I.

4/10/18

14

2449 Wt. W14957/M90 750,000 1/16 J.B.C. & A. Forms/C.2118/12.

APPENDIX. I
(Referred to 1.9.18).

18

2ND. REGIMENT - SOUTH AFRICAN INFANTRY.

DISTRIBUTION OF OFFICERS. 1/9/18.

HEADQUARTERS.

Lieut. Col.	H. W. M.	BAMFORD. OBE. MC.	Commanding.
Major.	L. F.	SPRENGER. DSO. MC.	2nd. in CommD
Capt.	L.	Greene DSO. MC.	Adjutant.
Lieut.	E. J.	RICHES.	Trspt. Offr
"	F. L.	MARILLIER.	Asst. Adjt.
2/Lieut.	S. G.	PHILLIPS. MC.	Intelligence Officer.

"A" COMPANY.

Capt. T. H. SYMONS MC.
Lieut. J. T. HUMPHREY.
2/Lieut. C. L. FRASER.
" C. S. GILLY.
" F. G. A. McCARTER.

"B" COMPANY.

Capt. L. M. JACOBS.
Lieut. H. W. HEELEY.
" E. J. BROOK.
2/Lieut. A. K. PARROTT.
" H. J. ALLEN.
" W. V. BOWES.

"C" COMPANY.

Capt. W. L. KING. MC. DCM.
Lieut. E. R. BEGLEY. MC.
2/Lieut. H. BERRY. (PERRY).
" C. W. ROBERTS.
" C. C. RAYMOND.
" E. L. FRANCIS.

"D" COMPANY.

Lieut. C. M. EGAN.
" M. E. WHELAN. MC.
2/Lieut. A. H. HUNDLEY.
" H. C. H. GUNN.
" R. H. LAZARUS.
" H. A. MARTIN.

ATTACHED.

Major W. A. BLOOMFIELD. V. C.
Capt. P. J. WALSHE MC. (R. C. Chaplain)
Capt. ~~SAMPSON~~ ~~MC.~~ G. A. BEYERS (M. O. S. A. M. C.)

COPY NO...1....

Appendix II (War Diary Sept. 1918)
(Referred to 2.9.18)

2nd. SOUTH AFRICAN INFANTRY.

OPERATION ORDER NO. 1 2/9/18.

1. The 2nd. South African Infantry will move by March Route to the AIQUINES AREA to day, the 2nd. Sept. 18.

2. The Battalion will parade ready to move off at 9-45a.m. on same ground as Church Parade was held yesterday the 1st. inst.

3. Battalion will parade in following Order in MASS.
   Head Quarters.
   "D" Company.
   "C" Company.
   "B" Company.
   "A" Company.

4. The Battalion will march in same order as on Parade followed by the Battalion Transport. Head Quarters to pass the starting point at the junction of the LUMBRES - ACQUIN ROAD and the MAIN BOULOGNE ROAD at 10a.m.

5. Dress will be FULL MARCHING ORDER and STEEL HELMETS . Mounte Officers will wear SAM BROWN BELTS.

6. On the March intervals of 100 yards will be maintained between Companies.

[signature]

Capt and Adjt.

Issued to at a.m.

A.B.C.D Companies.
Transport Officer.
Quarter Master.
War Diary.

Appendix III
(War Diary Sept. 1918).
(Referred to 12.9.18).

2ND. SOUTH AFRICAN INFANTRY.

COPY NO..9.. 20

ORDER NO.2.

11th. Sept. 1918.

I. The 2nd. South African Infantry will move tomorrow the 12th. September, 1918 to SENINGHEM.

II. A Billeting Party consisting of 2/Lt. S. C. Phillips M. C. and 1 N. C. O. from Headquarters and one from each Company will report to the Staff Captain, South African Brigade, at 8.0. a.m. tomorrow at SENINGHEM Church.

III. The following will be the order of march:-

Hdqrs.
"C" Company.
"D" Company.
"B" Company.
"A" Company.
Transport.

IV. Head of the column will pass the road junction of the main BOULOGNE Road and the COULEMBY - HARLETTES Road at 10.30 a.m.

V. Dress will be full marching order with steel helmets. All Officers except mounted Officers will wear equipment. Mounted Officers Sam Brown Belts.

VI. Lewis Gun Limbers will report to each Company at 9.30 a.m. together with an extra limber for all Officers kits, and mess kits , and Company Stores.
Transport for Headquarters will report at 8.0 a.m.

~~xxxx~~

VII. Marching out states will be handed to the Adjutant at the starting point at 10.25 a.m. .

VIII. Clear Billet Certificate will be handed in to the Orderly Room at SENINGHEM at 12 NOON.

IX. Acknowledge.

[signature]

Capt. & Adjutant.
2nd. Regiment. South African Inf.

1. "A" Coy.
2. "B" Coy.
3. "C" Coy.
4. "D" Coy.
5. Headquarters.
6. Transport Officer.
7. R.S.M.
8. Quartermaster.

Appendix XX IV (War diary Sept.)

SECRET.

2ND. SOUTH AFRICAN INFANTRY.

Copy No. 11. 21

(Referred to 22.9.18.)

ORDER NO. 3.

Reference.

21st. September, 1918

HAZEBROUCK Sheet $\frac{1}{100,000}$

LENS. Sheet $\frac{1}{100,000}$

1. The South African Brigade Group will move to the 1st Army Area to join the 66th Division on 22nd. Inst.

2. The 2nd. S.A.I. will move by rail from WIZERNES to TINQUES on Sunday 22nd instant.

3. Advance party of 1 N.C.O. from each Company and 1 N.C.O. from Battalion Headquarters under the command of Lieut. HUMPHREY. will leave LUMBRES by train at 12 Noon today, 21st instant.

4. Lieut. H.N. HEELEY will act as Battalion entraining officer and will report to Lieut. L.G. MACKAY (1st Regt.) at WIZERNES station at 5.45 p.m. on Sunday 22nd instant. Lieut. HEELEY will report to Adjutant for further instructions before leaving.

5. (a). The Regiment will move to WIZERNES by march route on Sunday 22nd instant.
(b). DRESS - FULL MARCHING ORDER.
(c). Starting point will be on road just E of present transport billets.
(d). Order of March -- Hdqrs., A, B, C, D.
(e) Head of column will pass starting point at 4.30 ~~a.~~ p.m.

6. Transport - 1st and 2nd Line - will entrain with Regiment and will be at WIZERNES Station at 6.15 p.m. on Sunday, 22nd instant.
Transport Officer will reconnoitre entraining place today, 21st instant. Before doing so he will report to Adjutant for further instructions.

7. Loading party of 1 Officer and 50 O.Rs will report to R.T.O. WIZERNES at 5.45 p.m. on Sunday 22nd inst.
This loading party will also act as unloading party at TINQUES.

8. Rations for 23rd instant will be carried.

9. Further instructions later.

Capt. & Adjutant.
2nd. Regiment. South African Inf.

1. File.
2. "A" Coy.
3. "B" "
4. "C" "
5. "D" "
6. Hdqrs.
7. Transport Officer.
8. Quartermaster.
9. S.A. Brigade.
10. War Diary.
11. " "

22

2nd. REGIMENT. SOUTH AFRICAN INFANTRY.

In continuation of Order No. 3. the following amendments and additional instructions are now issued:-

1. Para. 5. (e) for 4. 30 p.m. read 4. 0. p.m.

2. Loading party detailed in para. 7. will be furnished by "A" Company. This party will march at 2. 0. p.m.. Their packs will be carried by Transport.

3. All ranks must carry rations for consumption on night of 22nd and breakfast on 23rd.
Rations for 23rd/24th will be carried in bulk by the Quartermaster and will not be issued till arrival at destination.

4. Transport will march at 3. 0. p.m. All Lewis Guns, kit, and baggage to be ready outside Company Billets for Transport Officer by 2. 0. p.m. One man only per Company will proceed with Transport.

5. Blankets will be rolled in bundles of 10 and will be picked up by lorry outside Company billets at 2. 0. p.m. Quartermaster will arrange.

6. Tea will be ready at WIZERNES station to be issued immediately the Battalion arrives there.

7. Transport Officer will see that Water Carts are filled before leaving.

8. Marching out states will be sent to Orderly Room at 3. 0. p.m. These states to shew full distribution of Company.

9. Clean Billet Certificates to be handed to Adjutant at 4. 0. p.m. Major Sprenger and Medical Officer will inspect the area before leaving.

L Steen

Capt. & Adjutant.
2nd. Regiment. South African Infantry.

In the Field.
21/9/18.

Appendix V (War Diary Sept. 1918).

2ND. SOUTH AFRICAN INFANTRY. COPY NO.......
(Referred to 25.9.18).

SECRET.

23

Reference
Lens & Amiens Sheets
$\frac{1}{100,000}$

ORDER NO. 4.

27th September, 1918.

1. South African Brigade entrains tomorrow (Saturday), 28th September, 1918, for CORBIE AREA.

2. (a). 2nd. Regiment will parade at 7.55 a.m. on road running N.W. from "C" Company Billets to MONTS EN TERNOIS. The Regiment will proceed by march route to PETIT HOUVIN station and entrain there.

(b). Order of march will be

Headquarters.
A. Company.
B. "
C. "
D. "

Head of column will march at 8.0. a.m.

(c). Men unable to march with their companies will parade at 7.0. a.m. under 2nd. Lieut. Giddy at starting point mentioned in (a) and will proceed ahead of Regiment to the entraining point at PETIT HOUVIN.

(d). The probable length of train journey will be ~~four~~ 4-5 hours.

3. CAPT. L.M. JACOBS will proceed by train from PETIT HOUVIN at 10.25 a.m. tomorrow and will report to R.T.O. on arrival at CORBIE to act as South African Brigade detrainment Officer.

4. Rations for consumption on 28th and breakfast 29th will be carried on the man. Rations for 29th will be issued in CORBIE AREA.
All ranks to entrain with ~~waterx~~ water bottles full.

5. (a). All blankets will be rolled in bundles of 10 and deposited outside Battalion Headquarters Orderly Room by 7.0. a.m.

(b). Officers kits, and mess stores and all other Company luggage including field kitchen utensils to be at Battalion Headquarters Orderly Room at 7.0. a.m.

(c). One man only per company will travel on lorry as a loading and offloading man and to guard Company property. Lorry proceeds direct by road to CORBIE AREA, and will be offloaded immediately on arrival at destination.

(d). No Baggage whatever will be taken on the train.

6. (a). States shewing exact number of Officers and other ranks to entrain at PETIT HOUVIN will be handed to Adjutant at 7.0. a.m. at Orderly Room.

(b). Clean billet certificates will also be handed to Adjutant at 7.30. a.m.

[signature]

Capt. & Adjutant,
2nd. Regiment. South African Infantry.

Appendix VI

24

2ND. SOUTH AFRICAN INFANTRY. COPY NO........

ORDER NO. 5. 29th September, 1918.

(War Diary Sept. 1918 Referred to 29.9.18.)

Reference Map.

AMIENS. $\frac{1}{100,000}$

---

1. The Regiment moves by March Route to CHUIGNOLLES AREA Today.

2. The Battalion will parade at 2.0. p.m. in the following order on main road facing East:-

Headquarters.
D. Company.
A. Company.
B. Company.
C. Company.
Transport.

3. All kit and baggage to be stacked on the Main Road outside Company Billets by 1.30. p.m.

4. A Billeting party of 1 N.C.O. from each Company and 1 from headquarters, with bicycles; under Lieut. Begley and will report to Adjutant at 10. a.m.

5. All Company Commanders and the Transport Officer will report to the Adjutant at 9.0. a.m. for further instructions.

Capt. & Adjutant.
2nd. Regt. South African Infantry.

4 S A Inf Bn

Army Form C. 2118.

Instructions regarding War Diaries and Intelligence Summaries are contained in F. S. Regs., Part II. and the Staff Manual respectively. Title pages will be prepared in manuscript.

WAR DIARY
or
INTELLIGENCE SUMMARY.
(Erase heading not required.)

SEPTEMBER, 1918.

Vol 2

Place	Date	Hour	Summary of Events and Information	Remarks and references to Appendices
LUMBRES	1-9-18	—	Regiment came into being as an Administrative Unit. Strength Officers – 25 Other Ranks – 841. Church parades from 10.30 am to 11.30 a.m. Weather Showery.	
LUMBRES	2-9-18	—	41 Other Ranks posted to this Unit from late 3rd Regiment South African Infantry. Companies training from 9. am to 12.30 p.m. Showery weather. Battalion moving to ALQUINES tomorrow.	See Appendix No. 1
LUMBRES	3-9-18	—	Battalion left for ALQUINES at 10.30 a.m. Arrived ALQUINES at 2 p.m. Billets good. 35 Other Ranks posted to this Battalion from the late 3rd Regiment South African Infantry. Captain H. Ramsay Rae rejoined the Battalion. Weather Cloudy.	

25

Instructions regarding War Diaries and Intelligence Summaries are contained in F. S. Regs., Part II. and the Staff Manual respectively. Title pages will be prepared in manuscript.

WAR DIARY
or
INTELLIGENCE SUMMARY.
(Erase heading not required.)

Army Form C. 2118.

SEPTEMBER, 1918

Place	Date	Hour	Summary of Events and Information	Remarks and references to Appendices
ALQUINES	4/9/18	—	Training being carried out under Company arrangements from 9 a.m to 12.30 p.m. Draft of 4 other ranks arrived from Rouen also two other ranks arrived from Rouen, posted to this Unit from the late 3rd Regiment South African Infantry. Weather fine.	
ALQUINES	5/9/18	—	Training being carried out under Company Arrangements from 9. a.m to 12.30 p.m. Weather fine.	
ALQUINES	6/9/18	—	Training carried out from 9 a.m. to 12.30 p.m. Weather again showery.	
ALQUINES	7/9/18	—	Training carried out under Company arrangements. Weather fine.	26

Instructions regarding War Diaries and Intelligence Summaries are contained in F. S. Regs., Part II. and the Staff Manual respectively. Title pages will be prepared in manuscript.

WAR DIARY
or
INTELLIGENCE SUMMARY.
(Erase heading not required.)

Army Form C. 2118.

SEPTEMBER, 1918

Place	Date	Hour	Summary of Events and Information	Remarks and references to Appendices
ALQUINES	8/9/18	—	Weather very Showery. Church parades cancelled on account of rain. Reinforcing draft of 13 other ranks arrived from Rouen.	
ALQUINES	9/9/18	—	Weather Showery. Training carried out under Company arrangements. Lieut. Colonel D. M. MacLeod, D.S.O., M.C., D.C.M. arrived from England and assumed Command of the Battalion.	
ALQUINES	10/9/18	—	Weather dull. Companies carrying out Rifle Practice on Range at ESCOEUILLES from 9 a.m. to 1 p.m.	
ALQUINES	11/9/18		Weather Showery. Training cancelled for the day. Draft of 4 other ranks arrived from Rouen. Revd. Capt. W. Menzies rejoined the Battalion from England. S. A. Brigade withdrawn from 9th Division to-day	

(A9175) Wt W2358/P360 600,000 12/17 D. D. & L. Sch. 52a. Forms/C2118/13.

Instructions regarding War Diaries and Intelligence Summaries are contained in F. S. Regs., Part II. and the Staff Manual respectively. Title pages will be prepared in manuscript.

WAR DIARY
or
INTELLIGENCE SUMMARY.
(Erase heading not required.)

Army Form C. 2118.

SEPTEMBER – 1918.

Place	Date	Hour	Summary of Events and Information	Remarks and references to Appendices
ALQUINES	12/9/18	—	Weather again showery. Battalion moved off for COULOMBY at 4.30 p.m. and arrived at COULOMBY at 6.30. p.m. Billets unsatisfactory.	See App. No. [illegible]
COULOMBY	13/9/18	—	Weather fine. Commanding Officer's parade in forenoon. Recreational training in afternoon	
COULOMBY	14/9/18	—	Weather Dull. Gas and musketry training carried out by Companies at ESCOEILLES from 8-30 a.m. to 1 p.m. Recreational training in afternoon.	
COULOMBY	15/9/18	—	Weather fine. Gas and musketry training carried out by Companies at ESCOEILLES from 8.30 a.m. to 1 p.m. Draft of 5 Other ranks arrived from Rouen	

28

(A9475) Wt W2358/P360 600,000 12/17 D. D. & L. Sch. 52a. Forms/C2118/15.

Army Form C. 2118.

Instructions regarding War Diaries and Intelligence Summaries are contained in F. S. Regs., Part II. and the Staff Manual respectively. Title pages will be prepared in manuscript.

WAR DIARY or INTELLIGENCE SUMMARY.

(Erase heading not required.)

SEPTEMBER, 1918

Place	Date	Hour	Summary of Events and Information	Remarks and references to Appendices
COULOMBY	16/9/18	—	Weather fine. Battalion inspected by Brigadier-General at 11-30 a.m. Companies paraded at 10.30 a.m. and marched to parade ground for inspection. Company Competitions Commenced to-day.	
COULOMBY	17/9/18	—	Weather fine. B and D Companies carried out Rifle practice on Range at LUMBRES from 8.30 a.m to 1 p.m. A and C Companies delousing at Field Ambulance from 9 a.m to 12.30 p.m	
COULOMBY	18/9/18	—	Weather Showery. Companies carried out General training from 9 a.m. to 12.30 p.m Recreational Training in afternoon.	

29

Instructions regarding War Diaries and Intelligence Summaries are contained in F. S. Regs., Part II. and the Staff Manual respectively. Title pages will be prepared in manuscript.

WAR DIARY
or
INTELLIGENCE SUMMARY.
(Erase heading not required.)

Army Form C. 2118.

SEPTEMBER 1918.

Place	Date	Hour	Summary of Events and Information	Remarks and references to Appendices
COULOMBY	19/9/18	—	Weather Showery. Companies carried out General Training from 9 a.m. to 1 p.m. Lewis Gun Classes report to Lewis Gun Sergeant for instruction, from 9 am to 12.30 pm. Signallers report to Signalling Officer at Battalion H.Q. at 9 am for instruction. Lecture at Medical Inspection Room at 5 p.m. by Commanding Officer, to all Officers of the Battalion. Foot ball team representing the Battalion played 206 Squadron R.A.F and were beaten by 2 goals to one.	
COULOMBY	20/9/18	—	Weather Showery. Companies carried out General Training as laid down for 19th instant. Lewis Gun Classes and Signallers will report for instruction as laid down for 19th instant.	
COULOMBY	21/9/18		Weather showery in morning but cleared up towards midday. Billetting party left for AMBRINES, reporting to Brigade H.Q. General Training carried out by Companies from 8 a.m. to 1 p.m. Major E.G. CLERK and LIEUT. C.C. Mc KELLAR-BASSET arrived from England and are taken on Strength of Battn. Major E.G. CLERK assumes duties of Second-in-Command as from to-da[y]	30

(A9175) Wt W2358/P360 600,000 12/17 D. D. & L. Sch. 52a. Forms/C2118/15.

Instructions regarding War Diaries and Intelligence Summaries are contained in F. S. Regs., Part II. and the Staff Manual respectively. Title pages will be prepared in manuscript.

WAR DIARY
or
INTELLIGENCE SUMMARY.
(Erase heading not required.)

Army Form C. 2118.

SEPTEMBER, 1918.

Place	Date	Hour	Summary of Events and Information	Remarks and references to Appendices
COULOMBY	22/9/18	—	Weather Sulky. Battalion left for AMBRINES at 8-30 a.m. and proceeded by march route to WIZERNES where Battalion entrained at 3 p.M and was conveyed by rail as far as TINCQUES. Detrained at TINCQUES at 9.00 p.M and proceeded by march route to AMBRINES arriving there at 10-30 p.M. Billets unsatisfactory. Draft of 11 O/Rs arrived from Rouen and were taken on strength of Battalion. S A Infantry Brigade Group joined 66th Division to-day	See Appendix No. 5
AMBRINES	23/9/18	—	Weather Cold & Showery. Day spent in improving Billets. Officers reconnoitred training area	
AMBRINES	24/9/18	—	Weather Sulky. From 8 am to 9 am Company Inspection carried out. From 9 am to 1 pm General Training by Companies. Range utilized by C Company Lewis Gunners for Lewis Gun firing from 12 noon to 1 pm. All Sergeants and Lance-Sergeants report to R.S.M. Wilson, J. at 12 noon for instruction. Leaflets extending invitation to discuss peace terms at a place to be appointed in a neutral country dropped by enemy aircraft at 8.30 a.m	

Instructions regarding War Diaries and Intelligence Summaries are contained in F. S. Regs., Part II. and the Staff Manual respectively. Title pages will be prepared in manuscript.

WAR DIARY
or
INTELLIGENCE SUMMARY.
(Erase heading not required.)

SEPTEMBER, 1918.

Army Form C. 2118.

Place	Date	Hour	Summary of Events and Information	Remarks and references to Appendices
AMBRINES	25/9/18	—	Weather fine. From 8.30 am to 9.15 a.m Company Inspection and march to Training Area. From 9.15 am to 1 p.m General Training carried out by Companies. From 3 p.m. to 7 p.m. Range practice by A Coy. Lewis Gunners. All Signallers to report immediately after Company Inspection to Signalling Officer for instruction. Lieutenant C.C. McKELLAR-BASSET appointed Quartermaster as from to-day's date	
AMBRINES	26/9/18	—	Weather fine. Battalion left at 8.30 a.m on Route march returning at 12.45 p.m. Recreational training during the afternoon. Lecture on Tanks at 6 p.m to all officers of the Battn. Concert in evening by men of Battn.	
AMBRINES	27/9/18	—	Weather fair. Battalion leaving tomorrow for CORBIE AREA. Billeting party left at 7 a.m by lorry. Transport left at 8.30 a.m, by road, for VILLERS BRETONNEUX. Remainder of Battn on route march from 8.30 am to 1 p.m. Transferred from 1st Army to 4th Army as from to-day's date	See Appendix No. 4.

(A9175) Wt W2358/P360 600,000 12/17 D. D. & L. Sch. 52a. Forms/C2118/15.

32

Instructions regarding War Diaries and Intelligence Summaries are contained in F. S. Regs., Part II. and the Staff Manual respectively. Title pages will be prepared in manuscript.

WAR DIARY
or
INTELLIGENCE SUMMARY.
(Erase heading not required.)

Army Form C. 2118.

SEPTEMBER – 1918.

Place	Date	Hour	Summary of Events and Information	Remarks and references to Appendices
AMBRINES	28/9/18	–	Weather Showery. Battalion left at 11 a.m. to entrain at TINCQUES for CORBIE. Left TINCQUES at 3.30 p.m. and arrived at CORBIE at about 12.30 a.m. on morning of 29th instant. Had tea at Station (CORBIE) and then left by march route for VILLERS BRETONNEUX arriving there at 4 a.m. Battalion billeted by 5 a.m. in Cellars.	
VILLERS BRETONNEUX	29/9/18	–	Weather Showery. Battalion left for FOUCAUCOURT AREA at 2.30 p.m. by march route arriving at new Area at 7 p.m. Battalion billeted in Shacks and dug-outs recently vacated by enemy, in valley near RAINECOURT.	See Appendix No. 5
FOUCAUCOURT AREA	30/9/18	–	Weather Windy & Cold. Battn. busy Salvaging. One man accidentally wounded by German hand grenade.	

4th S.A. INFANTRY REGT. 1 - OCT. 1918 Ref. No. SOUTH AFRICAN SCOTTISH

D. M. MacLeod Lt. Col.
Commanding 4th Regt. S.A. Inf.
(S.A. Scottish)

33

W 5593/826 600,000 12/17 D. D. & L. Sch. 52a. Forms/C2118/15.

4th Regt: S.A. INFANTRY.

Daily State.

30/9/18.

I				II		III		IV		V		VI		VII		VIII	
AVAILABLE FOR GOING INTO ACTION				SURPLUS PERSONNEL TO BE LEFT AT DETAIL BATTN.		ADMIN. PORTION HD QRTS		ON LEAVE		ON COURSES		IN FIELD AMBLCE		EXTRA REGTLY. EMPLOYED AND OTHER DETACHED		TOTAL	
BN HD QRTS		FOUR COY															
O	OR	O	OR.	O	OR	O	OR	O	OR	O	OR	O	OR	O	OR	O	OR.
4	72	19	684	-	25	2	120	1	23	1	1	-	-	-	29	27	954.

Sgd. D. M. MacLeod.
LIEUT.-COL.
COMMANDING 4TH. REGT. SOUTH AFRICAN INF.

34

Appendix No 1

35

SOUTH AFRICAN SCOTTISH. COPY NO...........

ORDER NO. 1.

Reference Maps.-
HAZEBROUCK 5.a. 100000
Army Area Map No. 6. Monday, September, 2nd. 1918.

---

1. For the purpose of administration the South African personnel is now formed into

1st South African Infantry
2nd. South African Infantry
4th South African Infantry.
South African Light Trench Mortar Battery.

2. The 2nd. S.A.I., the 4th S.A.I. and S.A.I. T.M.B. will move to-day the 2nd. instant to the ALQUINES AREA. The 1st S.A.I. will remain for the present at BAYENGHEM.

3. On arrival at the new area the South African Scottish will be billeted as follows.-

Headquarters ALQUINES
JOURNY
HAUT -LOQUIN

Transport lines will be at JOURNY.

4. The Battalion will move off at 10 30a.m. Order of march will be as follows.-

"A" Company
"B" Company
"C" Company
"D" Company.

The transport will follow immediately in rear of Battalion.

5. All Officers' kit will be dumped near theguard tent by the road-side by 10 a.m. The Transport Officer will make arrangements to pick up the material. Officers' Mess Stores and Quartermaster's Stores will be picked up by Transport at 10 a.m.

6. On arrival at New Area Company Commanders will render to Battalion Orderly Room immediately (1) Marching in state (2) a statement showing (a) location of Officers' billets (b) distribution of Company.

[illegible signature]

2nd. Lieut. and Adjutant.

4th Regt. South African Infantry.
(South African Scottish)

IN THE FIELD.

Copies issued at 8 a.m. as under.-

1 - 4 All Coys.
5. 2nd. in Command.
6. Quartermaster.
7. Transport Officer.
8. Medical Officer.
9. Signalling Officer.
10. R.S.M.
11/12 War Diary.
13. File.

36

SOUTH AFRICAN SCOTTISH

COPY NO.........

ORDER NO. 2.

REFERENCE MAPS.-
HAZEBROUCK 5 a. 1/100000
CELLES 1/40,000

Thursday, 12th September, 1918.

---

1. The 4th Regiment South African Infantry will move by march route to-day, 12th September, from the ALQUINES AREA to the LUMBRES AREA and will be billeted in the villages of COULOMBY AND SENNINGHEM.

2. The order of march will be as follows.-

"A" company
"B" Company
"C" Company
"D" Company
Headquarters.

The starting point will be the road junction in ALQUINES at the Regimental Quartermaster's Stores as situated.

The head of column will pass the starting point at 2 p.m. Transport will march in rear of Battalion.

3. All Officers' kits will be dumped by 12 noon at the Headquarters of their respective Companies. Transport Officer will arrange to pick up Officers' kits, mess kits, Quartermaster's Stores material and Medical Officers equipment.

4. The Second in Command and Medical Officer will inspect billets during the morning. In addition clean billet certificates will be handed in by Company Commanders on passing the starting point.

5. On arrival at the new area Companies will render immediately to Battalion Orderly Room
(1) Marching in State
(2) The list of billets occupied showing Company Headquarters and all Officers. billets

6. Company Commanders will, as soon as possible after arrival, arrange to reconnoitre training areas in the vicinity of their Companies

7. DRESS. Dress for Officers will be steel helmets and Sam Browne belts. For other ranks steel helmets and full marching order.

8. Battalion Headquarters will be situated in COULOMBY.

2nd. Lieut. and Adjutant.
4th Regt. South African Infantry.
(South African Scottish)

IN THE FIELD.

Copies issued at 9 a.m. to ALL CONCERNED.

Appendix No. 3.

SECRET.

37

COPY NO.........

SOUTH AFRICAN SCOTTISH

ORDER NO. 3. (3)

Reference Maps.-
Hazebrouck 5.a. 1/100000.
Lens. 11. 1/100000.

Saturday, September, 21. 1918.

---

1. The 66th Division (less Artillery) is being concentrated in the LE CAUROY AREA, (First Army).

2. The South African Infantry Brigade Group will be transferred by rail to First Army on 22nd. September to join 66th Division,

3. The South African Scottish will entrain at WIZERNES, as under, on 22nd. inst. and will detrain at TINCQUES on 23rd. inst.-

"A" Company	11 a.m.	First train.
"B" Company	2 p.m.	Second train.
"C" Company	2 p.m.	do.-
"D" Company	2 p.m.	do.-
Transport	12 noon	do.-

Headquarters personnel will move and entrain with their respective Companies.

Field Kitchen with team will accompany "A" Company and will report to Battalion Entraining Officer at WIZERNES by 9 a.m. 22nd. inst.

4. Lieut. R. Hill is detailed as Battalion Entraining Officer and will report to Brigade Entraining Officer (Lieut. L. G. MacKay, 1st Regt.) at WIZERNES by 8.30 a.m. 22nd. inst.

5. The Battalion will move by march route to WIZERNES on 22nd inst. via SENINGHEM, BAYEN GHEM, thence along BOULOGNE - ST. OMER road to WIZERNES.

6. The order of march will be as under.-

"B" Company
"C" Company
"D" Company
Transport.

7. The starting point will be "B" Coy. Headquarters. Head of column will pass starting point at 8.30 a.m.

8. Clock hour halts will be observed.

9. Rations for consumption on the 23. inst. and 1 blanket per man will be issued at entraining point.

10. Packs will be dumped at respective Company Headquarters by 7.30 a.m. 22nd. inst., and will be transported to entraining point. Companies supplying their own loading and unloading parties.

11.. All Company Stores requiring to be carried by Regimental Quartermaster's stores must be handed in by 7. a.m. 22nd. inst,

12. "C" Company will supply a loading party of 1 Officer and 50 Other Ranks who will report to Battalion Entraining Officer at 11.30 a.m. at WIZERNES.

13. The Quartermaster will arrange for a meal to be provided at Entraining station where a Bivouacing area will be available with water.

14. All area stores belonging to this area will be handed in before moving excepting latrine screens which will be left standing.
If the day is wet, tents will not be struck but will be handed over standing.

15. All Officers' kits will be dumped at the Headquarters of their respective Companies by 7.30 a.m. 22nd. inst.
All Officers' mess kits must be dumped at Regimental Quartermaster's Stores by 8.a.m.

16. All salvage will be collected and handed into Quartermaster's Stores by 7.a.m. 22nd. inst.

17. The following will be required from Company Commanders at the starting point.-

(a) Clean billet certificate
(b) Marching out state.

18. The following will be required from Company Commanders on arrival.-

(a) Marching in state.
(b) List of Billets, showing Officers' Billets and Company Headquarters.

The situation of Battalion Headquarters will be notified later.

Sgd. F. G. [illegible]

Captain and Adjutant.

4th Regt. South African Infantry.
(South African Scottish)

IN THE FIELD.

Copies issued at 10 a.m.
by runners as under.-

1. South African Inf. Brigade.
2.-5 All Coys.
6. 2nd. in Command.
7. Quartermaster
8. Transport Officer
9. Medical Officer
10. Signalling Officer.
11. R.S.M.
12/13. War Diary.
14. File.

39

(A)

File

SOUTH AFRICAN SCOTTISH.

WARNING ORDER.

1. The 66th Division is being transferred from the 1st to the 4th Army, and will move from its present Area to the CORBIE AREA on the 27th and 28th Sept.

2. 1st. and 2nd. Line Transports of the S.A. Infantry Brigade Group will proceed by road on the 27th Sept. Personnel will entrain on the 28th Sept. Detailed instructions will be issued later for move on these dates.

3. All Q.M. Stores, Office material, (except that actually required for use on the 27th.) Officers kits (less blankets and shaving kit) must be loaded on the 1st and 2nd. Line Transports. One supply waggon of each Unit will be available to carry a certain amount of baggage. This can be arranged direct with O.C. Train Coy.

4. As cookers are proceeding by road it will be necessary to keep back Cooking utensils for use on the 27th and 28th.

5. A lorry will be provided on the 28th Sept. to convey Officers Mess kits, personal kits, and cooking utensils, left behind for the men. Further instructions will be issued regarding mens blankets.

6. Rations for consumption on the 28th Sept. are being issued to-day. Transport personnel must carry rations for consumption on 27th and 28th.

7. Rations for 29th Sept. will be issued on arrival in CORBIE AREA.

8. Any baggage carried on supply waggons will be dumped at Refilling point and must be collected by Units.

9. In view of the above all Officers surplus kit will be handed into Regimental Quartermaster's stores to-night by 10 p.m.

T.G. Maefie

Captain and Adjutant.

4th Regt. South African Infantry.
(South African Scottish)

26th Sept. 1918.

Cipies issued to.-

1 to 4 All Companies.
5. 2nd in Command.
6. Quartermaster
7. Transport Officer
8. Medical Officer
9. Signalling Officer
10. R.S.M.
11/12 War Diary.
13. File.

SECRET.

(A)

40

COPY NO........

SOUTH AFRICAN SCOTTISH.

ORDER NO. 4.

Reference Maps

Sheet 51 C.
LENS II 1/100000
AMIENS 17. 1/100000.

FRIDAY, SEPTEMBER 27th 1918.

1.. The 66th Division (less Artillery) accompanied by Div. M.T. Coy. (less 2 sections) will be transferred to Fourth Army from First Army commencing September 27th.

2. South African Brigade Group will move, personnel by train, transport by road to the CORBIE AREA.

3. The Battalion will move by march route to TINCQUES on Saturday, September 28th, the order of march for Companies being as under.-

"A" Company
"B" Company
"C" Company
"D" Company
Headquarters.

The starting point will be road junction I.3.d.2.2. Head of column will pass starting point at 11 a.m.

4. The South African Scottish will entrain at TINCQUES at 12.38 p.m.

5. Rations for consumption on 28th inst. will be carried on man. Rations for consumption on 29th inst. will be issued in CORBIE AREA. All waterbottles must be full on entraining.

6. No baggage whatsoever will be taken on the train.

7. All surplus baggage, i.e., Officers' bedding, mess kits and men's blankets requiring to be transported to New Area must be at the Regimental Quartermaster's Stores by 7 a.m. Blankets will be rolled in bundles of 10. All cooking utensils must be dumped at Regimental Quartermaster's Stores by 7.30 a.m.

8. 2nd. Lieut. D.A.R.Leathern is detailed as Battalion Entraining Officer and will report to Railway Transport Officer TINCQUES at 11 a.m.

9. Company Commanders will, on passing the starting point, render the following to the Adjutant.-

(a) Clean Billet Certificate.
(b) Marchingout state.

10. Company Commanders on arrival in new billets will render immediately to Battalion Orderly Room a marching in state.

T.G. Marfin

Captain and Adjutant.
4th Regt. South African Infantry.
(South African Scottish)

ISSUED TO ALL CONCERNED.

41

SECRET. COPY NO. 12

SOUTH AFRICAN SCOTTISH.

ORDER NO. 5.

Reference Map.

AMIENS 17. 1/100000. Sunday, 29th September, 1918..

---

1. The South African Scottish will move to-day by march route to RAINECOURT.

2. The route followed will be via LAMOTTE and X roads in I. 2. central.

3. Order of march for Companies will be as under.-

"A" Company..
"B" Company.
"C" Company
"D" Company.
Headquarters.
Transport.

4. Starting point will be Regimental Orderly Room.

5. Head of column will pass starting point at 2.15. p.m.

6. 100 yds. intervals will be maintained between Companies and also between the Battalion and Battalion Transport. 500 yds. intervals will be maintained between Battalions.

7. Clock hour halts will be observed.

8. All Officers' kits and mess kits must be handed into Quartermaster's ~~xxxxxx~~ stores by 1. 30 p.m.

9. Company Commanders will render immediately on arrival in New Area to Battalion Orderly Room a marching in state.-

Captain and Adjutant.

4th Regt. South African Infantry.
(South African Scottish)

IN THE FIELD.

Copies issued by runners at 11 a.m.
as under.-
1-4 All Coys.
5. 2nd. in Command.
6. Quartermaster.
7. Transport Officer.
8. Signalling Officer.
9. Medical Officer.
~~10. South African Brigade.~~
11. R.S.M.
12/13. War Diary.
14. File.

LIST OF OFFICERS

4th Regt. South African Infantry (South African Scottish)

as at 30th. September, 1918.

HEADQUARTERS.-

Lieut.-Col. D.M.MacLeod, D.S.O.,M.C.,D.C.M.,	Commanding Officer,
Major. E.G. CLERK,	2nd. in Command.
Captain L.W. Tomlinson, D.S.O.	
Captain L.W. Reid.	
Captain T.G. Macfie. M.C.,	Adjutant.
Lieut. C.C. McKellar-Basset.	Quartermaster.
Lieut. L.R. Johnston.	Transport Officer.
2nd. Lieut. P.C. Neille, M.C.,	Signalling Officer.

"A" COMPANY.-

Lieut. R.B.Marshall.	Officer Commanding.
Lieut. R. Hill.	
2nd. Lieut. E.A.Goodwin.	
2nd. Lieut. G.H.Wallace.	
2nd. Lieut. E.G.L. Smith.	

"B" COMPANY.-

Captain A. McI. Cameron.	Officer Commanding.
Lieut. E. Middleton.	
2nd. Lieut. J.K.Fowle.	
2nd. Lieut. N.J. Johnson.	
2nd. Lieut. J.J.Young, M.M.,	

"C" COMPANY.-

Captain C.M. Guest.	Officer Commanding.
2nd. Lieut. H.W. Backeberg, M.C.,	
2nd. Lieut. H. Pettman.	
2nd. Lieut. D.A.R. Leathern.	
2nd. Lieut. G.W. Gordon.	

"D" COMPANY.-

Captain W.H. Kirby, M.C.,	Officer Commanding.
2nd. Lieut. S.G. Thompson.	
2nd. Lieut. T.J.McLeod.	
2nd. Lieut. J. Peters.	

OFFICERS ATTACHED.-

Capt. H.R. Rae.	Musketry Officer.
Capt. B. Sampson. M.C.,	S.A.M.C. (M.O.)
Capt. and Revd. W. Menzies,	Chaplain.
Lieut. C.B. Barry.	attached to "D" Coy.

43

SOUTH AFRICAN SCOTTISH.

Copy No. 12

ORDER NO. 27.

Ref. Map.
NAMUR 1/100,000.

Saturday, 23rd November, 1918.

I. The South African Scottish will march by march route to-morrow 24th November, 1918 to HERMETON.

II. The route will be via AGIMONT - BAC DU PRINCE.

III. The order of Companies on the march will be as under.-

"C" Company
"D" Company
Headquarters Company
"A" Company
"B" Company
Transport.

IV. The Battalion will parade on the Square at 08.05 hours.

V. Baggage wagons will report to R.Q.M. Stores by 07.30 hrs.

VI. One blanket will be carried on the man; the second blankets will be rolled in bundles of ten and handed in to R.Q.M. Stores by 07.30 for conveyance by lorry. Only greatcoats, Officers' kits and usual boxes will be carried on Company G.S. wagons. Lorry will report at Church ROSSE at 10.00. The Quartermaster will arrange for a guide to meet it and for a loading party.

VII. 1st and 2nd. Line Transport will march with the Battalion.

VIII. Reveille will be at 06.00 hrs. to-morrow.

IX. Billeting N.C.Os. will report at Battalion Orderly Room to Lieut. J.Oates at 07.30.

T.G. Murfie
Captain and Adjutant.
South African Scottish.

Issued by Runners
as under at 22.45.
1.-4 All Coys.
5. 2nd. in Command.
6. Quartermaster.
7. Transport Officer.
8. Medical Officer
9. Signalling Officer.
10. R.S.M.
11/12 War Diary.
13. File.

WAR DIARY
or
INTELLIGENCE SUMMARY
(Erase heading not required.)

Instructions regarding War Diaries and Intelligence Summaries are contained in F. S. Regs., Part II. and the Staff Manual respectively. Title Pages will be prepared in manuscript.

October 1918. 2nd South African Infantry.

Place	Date	Hour	Summary of Events and Information	Remarks and references to Appendices
FRAMERVILLE + Line of March	1.10.18		Battalion moves off at 9.30 am followed by 199th Bgde via BRAY - CARNOY to Camp in valley near and S.W. of MAMETZ WOOD. During march owing to slow pace. Camp consists of Shacks and cubby hole in side of hill.	Appendix I Order No. 6
Camp near MAMETZ WOOD.	2.10.18 to 3.10.18		Bgde in XIII Corps. Attack practice during afternoon (2.10.18). 2/Lt. FERNIE D.C.M. joins from England (2.10.18). Bath during the day (3.10.18). Some rain and considerable artillery activity in distance.	
MAMETZ Wood - line of March - NURLU.	4.10.18		Battn moves off 8.45 am to "Shack" billets in camp near BOULEAU Wood West of GUILLEMONT arriving 11.30 am. Coys carry out attack practice 2.0 pm to 4.0 pm. Orders received 4.45 pm to be ready to move at moments notice. Battn moves 8.0 pm to NURLU arriving 12.45 am (5.10.18). Fine straggling. [illegible] the march owing to the "strenuousness" of the day. Lieuts. PARROT, FRASER, RAYMOND proceed to L.G., General Musketry and Musketry course respectively at IV Army School.	Appendix II Order No. 7. Appendix III Order No. 8
NURLU + Line of March	5.10.18		Head of Battn passes starting point 1000x E. of Village 9.40 am. Battn reaches camp in open field just W. of RONSSY about 1.0 pm. Bivouacking 50 tents and 30 trench shelters. Route via LIERAMONT and VILLERS FAUCON. Cold and dusty march. Draft of 3 officers (Capt. T.G. WALSH M.C., 2/Lt. S.H.A. LOWE, 2/Lt. R.H. HEWAT) and 53 O.Ranks arrives. Lieut PHILLIPS proceeds to S.O.S. course IV Army. B. team under Lieuts BEGLEY and ALLEN (with Major BLOOMFIELD V.C. attached) proceed to reinforcement Camp at MOISLANS.	Appendix IV Order No. 9

45

2449 Wt. W14957/M90 750,000 1/16 J.B.C. & A. Forms/C.2118/12.

(2)

WAR DIARY
or
INTELLIGENCE SUMMARY

Instructions regarding War Diaries and Intelligence Summaries are contained in F. S. Regs., Part II. and the Staff Manual respectively. Title Pages will be prepared in manuscript.

October 1918 *(Erase heading not required.)* 2nd South African Infantry

Army Form C. 2118.

Place	Date	Hour	Summary of Events and Information	Remarks and references to Appendices
RONSSY CAMP.	6.10.18		Summer time changes to winter time during night 5th/6th. Order received 8.45 am that Battn on fighting strength were to move forward to occupy LE CATELET – NAUROY Line E of BONY. This was cancelled and Battn "stand-by". 2/Lieut. BONTHUYS from England posted to Battn.	
RONSSY CAMP to LINE OF MARCH	7.10.18		Battn moves off 9.40 am to LE CATELET – NAUROY LINE with a view to impending attack (8.10.18). All surplus personnel (including MAJOR SPRENGER, Lieuts MORILLIER, LAZARUS, BOWES, HEWAT, LOWE) and transport remain behind at RONSSY. Battn moved to assembly position during night vide narrative Appendix VI	Appendix V; Order No 10; Appendix VI
BEAUREVOIR	8.10.18		Battn attacks. See Appendix VII (orders for attack) and Appendix VI (Narrative of attack.)	Appendix VII (Order No 11) & Appendix VI (narrative)
SERAIN – MARETZ – MAUROIS and HONNECHY.	9.10.18		Battn attacks. See Appendices VIII and VI	Appendix VIII (Order No 12) Appendix VI
MAUROIS – HONNECHY to LE CATEAU	10.10.18 to 19.10.18		See Appendices 10.10.18 IX Relief & occupation of Line. 15.10.18 X Minor operation bridges W. of LE CATEAU. 16.10.18 XI Relief in Line & concentration 17.10.18 XII attack by Battn 18.10.18 XIII attack by Battn 19.10.18 XIV Relief of Battn } To be read in conjunction with Appendix VI. Report on operations from 7.10.18 to 19.10.18.	Appendices IX, X, XI, XII, XIII, XIV, [illegible] and VI

2449 Wt. W14957/M90 750,000 1/16 J.B.C. & A. Forms/C.2118/12.

(5)

Instructions regarding War Diaries and Intelligence Summaries are contained in F. S. Regs., Part II. and the Staff Manual respectively. Title Pages will be prepared in manuscript.

WAR DIARY
or
INTELLIGENCE SUMMARY
(Erase heading not required.)

Army Form C. 2118.

October 1918 — 2nd South African Infy

Place	Date	Hour	Summary of Events and Information	Remarks and references to Appendices
REUMONT & LINES of Brown to SERAIN	20.10.18		Battn moves at 10.30 am via MAUROIS - MARETZ to SERAIN. Road one continual stream of traffic making march very difficult. Cold and raining. Battn billeted in houses vacated by civilians. Very comfortable.	App.
SERAIN	21.10.18 to 31.10.18		Battn cleans up, makes up deficiencies, reorganizes on basis of three platoons per Coy and carries out, owing to shortage of Lewis Gunners and Signallers, special training in specialist subjects. Officers are posted to Coys vide Appendix XVI. Lieut. PARROTT rejoins ex Course 25.10.18. 2/Lt. C.K. MARTIN rejoins from England 26.10.18. 2/Lts. R. HASKIS and P.H. HAVILAND from England are posted to Battn and to Coys. 2/Lt. C.C. RAYMOND rejoins from course 30.10.18. Battn participates in Divisional Attack Scheme 31.10.18.	Appendix XVI (Posting to Coys. of Officers)

Battn Strength as at 31.10.18.

With Battn	18	395
Field Ambulance	1	5
On Courses	1	8
On Leave	1	31
Detached Duties		21
	21	460

J. F. Jennings [illegible]
Major
Comdg 2nd S.A.I.
Field 1.11.18.

47

2449 Wt. W14957/M90 750,000 1/16 J.B.C. & A. Forms/C.2118/12.

SECRET.

2ND. SOUTH AFRICAN INFANTRY.

Reference-MAPS.

ORDER NO. 6. 1ST. OCTOBER, 1918.

AMIENS 17-Q/100,000
LENS. 11-1/100,000

48

1. The South African Brigade Group will move by March Route ~~xxxxxxxx~~ to billets in the MONTAUBAN AREA today.

2. The Battalion will parade ready to move off at 9.30 a.m. The head of the column crossing starting point at TRANSPORT LINES at this time.

3. The Battalion will parade in the following order:-

Headquarters,
"A" Company.
"B" Company.
"C" Company.
"D" Company.
Transport.

Interval of 100 yards between companies will be observed.

4. DRESS - FULL MARCHING ORDER AND STEEL HELMETS: Mounted Officers will wear Sam Brown Belts.

5. ADVANCE PARTIES will meet Staff Captain at X roads W of "M" in MARICOURT at 10.30. a.m.

6. MARCHING OUT STATES and Billet Certificates will be handed to the Adjutant at 9.25 a.m. at head of column.

7. BLANKETS will be rolled in bundles of 10 and stacked on road outside Company Headquarters by 8.30. a.m. together with all Officers kits, mess kits, etc.

8. One other rank will be left in charge of this kit by each Company and see it loaded.

Capt. & Adjutant.
2nd. Regiment, South African Infantry.

SECRET.

2nd. SOUTH AFRICAN INFANTRY.

Reference. ORDER NO. 7. 3rd October, 1918.

LENS 11. 1/100,000
Sheet. 57c. 1/40,000

1. The South African Brigade will move by march route tomorrow, 4th October, 1918, to the COMBLES AREA.

2. The Battalion will parade ready to move off at 8.40 a.m. in the following order:-

Headquarters.
"D" Company.
"C" Company.
"A" Company.
"B" Company.

3. (a). Starting point on road opposite West Edge of Catepillar Wood (S.20. c. 2. 7.)
(b). DRESS - Full marching order.
Mounted Officers with sam brown belts.
(c). Head of column will pass starting point at 8.45 a.m.
(d). Interval of 100 yards to be observed between Companies and Transport.
(e). Transport will move at intervals of 25 yards between every 5 vehicles.

4. All blankets to be rolled in bundles of 10 and stacked on road near Company Billets, together with officers' kits, mess kits, etc, by 6.0. a.m.

5. Marching out states and clean billet certificates to be handed to Adjutant at starting point at 8.40. a.m.

6. All men unable to march with their Companies will parade at 7.0. a.m. under 2/Lt. R.D. Birrell at starting point mentioned above and will go on in advance.

7. Only one man per Company will be left as a loading and offloading party for the lorries.

8. Transport Officer will ensure that water carts are filled prior to departure.

9. Route: Via MONTAUBAN, SOUTH EDGE OF BERNAFAY WOOD, GUILLEMONT to COMBLES.

Capt. & Adjutant.
2nd. Regt. South African Infantry.

2ND. SOUTH AFRICAN INFANTRY. **SECRET.**

Appendix VI (Reference 4.10.18)

ORDER NO. 8.

Reference.
Sheet 57c 1/40,000
62c 1/40,000

4TH. OCTOBER. 1918.

50

1. The South African Brigade will move by march route this evening 4th October, 1918, to the NURLU AREA.

2. The Battalion will parade ready to move off at 7.30 p.m. in the following order:-

Headquarters;
"A" Company.
"B" Company.
"C" Company.
"D" Company.
Transport.

3. (a). Starting point on road opposite Battalion Guard tent.
(b). DRESS- Full marching order.
Mounted Officers with Sam Browne Belts.
(c). Head of column will pass starting point at 7.30. p.m.
(d). Interval of 100 yards to be observed between Companies and Transport.
(e). Transport will move at intervals of 25 yards between every 6 vehicles.

4. All Blankets to be rolled in bundles of 10 and stacked at R.Q.M. Stores together with Officers kits, mess kits, etc, by 6.30. p.m.

5. All men unable to march with their Companies will parade at 7.0. p.m. under 2/Lieut. G.S. Fernie DCM. at starting point mentioned above. and will go on in advance.

6. Only one man per Company will be left as a loading and offloading party for the lorries.

7. Transport Officer will ensure that water carts are filled prior to departure.

8. Route: Via COMBLES: BOUCHAVESNES: MOISLAINS: to NURLU.

L. Greene

Capt. & Adjutant.
2nd. Regt. South African Infantry.

2ND. SOUTH AFRICAN INFANTRY. SECRET.

Appendix IV

ORDER NO. 9.

Reference.

62c 1/40,000.

5TH. OCTOBER 1918. (Reference to 5.10.18)

51

1. The South African Brigade will move by march route at 9.0. a.m. 5th instant. to the RONSSOY AREA.

2. The Battalion will parade ready to move off at 9.0. a.m. in following order:-

Headquarters,
"A" Company.
"B" Company.
"C" Company.
"D" Company.
Transport.

3. (a). Starting point on cross roads at Battalion Headquarters.
(b). DRESS- BATTLE ORDER.
(c). Head of column will pass starting point at 9.0. a.m.
(d). Interval of 100 yards to be observed between Companies and Transport.
(e). Transport will move at intervals of 25 yards between every 6 vehicles.

4. All blankets and grey coats to be rolled in bundles of 10 and stacked at R.Q.M. Stores by 7.30. a.m.

5. ROUTE: via LIERAMONT: VILLERS FAUCON.

6. "B" Teams and spares will return to MOISLAINS under orders of Major CLERK, 4th S.A.I. and report to billet Warden for Accommodation. Major CLERK will remain in command of these teams.

7. Companies will furnish a return to this office by 14.00 o'clock, 5th October,1918, shewing distribution of personnel going into action.

8. Personnel of "B" teams must be rationed for consumption 5th instant.

9. All surplus kit will be dumped at Brigade Headquarters at NURLU under Guards to be detailed from Battalion "B" Teams.

Capt. & Adjutant.
2nd. Regt. South African Infantry.

Appendix V

SECRET

(Reproduced 1/0 7.10.18).

52

2ND. REGIMENT. SOUTH AFRICAN INFANTRY.

ORDER NO. IO.

7TH. OCTOBER. 1918.

I. The South African Brigade will move by march route at 9.40.a.m. 7th instant, to CATLLET NAURCY LINE.

2. The Battalion will parade ready to move off at 9.40.a.m. to BONY, in following order:-

Headquarters,
"B" Company.
"C" Company.
"D" Company.
"A" Company.

3. (a). Starting point on the road apposite Battalion Orderly Room.
(b). DRESS-BATTLE ORDER WITH BLANKETS.
(c). Head of column will pass starting point at 9.40.a.m.
(d). Interval of IOO yards to be observed between companies.

4. All great coats to be rolled in bundles of IO, and stacked at R.Q.M. Stores, by 9.30.a.m. together with tents vacated.

5. All surplus personnel and Transport will remain behind under the charge of Major L.F.Sprenger. D.S.O. M.C.

6. Transport will be Brigaded and will be under the charge of Lieut. Johnson ,4th South African Infantry., who is acting as Brigade Transport Officer.

7. All Lewis Gun limbers and kitchens ., also limber to load picks and shovels, very lights,etc, will march behind the Regiment.

(Signed) L.Greene ~~DSO. MC.~~
Capt. & Adjutant.
2nd.Regiment,South African Infantry.

53 Appendix VI

2ND. REGIMENT. SOUTH AFRICAN INFANTRY.

REPORT ON OPERATIONS CARRIED OUT BY THE BATTALION 8.10.18 TO 19.10.18.

(Referred to 7.10.18 to 19.10.18)

Ref.
MONTBREHAIN.
Edition IA.
1.20,000.

On the 7th October, 1918, the Battalion lying in the HINDENBURG LINE at BONNY, on receipt of orders pushed via GRAND COURT - MUSHROOM VALLEY - LA MOTTE FARM to Railway Line South of BEAUREVOIR. The Battalion was to form up EAST of BEAUREVOIR on an assembly line running from B.10.b.o.4. to B.11.c.5.o. (BLACK LINE) for an impending attack. About 01.00, 8th October, the enemy placed a somewhat heavy barrage West of this line considerably hampering the process of assembly. This latter, however, was eventually completed about 03.30. The Commanding Officer, Lt.Col. H.W.M.Bamford, OBE, MC., becoming a casualty.

The Battalion took up its frontage with the normal formation viz:- A on right, B on left, supported by C and D Companies respectively, the assembly being covered by the 25th Div. Troops who were immediately EAST of the forming up line which had previously been taped out.

The RED LINE, U.25.b.1.9. to U.26.c.2.5., was the objective, the Battalion Northern boundary running from B.10.b.o.4. to U.25.b.1.9. and the Southern boundary B.11.c.5.o. to U. 26.c.2.5.

Supported by the 1st South African Infantry and with the 4th South African Infantry on its left at zero viz:- 05.10. 8.10.18, the line moved forward to the attack in normal formation.

The creeping shrapnel barrage was well timed and beautiful in its execution.

Heavy machine gun fire was experienced on the first crest reached and after a bit of a fight a round number of machine guns were captured, many of the enemy being killed and captured in the Sunken Roads and trenches in B.10.b., B.11.a., B.5.d., B.11.c.

In the USIGNY RAVINE considerable opposition was experienced, the enemy bringing a great number of machine guns and much sniping to bear. These however were well in hand when the timely arrival of a tank helped to finish up this particular portion of the front.

Although resistance was stubborn the advance forward was brisk, the troops of the 25th Division being unable to maintain the pace resulting in somewhat thick machine gun fire coming from PONCHAUX to the right rear.

The Copse in B.6.b., needed careful handling before it was cleared with the capture of quite a strong garrison of enemy machine gunners and snipers.

The right front Company was suffering severe casualties, not an officer being with this Company at this stage.

The high ground immediately WEST of U.25. Central offered sufficient resistance to allow the men to have a breather before proceeding further. Here also the outer fringe of heavy machine gun fire from PETIT FOLIE AND DES FOLIES FARMS begun to have effect.

The line was now reinforced by the two support Companies viz. C and D and the advance was continued by short rushes covered by fire from Lewis Guns and riflemen. Four enemy field pieces firing over open sights at point blank range were the cause of a number of casualties, but LIEUT. E.J.BROOK with SGT. HINWOOD and a few men with a determined rush pushed forward and captured the guns on the RED LINE. The crews surrendering.

The objective was now reached but PETIT FOLIE FARM still a source of annoyance, needed investigation. By a flanking movement carried out by men on the left flank under the direction of CAPT. JACOBS the Farm was enveloped and the garrison either killed or captured. The Farm was held until the 4th Regiment, South African Infantry, moved up when our garrison was relieved.

The RED LINE was captured about 0630 and the work of consolidation proceeded with immediately, covering parties in the shape of Lewis Gun posts being pushed out well in front.

The 199th Brigade now passed through on the way to the 2nd objective - the GREEN LINE, which included the village of SERAIN and the high ground in U.13. 14. and 26. The four field pieces captured were reversed and fire opened on the enemy, about 40 rounds being expended. (Nos. of Guns K.16. (1). 10330. K.16. (2). Or. Nr. 15014. K.16. (3). Nr. 21846. K.16. (4). Nr. Nr. 15027.)

The total captures of the Battalion in addition to the four field guns, above were between 450 to 500 prisoners, excluding a large party who were used as Stretcher Bearers, two anti tank guns, twelve heavy and 7 light machine guns.

After consolidation Companies were reorganized and stragglers collected. Officers casualties were Lt. Col. H. W. M. Bamford. O.B.E. M.C. (wounded) 7.10.18): 2/Lieut. R. G. A. McCarter (Killed A Coy. 8.10.18.): Capt. T. H. Symons M.C.; 2/Lieut. O. S. Giddy, 2/Lieut. E. D. Birrell, all wounded and of "A" Company. 2/Lieut. G. S. Fernie, "B" Company, wounded. 2/Lieuts. C. W. Roberts and N. L. Francis, both of "C" Company, wounded and Lieut. C. M. Egan and 2/Lieut. H. C. H. Gunn of "D" Company, wounded.

Above casualties left "A" Company without an Officer, the command of which was taken over by LIEUT. H. W. HENRY of "B" Company.

Casualties to other ranks were moderately light.

The shrapnel barrage was excellent and most effective many of the enemy being found dead in their cubby holes all hit in the head.

The work of evacuation was proceeded with during the afternoon and the men after a most successful day settled down for the night.

Some alteration of the disposition was necessary and about 23.00 "B" Company moved to the left and took over portion of frontage of 4th South African Infantry. This Battalion also side slipped to left by one Company. "A" Company took over line vacated by "B" Company.

Enemy aeroplanes came over in large numbers and were most persistent in bombing during the whole night, the whole area captured by the Battalion. No casualties resulted.

On the afternoon of the 8th October, 1918, MAJOR L. F. SPRENGER, DSO. MC. on instructions received, took over command of the Battalion.

9.10.18.

Ref:
1.) Sheet 57B. S. E.
1. 20000
2.) Sheet 57B.
1. 40000

Orders were received at 05.30., 9.10.18., that the 199th. Brigade were attacking MARETZ and that as soon as they had secured their objective the Battalion with the 4th South African Infantry on left supported by the Ist. South African Infantry would leapfrog and continue the attack.

The Battalion objective ran from P.17.c.0.0. to P.23 central, the Northern boundary running O.36.b.6&15. - P.26. central - P.17.c.o.o. and the Southern boundary V.1.a.20.05 - P.32 central - P.23 central.

Rations having arrived very late the previous night had not yet been issued but the men realizing the urgency of a quick move co-operated in a splendid manner and the Battalion moved off in column of fours in the order C.D.A.B. Hdqrs. via SERAIN - U.21.d.7.9. then along main road to MARETZ until about U.12. a.5.5. where we formed up in normal formation in rear of the Support Battalion of the attacking Brigade.

A think mist made visibility poor but about 10.00 the preceding Brigade being more or less on their objective the Battalion with C on left, D on right, supported by A and B respectively moved forward to the attack.

On emerging from the Eastern outskirts of MARETZ Heavy Machine Gun fire was encountered from the hedges and undergrowth in P.25.a. b. and c. the enemy artillery shooting being also fairly accurate.

The 4th South African Infantry not having come up into line the advance Companies halted but about 10.30. the 4th having come abreast the attack was pushed forward. The resistance on the left was finally overcome, many Machine Guns and a number of prisoners being taken.

Enemy machine gunners well placed tactically and at points from which oblique fire could be directed were a constant source of annoyance to our advance. These were, however, mopped up one by one and the Battalion moved up towards the wood in P.26.d. and P.27.a.

Here enemy opposition was again strongly felt but with careful handling machine gunners and snipers were gradually overcome and the Eastern edge of the wood with the assistance of two armoured cars was reached. D and B Companies on the right, South of the Wood, being more in the open were more severely dealt with by both Artillery and anti-tank gun fire.

The enemy appeared to have concentrated more strongly still on the Railway line and here the advance was held up for at least half an hour.

To add to the difficulty the 4th South African Infantry on left veered off due North towards BERTRY and the troops of the Division on our right unable to keep pace with our advance were out of touch.

The right flank on account of resistance offered and numbers of enemy, being the most dangerous flank was held up longer than the left. To overcome this difficulty "B" (Support Company on right) was ordered to move up to assist the advance and our line was eventually established on the Railway.

In this area many Machine Guns and prisoners were taken, a good number of the enemy being shot.

The villages (MAUROIS AND HONNECHY) immediately ahead of us appeared to be quiet and many of the houses were flying white flags.

After some deliberation and a reconnaissance had been made, orders for the advance to continue were given and the Battalion, now with three Companies in the line and one in support on the right moved through the two villages with but little opposition and the objective was reached at 13.00.

With both flanks out of touch, however, the line occupied overlapped the objective considerably.

On the left the line ran from P.16.d.9.0.55 - the CEMETRY- P.17.c.65.55. to P. 23.d.6.6.

Lewis Gun posts were established at P.29.b.8.7. and P.29.b.2.5. by the right flank Company Commander and a number of stragglers collected by CAPT. WALSH were brought up and placed in position about P.29.c.2.8. and a post of 8 men detailed to proceed to occupy the station at P.29.d.2.4.

The right flank was now comparatively secure and a Company of the Division on the right coming up about two and a half hours later through HONNECHY were disposed of on this flank, our line being considerably shortened.

About 16.30. also the 4th Regiment pushed out posts across to the Battalion left flank and the line was now more or less continuous although still lying somewhat far back on the right.

Battalion Headquarters were established in the Cemetery on the objective being gained and about 13.10 a number of Cavalry, about 35 strong came up and stood by in the field West of the Cemetry.

On making a reconnaissance into REUMONT on one of these Cavalry Horses, MAJOR SPRINGER found a number of the enemy riding eastwards on bicycles and in trying to draw up to them was fired on by snipers and the horse killed.

No move forward was made by the cavalry until about 16.00 when large numbers came up and proceeded to move up to a line running from about P.18.c.8.3. to P.23.d.9.3. on the right and the line of the RIVER EROLUIN N.W. of BEAUMONT on the left.

Prior to their arrival enemy guns firing over open sights were plainly visible on the high ground beyond BEAUMONT and the enemy infantry rapidly retiring with some mounted men, motors and vehicles of all description. This was about 14.00 and was confirmed by an aeroplane dropping a message saying "All clear ahead."

Excellent targets were afforded to Machine Gunners but they apparently had been unable to maintain our pace.

The Battalion captures during the day included about 150 prisoners, 20 odd machine guns several anti-tank guns and a Staff motor car. The houses in MAUROIS AND HONNECHY had hardly been demolished at all and the enthusiasm of the civil inhabitants on our entry was unbounded. Our casualties were moderate only. 2/Lieut H. PERRY. "C" Company, being the only Officer casualty.

Our advance was without barrage of any description but our aeroplanes in dozens dominated the air.

The cavalry appeared, although much manoeuvring took place, to attain no particular object and suffered a large number of casualties to both men and horses.

On the afternoon of the 10th the Battalion moved up and occupied a line running from Q.1.d.6.9. to Q.8.b.2.9. with B.A.D. running from right to left and "C" Company along the road bank in Q.1.d.

Being out of touch with 50th Division on right, patrols were sent out but connection was not attained until the next morning.

Kitchens were brought up to "C" Company lines and hot meals with ample rations were the order of the day.

The men dug in and and although subjected to spasmodic shelling by 5.9s and gas, suffered only three casualties during the next 3 days.

14.10.18. On the evening of the 14th the Battalion was relieved by the 4th South African Infantry, the Regiment moving forward on relief to the front line.

Here it relieved the 2nd Northumberland Fusiliers the line running roughly from K.33.b.9.1. to Q.8.b.1.6., D.C. and B being in the line from left to right with A Company in support in Q.2.b.

Touch was established by a liason post with troops on right and connection established with 1st Regiment who were in the line on the outskirts of the village N.W. of LE CATEAU.

15.10.18.
Ref.
Notes & Town
Plan of
LE CATEAU
1.5000.
Oct.1918.

In view of an impending attack on LE CATEAU it was deemed of vital importance that the two bridges in the western outskirts of LE CATEAU over the river SELLE, then commanded by the enemy, should be captured and bridge-heads established on the EAST bank of the river.

The bridge in K.4.b.2.9. was assigned to the Battalion and orders were issued for an Officer (2/LIEUT. R.D.HEWAT with one Lewis Gun Section and one rifle section to establish posts in the houses EAST of the bridge on both sides of the road.

LIEUT. HEWAT was unable on account of the constant machine gun fire, to use the debris of the bridge which had been blown up, so taking to the water waded across, his men following one by one until the EAST bank was reached, two bombs being thrown at them on their way across.

The first section across was placed in position in a house at the corner of the street viz:- Q. 4. b. 20. 8. 5. While getting the next section into position at the opposite corner of the street the first section was attacked, one man being killed, one wounded and two being captured. LIEUT. HEWAT'S Section was attacked repeatedly by enemy bombers but successfully beaten off.

16. 10. 18. About 06. 00 an enemy patrol, 11 strong, was allowed to come within 15 yards when fire from rifles and the Lewis Gun opened, the entire patrol, it is believed being wiped out.

Another patrol attacked the 1st Section in Q. 4. b. 20. 85. which now, only half strength, retired to the West Bank of the river.

LIEUT. HEWAT with only 7 men left maintained the position until the following morning viz: the 17th. When the attack commenced, they were heavily engaged, three machine guns being concentrated upon the house they were in, making movement impossible.

Late that afternoon they were relieved by the Battalion mopping up LE CATEAU and LIEUT. HEWAT with his small party having held out for over 36 hours returned and reported back to Battalion Headquarters.

16. 10. 18.
Ref.
SHEET. 57B. N.E.
Edition 2a.
1. 20000.

In the meantime and during the evening of the 16th the Battalion was relieved by Companies of the Dublin Fusiliers and Innerkillings and concentrated in the two cuttings in K. 26. b. and d.

Orders were received that the Battalion would attack the following morning (17. 10. 18) the boundary being on the North a line from the SELLE at a point K. 29. a. 2. 3. to level crossing at K. 29. c. 8. 9. and Southern boundary a line running K. 29. c. [illegible]. 70. - K. 35. b. 00. 75. - K. 29. c. 8. 9. to K. 35. b. 70. 65. and the assembly being the EAST bank of the SELLE. [handwritten: -K.35.b.70.65 the objective being the line] The 4th South African Infantry were to be on the right and the 1st South African Infantry, less one Company, in support. One Company, 1st South African Infantry, under CAPT THOMPSON was attached to the Battalion, his duty being, once the objective was gained, to occupy the rectangle North of the Battalion's left boundary. This area was bounded on the West by the SELLE, on the East by the Railway line and on the North by the River RICHEMONT. His orders were to further strengthen his position by a strong defensive flank along the RICHEMONT between the points K. 22. d. 7. 0.15 and K. 23. c. 10. 25.

Bridges were being constructed by the Engineers during the night and these, four in number, on the Battalion's sector of

17. 10. 18. assembly being completed about 02. 00. the Battalion led by guides of the 1st South African Infantry moved to the assembly point, the assembly being completed at 04. 45.

LIEUT. M.E. WHELAN. M. C. "O. C." D. Company just prior to moving forward was unfortunately severely wounded, succumbing to his injuries the following day (18. 10. 18.)

The Battalion on forming up was disposed of as follows. B and D Companies on the right and left respectively on the EAST bank of the river SELLE "C" Company, in support, on the WEST bank and "A" Company in reserve about 75 yards west of "C" Company. The 4th South African Infantry assembled on our right two companies being EAST and two companies WEST of the SELLE.

The attack was so planned that LE CATEAU itself would not be taken by a direct attack - it was to be envelloped, the South African Brigade attacking from the North and the 50th Division from the South: LE CATEAU to be mopped up by a Battalion of the 198th Brigade.

At zero (05. 20.) the 50th Division moved forward to attack their first objective viz. the road running from Q. 4. b. 50. 00. through Q. 10. b. and d., and Q. 17. a. and c.

Zero hour for the South African Brigade, viz., 08.05. had been so timed that the advance of the 50th Division to its 2nd objective would effect a junction with the advance of the South African Brigade at the point K.35.c.85.30.

A heavy mist obscured everything and from 05.20. to 08.05. the Battalion lying on the assembly point where they had dug in was subjected to heavy shelling and intense Machine Gun fire.

At 08.05. the Battalion advanced to the attack in the face of heavy machine gun fire and was immediately confronted by thick uncut wire.

The surmounting of this obstacle and two further belts of wire made progress most difficult and was accentuated by the dense fog thickened by smoke shell. This mist, however, was of most valuable assistance in screening our movements from the enemy.

A message timed 09.15. from CAPT JACOBS stated that the objective had been gained but that the line was being subjected to heavy infilade fire from both flanks as well as from the houses in LE CATEAU to the right rear.

Unable to dig in in the open under this Machine Gun barrage the line retired to the Railway line and here proceeded to dig in (10.30.)

Enfilade fire from both flanks was still most persistently heavy, enemy "whizz bangs" being most accurate in their shooting on the Railway Line.

The 1st Regiment Company under CAPT. THOMPSON in proceeding to carry out its task was met with such intense machine gun fire that this combined with the wire obstacles made progress almost impossible. They however persisted and receiving assistance from "A" Company, 2nd. South African Infantry, who had been ordered to reinforce them proceeded to the objective. Unable however to maintain the position the Company fell back forming a defensive glank along the Regimental northern boundary. All the officers of this Company during the course of the day were wounded.

From the Sunken Road East of the Railway enemy trench mortars were busy and enemy infantry and Machine Gunners were busy the whole day in dribbling forward in their endeavour to regain the Railway.

BAILLON FARM and the signal box on the Railway cutting in K.29.c.8.3. were points which needed constant attention.

RICHEMONT MILL and the high ground N.E. of MONTAY were the source of intense discomfort to the line. Machine Gun fire from these points being heavy and continuous.

The line now settled down to a most wearisome night, standing to almost the whole time. Enemy bombing and machine gun patrols were numerous, his machine guns and trench mortar fire accurate and intense and his artillery fire with light, heavy and gas shells was almost continuous.

In connection with the advance of the Battalion at zero hour the following points as tending to increase the difficulty of the advance are worthy of mention:-

(1). Assembly took place at point blank range of enemy machine gunners. One machine gun being less than 40 yards away. (LIEUT. E.J. BROOK was killed during the assembly, his riddled body being found about five yards from the muzzle of one of these guns).

(2). Two sunken roads running parallel to the Railway line, these roads being a veritable nest of machine gunners, bombers and enemy snipers.

(3). Three belts of double apron wire entangelments which were not cut at all and the presence of which was unknown by the advancing troops.

(4). The persistent and heavy Enfilade fire from both flanks and also from the houses in LE CATEAU to the right rear.

The discovery during the advance however, of an old communication trench running from the centre of our advance to the Railway Line became practically the means by which the success of the advance was assured.

The Battalions captures during the day were about thirty machine guns, three officers and about 150 prisoners besides which many of the enemy were killed.

The Battalion casualties in other ranks were somewhat heavy in both killed and wounded ~~and in~~ Officers, Casualties LIEUT. E.J. BROOK, "B" Company, Killed; CAPT L. GREENE DSO, MC, (Adjutant) wounded; LIEUT. H.W. HENRY "A" Company, wounded and 2/LIEUT. H.R. LAZARUS "D" Company, wounded.

During the afternoon (17.10.18) LE CATEAU was eventually mopped up which somewhat relieved the tension on the right.

18.10.18. After a very hard day on the 18th under constant machine gun, trench mortar and artillery fire arrangements were made for the capture of the original objective and this was successfully carried out and the line consolidated about

19.10.18. 04.30. on the 19th October, 1918.

CAPT. W.L. KING. MC. DCM. O.C. "C" Company was wounded during this operation.

The Battalion was relieved during the night by the 18th Kings Liverpools and the Regiment after twelve days under the most trying of ~~xxxxxx~~ conditions during which time it had participated in three successful attacks marched back to billets in BEAUMONT.

During the operations between the 17th and 19th the following points of interest are worthy of note:-

(1). Great difficulty of communication other than by runners owing to thick fog. Dangerous and hazardous task of runners when it is known that in one Company alone five runners were casualties (wounded).

(2). Necessity of closer liason work with both artillery and machine guns who should keep touch with infantry.

(3). The excellent work carried out by the Regimental Aid Posts which, in so far as this Battalion is concerned, was never more than about 500 yards away from Battalion Headquarters.

(4). The unfailing regularity of the delivery of rations under the most trying conditions.

(5). The excellent spirit of cheerfulness, courage and tenacity of Officers, N.C.Os., and other ranks which made success possible even though worn out by want of sleep and fatigue and in the face of the strongest enemy opposition. The complete confidence existing between Officers and men cannot be over-estimated.

(6). The doggedness of the German machine gunners resistance.

A further point of interest may be cited viz:-

When the line was withdrawn on the morning of the 17th to the railway line several wounded, who could not be brought back at the time but were recovered during the night 17th/18th, were left lying on the objective. The enemy who returned to the position found one of our N.C.Os. and examined his identification. Hearing that he was a South African they immediately rubbed his hands for him and gave him a drink of rum before passing on.

BATTALION CASUALTIES-NIGHT 7.10.18/NIGHT 20.10.18.

OFFICERS:-

Killed in Action.	2.	
Died of wounds.	1.	
Wounded.	14.	17.

OTHER RANKS.

Killed in Action.	56.	
Died of wounds.	17.	
Wounded.	317.	
Wounded (Gassed)	13.	
Unaccounted for	10	
Wounded and at duty.	7.	420.

TOTAL: 17 OFFICERS. 420. OTHER RANKS.

Field.
26. 10. 18.

L. F. Sprenger
Major.
Commanding 2nd. Regt. South African Infantry.

COPY NO.....Appendix VII
(Reference to 8.10.18.)

61

2nd. SOUTH AFRICAN INFANTRY.

ORDER NO. 11.

7th October, 1918.

Reference.

[illegible]RAIN. Sheet. 1/40,000.

---

1. (a). With a view to increasing the breach in the enemy's defences, major operations are about to be taken in a general North-Easterly direction.

(b). The South African Brigade will attack the RED LINE with the 2nd Regiment on the Right, the 4th Regiment on the Left and the 1st Regiment in support.

After the capture of the RED LINE, troops of the 198th Brigade will pass through the South African Brigade in order to seize the GREEN LINE (including SERAIN and the high ground in U. 13, U. 14, and U. 26)

(c). The Capture of SERAIN will be carried out in conjunction with the 2nd. American Corps, who will take PREMONT.

11. **INFORMATION.** The 2nd. Regiment will attack in normal formation with
"A" Company on the Right.
"B" Company on the Left.
"C" Company in Support.
"D" Company in Reserve.

111. **BOUNDARIES.** The Battalion boundaries are shown in RED on the map already handed to Company Commanders.

The NORTHERN boundary is now altered and runs from U.10 b. 2.2 in a straight line N.E. to U.15 d. 10.00.

The SOUTHERN boundary remains the same as already indicated.

1V. **ASSEMBLY.** (a). The position of Assembly for the assault is that approximately shewn on the reference map in BLACK.

The Support and Reserve Companies will form up immediately in rear of the front Companies, i.e. "C" Company behind "A" Company, "D" Company behind "B" Company.

The 1st. Regiment will be formed up immediately in rear of the 2nd. and 4th. Regiments along the N.E. edge of BEAUREVOIR VILLAGE.

(b). The BLACK Line referred to is immediately in rear of our present front line now held by troops of the 25th Division.

(c). Company Commanders will arrange to thoroughly reconnoitre the position of Assembly and also the necessary lines of approach both by Officers and N.C.Os.

(d). "A" and "B" Companies will each detail one, and "C" and "D" Companies two, reliable N.C.Os. to reconnoitre the routes between MUSHROOM QUARRY and their positions of assembly. These N.C.Os. will be prepared to guide the Tanks allotted to the Battalion from their positions of readiness to the assembly positions on Y/Z night. The N.C.Os. will travel in the tanks during the attack for the purpose of keeping touch between the Tanks and the Infantry.

(e). On Y/Z night the Battalion will complete the assembly by ZERO minus 2 hours.

V. ATTACK.

(a). The Battalion will attack in normal formation preceded by the Tanks and will closely follow the creeping barrage to the objective (RED LINE).

(b). When the 199th Brigade has passed through the Battalion on the RED LINE, "A" Company will send Two Platoons to occupy and hold the high ground in U. 26 a. and b.

"C" Company will detail Two Platoons to take the place of the Two Platoons of "A" Company in the RED LINE.

(c). The 1st Regiment will be following in support of the 2nd. and 4th Regiment and will occupy a position approximately along the line of the track running through G.1.a., U.24.c., T.30.d., D.4.a..

VI. ARTILLERY.

(a). The attack on the RED LINE will be made under cover of a strong barrage. This barrage will come down and rest for three minutes 200 yards in front of the Infantry forming-up tapes. It will then move forward by lifts of 100 yards in three minutes for 1200 yards, and then slow down to 100 yards in 4 minutes until it reaches a line 300 yards in front of the RED LINE.

A protective barrage will dwell 300 yards in advance of the RED LINE for 30 minutes, when it will lift and the second phase of the attack (i.e. by the 199th Brigade) will commence.

(b). The attack on the RED LINE will be further supported by a section of mobile Field Artillery which will move forward in support of the Battalion and give supporting fire over open sights.

VII. FLANKING TROOPS.

The 7th Brigade (28th Division) will be on our Right.

4th Regiment on our Left.

VIII. MACHINE GUNS.

(a). 28th M.G. Battalion will co-operate.

(b). On this Battalion front four guns will deal with USIGNY RAVINE (B.12.a.). These and 16 other guns will then concentrate in the valley in B.6 central after the assaulting troops have passed there. They will then be prepared to deal with any counter attack from a North-Easterly direction.

(c). Four further Machine Guns will advance with the Battalion and deal with the REDOUBT about U.24 central. On capture of RED LINE these guns remain laid on above target till further orders.

IX. CONSOLIDATION.

The objective on line gained will be consolid(at)ed at once. The importance of continuing this work, even although other troops have passed through any particular line cannot be too strongly impressed on all concerned.

(b). Strong points will be constructed near the following positions

1. Cross Tracks U.24.c.
2. U.26.a. } Protecting Right Flank.
3. U.26.b. }

(c). To assist in the construction of above strong points a Section or Sections of 430th. Field Company R.E. will be attached.

63

Page Four.

XX. SYNCHRONISATION OF WATCHES.

Each Company will send an Officer to Battalion Headquarters at 9.0 p.m. tonight to ascertain correct time.

Zero hour will be notified to this Officer.

XXI. S.O.S.

The S.O.S. Signal is

GREEN
GREEN
RED.

(Sgd) W.H.M. Bamford.
~~Lieut. Colonel.~~
Commanding 2nd. Regiment, South African Inf.

1. File.
2. O.C. "A" Coy.
3. O.C. "B" Coy.
4. O.C. "C" Coy.
5. O.C. "D" Coy.
6. O.C. Hdqr. Coy.
7. War Diary.
8. War Diary.

Appendix VIII

2ND. REGIMENT, SOUTH AFRICAN INFANTRY.

Sheet. 57B S.E.
Edition 2:
1:20,000.

ORDER NO. 12.

9TH. OCTOBER. 1918.

The Battalion will carry out an attack this morning.

The Battalion will pass through the 198th. Brigade on their reaching the 1st Objective East of MARETZ; and will then leapfrog and attack in normal formation, with the Northern and Southern boundaries and objective as shown on attached map. "D" Company will be on right, "C" on left, supported by "B" and "A" respectively.

L. F. Sprenger.
Major,
Commanding 2nd. Regt. South African Infantry.

64

2ND. REGIMENT. SOUTH AFRICAN INFANTRY. Appendix IX

ORDER NO. 13. 14TH. OCTOBER 1918.

65

Reference:

SHEET 57B.
1/40,000.

1. The 2nd. South African Infantry will relieve the 2nd Northumberland Fusiliers (198th Brigade) tonight.

2. The relief will be as follows:-

"D" Company	relieves	"D" Company 2nd. Northumberland Fusiliers, Left Flank.
"C" Company	relieves	"C" Company; 2nd. Northumberland Fusiliers, centre.
"B" Company.	relieves	"B" Company 2nd. Northumberland Fusiliers, Right Flank.
"A" Company	relieves	"A" Company 2nd. Northumberland Fusiliers, remaining in Support.

3. Battalion Headquarters will remain as at present.

4. Parties from B., C., and D companies will proceed to the line during the afternoon and reconnoitre their respective Company frontages and will make arrangements for guides to meet them and to guide ~~them to~~ the various night posts to their positions.

5. One Field Kitchen will accompany "C" and "D" Companies to their day quarters and will remain there.
Arrangements are being made for rations to be delivered daily in the vicinity of their headquarters.

6. A Field Kitchen and the water cart will remain where it is at present for "A" and "B" Companies. "B" Company will arrange parties to fetch their hot meals and rations daily.

7. Completion of relief will be notified to Battalion Headquarters by the code word "TANNER".

8. Offensive patrols must be pushed forward during the night and ~~xxxxxxxxxx~~ thoroughly reconnoitre the bridges this end of the River and the River itself, and where possible push forward and gain contact and continuation if possible.

9. "B" Company will gain touch with the Battalion on their right and form a liason post with them.

10. Acknowledge.

ISSUED AT 16.35.

L. F. Sprenger (signature)
Major.
Commanding 2nd. Regt. South African Infty

Appendix X

66

2nd. REGIMENT. SOUTH AFRICAN INFANTRY.

ORDER NO. 14

Reference:
Town Plan of LE CATEAU.
I. 5000.

1?th. OCTOBER 1918.

1. "C" and "D" Companies will tonight establish Bridge Heads East of the river SELLE.

2. "C" Company will force a crossing across the Bridge in Q. 4. B. 15. 90. and establish posts in the houses on both sides of the Road so as best to command the approaches to the Bridge.

3. "D" Company will force a crossing across the Bridge at K. 34. a. 95. 10. and establish posts on both sides of the as best to command the approaches.

4. The parties from each Company will be commanded by an Officer and consist of two sections. One a Rifle Section of an N. C. O. and at least 7 other ranks. The other a Lewis Gun Section of an N. C. O. and at least 6 other ranks. One runner with each officer.

5. Each man must be armed with rifle and bombs and will carry "Iron Rations" a day's ration and filled water bottle.

6. These posts once established will hold on to their positions until further orders.

7. The posts must be strengthened and enemy prevented at all costs from approaching bridges.

8. The posts must make every endeavour to establish themselves without disclosing themselves to the enemy.

9. All posts must keep a vigilant look out to prevent the enemy coming over unawares from the rear or flank.

10. These posts must not disclose themselves unless absolutely compelled to do so;

11. In order to support these Bridge heads, Posts must be established in the houses on both sides of the Road West of the River.

12. The latter posts will be armed and equipped in same manner as the Bridge Head posts.

13. These posts must endeavour by continual sniping to themselves prevent the enemy from approaching the Bridges and so aid the Bridge Head posts from unnecessarily disclosing themselves, once they are in position.

14. These Bridge Head posts and covering posts must be established before daylight.

15. As soon as the Bridge Heads are established the Officer in charge in each case will notify the Company Commander to this effect by Runners.

16. Each Company Commander will notify Battalion Headquarters of the establishment of these Bridge Heads by the code word "MATURED"

17. Acknowledge.

L. F. Sprenger

Major.
Commanding 2nd. Regt. South Afr. Inf.

ISSUED AT 18. 30.

Appendix XI

67

2ND. REGIMENT. SOUTH AFRICAN INFANTRY.

ORDER NO. 15.

16TH. OCTOBER 1918.

Reference: (1) 57 B S.E. } Ed. 2a 1:20000
(2) 57 B N.E. }

---

1. The Battalion will be relieved tonight by the Dublin Fusiliers (198th Brigade)

2. Companies on relief will move and concentrate in the two ravines in K.26.a. and d. in readiness to move forward to assembly position during the night for the attack taking place tomorrow morning.

3. Kitchens and water cart will return to the 1st Line of Transport.

4. Companies will notify completion of reliefs and assembly (as in (2). above by code word "LIAR" to Battalion Headquarters.

5. Battalion Headquarters will move at 7.0.p.m. to K.33.a.8.4.

L.F. Sprenger
Major.
Commanding 2nd. Regt. South African Infty.

2ND. REGIMENT. SOUTH AFRICAN INFANTRY. Appendix XII

Reference:

ORDER NO. 16

16TH. OCTOBER 1918.

68

SHEET 57 B. N. E
I/20000.

I. The 2nd. South African Infantry with the 4th South African Infantry on their right, will attack on the North of LE CATEAU tomorrow morning the 17th instant.

2. The 2nd. South African Infantry will form up on the assembly points as soon as the attack carried out this evening by the Ist South African Infantry has gained the objective and the necessary bridges are across the River SELLE.

3. The order of assembly will be "B" and "D" Companies on the East bank of the river, "B" Company on the Right, "D" Company on the Left. "C" Company will be in support on the West Bank of the River, "A" Company will be behind "C" Company in reserve.

4. The forming up line will be the East Bank of the River from K.29.c.oo.70. - K.29.a.20.30.

5. Guides from the Ist S.A.I. - one per company-will report to the Companies and Guide them to the vicinity of their assembly positions when companies will take up their positions as above mentioned.

6. Completion of assembly will be notified to Battalion Headquarters by the code word "RATIONS"

7. At Zero the 50th Division will attack on the right of LE CATEAU at the same time a barrage will fall in front of the assemblying positions and then move forward to Railway and then play on strong points. The attack by this Battalion will not take place on the opening barrage but will take place at Zero plus I65 minutes.

8. The barrage will return to the front of the assembly positions at ZERO plus I50 minutes and play there for I5 mins. until the starting time ZERO plus I65 minutes and then it will move forward at the rate of I00 yards in 3 minutes up to the final objective marked B L U E on the maps, it will then move on to selected points.

9. As soon as the final objective marked BLUE is reached the Battalion will dig in and consolidate.

I0. Section of R.E. will then push forward and help in consolidating certain selected points at K.29.c.8.9.

II. Should the 50th Division fail to reach their objective the attack on our front will still take but the final objective will be the railway line RED LINE.

I2. Battalion Headquarters will move on completion of assembly to K.28.c.3.3.

I3. The code word to notify companies that the 50th Division has failed and that our objective is limited will be "REFUSAL"

I4. Acknowledge.

L.F. Sprenger
Major.
Commanding 2nd. Regt. South African Infty.

69

2ND. REGIMENT. SOUTH AFRICAN INFANTRY. Appendix XIII.

Ref. Sheet 57.B. N.E. 1.20000. _ORDER NO. 17_ 18 OCTOBER 1918.

Tonight 2nd and 4th will attack from their present Line with the objective K.36.a.I.9. to K.29.central,. Lancashire Fusiliers are reported to be holding cross roads at K.36.a.I.9. 4th Regiment will attack on right, 2nd. Regiment on left.

There will be no artillery preparation or barrage.

Zero hour will be arranged between CAPT. JACOBS, ZERM, and CAPT. GUEST, ZESA, who will advise their respective Battalion Headquarters what time zero will be.

The attack will pivot on K.29.c.9.9. and interlocking posts will be established on flanks of both Battalions during attack and on consolidation of objective.

2nd. Regiment will attack with ~~two~~ three Companies leaving one Company in Support on Railway line.

Disposition of troops when on objective and consolidated will be indicated on MESSAGE MAPS (Attached).

L. J. Sprenger [signature]

Major,
Commanding 2nd. Regt. South African Infty

2ND. REGIMENT. SOUTH AFRICAN INFANTRY.

ORDER NO. 18

Reference:
SHEET 57.B. N.E.
1/20000

19TH. OCTOBER 1918.

70

I. The Battalion will be relieved tonight by "A" Coy, 18th Kings Liverpool Regiment.

2. Companies will each send one guide to be at Battalion Headquarters by 7.15. p.m.

3. Companies will be relieved by platoons of above Regiment ("A" Company) as are ~~allotted~~ allocated to guides.

4. On relief Battalion will move to Billets in REUMONT.

5. Companies will, when relieved, proceed by road to K.33.a.4.5. ,then K.32.d.20.45. then along road into REUMONT.

6. All Lewis Guns, Lewis Gun drums, picks and shovels, both full and empty will be brought out.

7. All ranks will carry full compliment of ammunition.

8. Companies will notify Battalion Headquarters (CHATEAU SEYDOUX) of completion of relief when passing.

9. Two limbers will be drawn up alongside road at K.33.a.1.2. on which Companies will load Lewis Guns, etc, when passing.

10. Guides will meet Companies at EASTERN entrance to REUMONT to show them to their billets.

11. Probable time of commencement of relief will be about 20.45.

12. Hot meal will be provided at REUMONT.

13. Acknowledge.

L.F. Sprenger.
Major.
Commanding 2nd. Regt. South African Infantry.

ISSUED AT 17.45.

2ND. REGIMENT. SOUTH AFRICAN INFANTRY. *Appendix XV*

ORDER NO. *19*

20TH OCTOBER 1918.

71

Reference
SHEET 57B. Edition Ia.
1/40000.

I. The Battalion will move by march route to SERAIN today in following order,

Headquarters,
"A" Coy.
"B" Coy.
"C" Coy.
"D" Coy.

2. Head of column will pass Battalion Headquarters at 10.30. a.m.

3. Packs, blankets, great coats, will be stacked outside Company Billets by 9.0. a.m. and will be picked up by lorry.

4. Transport will move under Brigade arrangements.

5. Guides to lead Companies to Billets will meet Companies about 1000 yards N.E. of SERAIN on main SERAIN -MARETZ road.

6. Marching out state will be handed to Adjutant at head of column at 10.30. a.m.

L.T. Sprenger.
Major.
Commanding 2nd. Regt. South African Inf

ISSUED AT 7.0. a.m.

72

2ND. REGIMENT. SOUTH AFRICAN INFANTRY.

31st. October, 1918.

NOMINAL ROLL OF OFFICERS IN ORDER OF COMPANIES.

Headquarters.

Commdg. Officer	MAJOR.	L. [illegible]	SPRINGER.	D.S.O. M.C.
Adjt.	CAPT.	F. G.	WALSH.	M.C.
Transport Officer	LIEUT.	E. J.	RICHES.	
Intelligence Officer	2/LIEUT.	H. A.	MARTIN.	

"A" Company.

LIEUT.	J. T.	HUMPHREYS	(On Leave)
2/LIEUT.	S. G.	PHILLIPS.	M.C.
2/LIEUT.	W. V.	BOWES.	
2/LIEUT.	H. J.	ALLEN.	
2/LIEUT.	C. H.	FRASER	(On Course)

"B" Company.

CAPT.	L. M.	JACOBS.
2/LIEUT.	A. M.	PARROTT.
2/LIEUT.	A. H.	HUMBLEY.
2/LIEUT.	P. H.	HAVILAND.

"C" Company.

LIEUT.	[illegible] R.	BAILEY.	M.C.
2/LIEUT.	C. K.	MARTIN.	
2/LIEUT.	C. C.	RAYMOND.	
2/LIEUT.	R. D.	HEWAT.	

"D" Company.

LIEUT.	F. L.	MARILLIER.
2/LIEUT.	F.	BOTHUYS.
2/LIEUT.	R.	HASKIS.

ATTACHED.

CAPT.	M. M.	ADAMS.	MEDICAL OFFICER.
CAPT.	P. J.	WALSHE M.C.	R.C. CHAPLAIN.
CAPT.	G. W. R.	TOBIAS. M.C.	C OF E. CHAPLAIN.

War Diary
for
Month of
January 1919.

2nd Regt. - S.A. Infantry.

Vol 38

WAR DIARY
or
INTELLIGENCE SUMMARY.
(Erase heading not required.)

Army Form C. 2118.

Instructions regarding War Diaries and Intelligence Summaries are contained in F. S. Regs., Part II. and the Staff Manual respectively. Title pages will be prepared in manuscript.

(1)

January 1919 — 2nd Regiment South African Inf.

Place	Date	Hour	Summary of Events and Information	Remarks and references to Appendices
MARCHE.	1/1/19.		TRAINING. NIL.	
			RELINQUISHMENT. CAPT. F. G. WALSH MC relinquishes	
			Temporary Command as from 31-12-18.	
Do.	2/1/19.		TRAINING. As per programme	
Do:	3/1/19.		TRAINING As per programme.	
"	3/1/19.		Lieut D. H. ELIAS with one platoon of A Company	
			proceeded to MELREUX to relieve the	
			1st Regiment guards. (Brigade Order S.C.A. 417.)	
Do.	4/1/19.		TRAINING.	
		09.00 09.30	Company Inspections	
		09.30	Inter-platoon cross country run.	
			APPOINTMENTS – Commissions.	
			Authority is granted for the undermentioned	
			Officer to wear badge of rank as set	
			against his name.	2
			MAJOR C. R. HEENAN D.S.O to be LIEUT. COLONEL.	

(A9475) Wt W2358/P360 600,000 12/17 D. D. & L. Sch. 52a. Forms/C2118/15

Army Form C. 2118.

Instructions regarding War Diaries and Intelligence Summaries are contained in F. S. Regs., Part II. and the Staff Manual respectively. Title pages will be prepared in manuscript.

(2)

WAR DIARY
or
INTELLIGENCE SUMMARY.
(Erase heading not required.) 2nd Regiment. South African Inf.

Place	Date	Hour	Summary of Events and Information	Remarks and references to Appendices
MARCHE	4/1/19.		CAPT F.L. MARILLIER & 2/Lt. M. KING proceed on leave to the United Kingdom.	
Do:	5/1/19.		CHURCH PARADES. Church of England, Presbyterians, Dutch Reformed, Wesleyans, Baptists & Congregationalists	
			STRENGTH. INCREASE.	
			The undermentioned Officers are taken on strength of Regiment as from 4/1/19. and posted to Companies as shewn.	
			MAJOR. J.W. WEBBER. —	
			CAPT. W.L. KING. MC. DCM to B Coy.	
			2/LIEUT J.S.D. SCANLAN. " C Coy.	
			2/LIEUT R.H. LAZARUS. " D Coy.	
			TRANSFERS – OFFICERS.	
			CAPT. F.H. THERON from Hdq Coy to "D" Coy.	
			" L.M. JACOBS " B " " Hdq "	
			2/LIEUT H. WINSHIP " A " " C "	3

(A9175) Wt W2353/P360 600,000 12/17 D. D. & L. Sch. 52a. Forms/C2118/15

Instructions regarding War Diaries and Intelligence Summaries are contained in F. S. Regs., Part II. and the Staff Manual respectively. Title pages will be prepared in manuscript.

3/

WAR DIARY
or
INTELLIGENCE SUMMARY.
(Erase heading not required.)

2nd Regiment South African Inf.

Army Form C. 2118.

Place	Date	Hour	Summary of Events and Information	Remarks and references to Appendices
MARCHE	5/1/19		RELINQUISHMENTS.	
			CAPT. F.L. MARILLIER relinquishes command of D Coy from 26/12/18	
			" J.T. HUMPHREY " " " B " 4/1/19.	
			COMMAND.	
			CAPT. F.H. THERON assumes command of D Coy as from 26/12/18	
			" W.L. KING M.C. DCM " " " B " " 4/1/19.	
Do.	5/1/19		POSTAL CENSORSHIP.	
			Regimental censorship of letters will be discontinued forthwith.	
Do.	6/1/19		TRAINING. As per programme.	
"	"		APPOINTSMENTS.	
			CAPT. L.M. JACOBS. D.S.O. is appointed second in command of this Unit as from 2-1-19.	
Do.	7/1/19		TRAINING. As per programme.	
			APPOINTSMENTS. A/CAPT. J.T. HUMPHREY is appointed additional A/CAPT. as from 4th January 1919.	4

(A9175) Wt W2358/P360 600,000 12/17 D. D. & L. Sch 52a. Forms/C2118/15

Instructions regarding War Diaries and Intelligence Summaries are contained in F. S. Regs., Part II, and the Staff Manual respectively. Title pages will be prepared in manuscript.

4.

WAR DIARY
or
INTELLIGENCE SUMMARY.
(Erase heading not required.) 2nd Regt. South African Inf.

Army Form C. 2118.

Place	Date	Hour	Summary of Events and Information	Remarks and references to Appendices
MARCHE	7/1/19		RELINQUISHMENTS.	
			A/CAPT. F.L. MARILLIER relinquishes the rank of A/Capt. as from 26-12-1918.	
	Do.		2/Lt. A.H. HUNDLEY. proceeded on leave to the United Kingdom.	
Do.	8/1/19.	09.00 10.30	TRAINING. Under Company arrangements.	
		11.00	Brigade Football Match (RUGBY) v. Australians	
Do.			POSTINGS.	
			2/Lt. A RYDER. M.M. having rejoined from BASE is posted to "C" Coy.	
Do.			HONOURS & AWARDS.	
			2/Lt. M. KING has been awarded the D.C.M.	
Do.			APPOINTMENTS.	
			2/Lt. S.G PHILLIPS M.C to be Temp. Lieut.	
Do.	9/1/19.		TRAINING. ROUTE MARCH.	

(A9175) Wt W2358/P360 600,000 12/17 D. D. & L. Sch. 52a. Forms/C2118/15

Instructions regarding War Diaries and Intelligence Summaries are contained in F. S. Regs., Part II, and the Staff Manual respectively. Title pages will be prepared in manuscript.

5

WAR DIARY
or
INTELLIGENCE SUMMARY.
(*Erase heading not required.*)

Army Form C. 2118.

2nd Regiment South African Inf.

Place	Date	Hour	Summary of Events and Information	Remarks and references to Appendices
MARCHE	9/1/19		STRENGTH — DECREASE. 67 OR^s having been despatched to BASE for the purpose of demobilization are struck off strength of Regiment from date.	
Do			CAPT. J. T. HUMPHREY proceeded to the United Kingdom on Draft conducting duty.	
Do	10/1/19		TRAINING. As per programme.	
Do:	11/1/19		Do: Under Company arrangements.	
			STRENGTH: INCREASE. A Draft of 48 OR^s having joined from BASE is taken on strength as from 10-1-19.	
Do:	12/1/19		Church Parades.	
Do:	13/1/19		TRAINING. Ceremonial Parade.	
Do:	14/1/19		Do: As per programme.	
Do:	15/1/19		Do: Do:	
			STRENGTH INCREASE. Two Officers & 8 other ranks having joined from BASE are taken on strength as from 14-1-19.	6

(A9475) Wt W2358/P360 600,000 12/17 D. D. & L. Sch. 52a. Forms/C2118/15

Instructions regarding War Diaries and Intelligence Summaries are contained in F. S. Regs., Part II. and the Staff Manual respectively. Title pages will be prepared in manuscript.

Army Form C. 2118.

WAR DIARY
or
INTELLIGENCE SUMMARY.
(*Erase heading not required.*)

6/ 2nd Regiment South African Inf.

Place.	Date	Hour	Summary of Events and Information	Remarks and references to Appendices
MARCHE	15/1/19.		POSTINGS.	
			2/Lieut F J ROBERTSON to "D" Coy	
			" R.T. EDMONSTON " "D" "	
Do.	16/1/19.		TRAINING. As per programme.	
"	"		Strength.	
			Offs. O.Rs.	
			With Regiment 36 1037	
			Field Ambulance 1 9	
			On Course 1 21	
			On Leave 4 32	
			Detached Duties 4 97	
			Total 46 1196	
Do:	17/1/19.		TRAINING. Under Company arrangements.	
			STRENGTH - INCREASE.	
			The undermentioned Officer having arrived from	
			U.K. is taken on strength of Regiment as from 16-1-19.	

(A9175) Wt W2358/P360 600,000 12/17 D. D. & L. Sch. 52a. Forms/C2118/15

Army Form C. 2118.

Instructions regarding War Diaries and Intelligence Summaries are contained in F. S. Regs., Part II. and the Staff Manual respectively. Title pages will be prepared in manuscript.

WAR DIARY
or
INTELLIGENCE SUMMARY.
(*Erase heading not required.*) 7. 2nd Regiment. South African Inf.

Place	Date	Hour	Summary of Events and Information	Remarks and references to Appendices
			Cnt.	
MARCHE. x	17/1/19.		2/Lt D. V. Scully posted to Headquarters (Sig. Officer)	
Do.	18/1/19.		TRAINING. As per programme.	
"	"		STRENGTH - INCREASE.	
			The undermentioned Officer having arrived from the United Kingdom is taken on strength as from 17-1-19.	
			2/Lt T. A. BROOKS posted to A "Coy"	
"	x 17/1/19.		2/Lt F. J. ROBERTSON with one platoon of D. Company proceeded to "Melreux" to relieve the 4th Regiment guards.	
"	19/1/19.		CHURCH PARADES. Church of England, Presbyterians, Dutch Reformed, Wesleyans, Baptists, Congregationalists, Roman Catholics.	
"	20/1/19.		TRAINING. CROSS COUNTRY RUN.	
"	21/1/19		TRAINING. Route March.	
"	22/1/19		TRAINING As per programme.	
"	23/1/19.		TRAINING As per programme.	∞
"	24/1/19		TAINING As per programme.	

(A9175) Wt W2358/P360 600,000 12/17 D. D. & L. Sch 52a. Forms/C2118/15

Instructions regarding War Diaries and Intelligence Summaries are contained in F. S. Regs., Part II. and the Staff Manual respectively. Title pages will be prepared in manuscript.

WAR DIARY
or
INTELLIGENCE SUMMARY.
(Erase heading not required.)

Army Form C. 2118.

8. 2nd South African Inf

Place	Date	Hour	Summary of Events and Information	Remarks and references to Appendices
MARCHE.	25/1/19		TRAINING. Companies at disposal of Company Commanders	
"	26/1/19		CHURCH PARADES. Church of England. Roman Catholics Presbyterians and Dutch Reformed.	
"	27/1/19		TRAINING. Route March. Warning order for move to HUY recieved.	
"	28/1/19		TRAINING. Under Company arrangements.	
"	"		DEMOBILIZATION. Extract from D.R.O. Men undergoing Field Punishment will not be demobilized when their turn comes but will complete their punishment first.	
"	"		Lieut Elias, 2/Lt Ryder, 2/Lt Hunsley and 2/Lt Balfe and 108 other ranks proceeded by Motor Lorries to VERVIERS today to report to 2ND Cav. Division.	
"	29/1/19		TRAINING. Route March	
"	30/1/19		TRAINING. Physical & Recreational training carried out under Company arrangements.	
"	31/1/19		TRAINING As per programme.	9

C.R. Heenan LIEUT.-COL.
COMMDG. 2nd SOUTH AFRICAN INFANTRY

(A9175) Wt W2358/P360 600,000 12/17 D. D. & L. Sch. 52a. Forms/C2118/15

Vol. 39.

Instructions regarding War Diaries and Intelligence Summaries are contained in F. S. Regs., Part II. and the Staff Manual respectively. Title pages will be prepared in manuscript.

WAR DIARY
or
INTELLIGENCE SUMMARY.
(Erase heading not required.)

(1) February '19. 2nd Regt. S. African Infy.

Army Form C. 2118.

6

Place	Date	Hour	Summary of Events and Information	Remarks and references to Appendices
Marche	1/2/19		TRAINING. As per programme.	5
	2/2/19		TRAINING As per programme —	
	3/2/19		TRAINING As per programme CHURCH PARADES. C of E. R.C. Presbyterian & D.R.	
	4/2/19		TRAINING As per programme	
	5/2/19		The undermentioned officer proceeded to England as Draft Conductor	
			2nd Lt. W. J. Willard	
			TRAINING As per programme	
	6/2/19		TRAINING Companies at disposal of Company Commanders.	
			DEMOBILIZATION Arrangements can be made for discharge of any officer or a	
			N.C.O. or men in England under certain condition	
	7-2-19		TRAINING. As per programme	
	8-2-19		" Under Company arrangements.	
	9-2-19		Church Services	
	10-2-19		Training. Under Company arrangements.	
	11-2-19		Under Company Arrangements.	
			2/Lt. K. Poole having proceeded to the United	10

(A9175) Wt W2358/P360 600,000 12/17 D. D. & L. Sch. 52a. Forms/C2118/15

Instructions regarding War Diaries and Intelligence Summaries are contained in F. S. Regs., Part II. and the Staff Manual respectively. Title pages will be prepared in manuscript.

WAR DIARY
or
INTELLIGENCE SUMMARY.
(Erase heading not required.)

Army Form C. 2118.

2/

2nd Regt S. African Inf.

Place	Date	Hour	Summary of Events and Information	Remarks and references to Appendices
Marche	11-2-19		Kingdom for discharge is struck off strength of Regiment from date. 10-2-19.	
"	12-2-19		Training, under Company Arrangements.	
"	"		The undermentioned officers having reported from Base are taken on strength of Regiment.	
			2/Lt L.B. TEDDER posted to A. Company.	
			2/Lt W.A. ARENHOLD " " B "	
"	13-2-19		Companies to prepare themselves for the inspection by the Prime Minister of South Africa.	
			The Battalion paraded in close column of Companies on the square by Rue de Porte Haute.	
			Dress - Fighting order with Steel Helmets	
			50 OR's under Capt King acted as guard of honour.	
			After the inspection the Battalion marched passed in column of route followed by the Transport.	

(A9475) Wt W2358/P360 600,000 12/17 D. D. & L. Sch. 52a. Forms/C2118/15

Instructions regarding War Diaries and Intelligence Summaries are contained in F. S. Regs., Part II. and the Staff Manual respectively. Title pages will be prepared in manuscript.

WAR DIARY
or
INTELLIGENCE SUMMARY.
(Erase heading not required.)

Army Form C. 2118.

3. 2nd Regt South African Inf.

Place	Date	Hour	Summary of Events and Information	Remarks and references to Appendices
MARCHE.	14-2-19		TRAINING. Under Company Arrangements.	
"	15-2-19		" " " "	
"	16-2-19		Church Services	
"	16-2-19		The 4th Regiment & Brigade Headquarters proceeded by Motor Lorries to the HUY AREA.	
"	17-2-19		Companies moved into new billets	
"	18-2-19		TRAINING. Under Company arrangements.	
			Relinquishment.	
			CAPT. F.H. THERON ceases to command "D" Company with effect from 1st Feb. 1919	
			APPOINTMENT.	
			Lt. F.L. MARILLIER is appointed to Command "D" Company with effect from 1st Feb 1919.	
"	19-2-19		TRAINING. Under Company Arrangements.	
"	20-2-19		TRAINING. As per programme.	
"	21-2-19		TRAINING. As per programme.	12

(A9175) Wt W2358/P360 600,000 12/17 D. D. & L. Sch. 52a. Forms/C2118/15

Instructions regarding War Diaries and Intelligence Summaries are contained in F. S. Regs., Part II, and the Staff Manual respectively. Title pages will be prepared in manuscript.

Army Form C. 2118.

WAR DIARY
or
INTELLIGENCE SUMMARY.
(Erase heading not required.)

4.

2nd Regiment. S. A. Infantry.

Place	Date	Hour	Summary of Events and Information	Remarks and references to Appendices
MARCHE.	22/3/19.		TRAINING. Under Company arrangements.	
"	23/3/19.		CHURCH PARADES.	
"	24/3/19.		TRAINING. As per programme.	
"	25/3/19.		Regimental Cross-country run.	
"	26/3/19.		TRAINING. Under Company arrangements.	
"	27/3/19.		TRAINING. do. do. do.	
"	28/3/19.		TRAINING. Route March.	
"				

C H Heeman [signature] LIEUT.-COL.
COMMDG. 2nd SOUTH AFRICAN INFANTRY

13

66TH DIVISION
SOUTH AFRICAN INFY BRIGADE

4TH STH AFRICAN INFY REGT

~~JAN - FEB 1919~~

1918 SEP — 1919 FEB

FROM 9 DIV

Instructions regarding War Diaries and Intelligence Summaries are contained in F. S. Regs., Part II. and the Staff Manual respectively. Title pages will be prepared in manuscript.

4th S.A.I

WAR DIARY
or
INTELLIGENCE SUMMARY.
(*Erase heading not required.*)

Army Form C. 2118.

October 1918. Vol I

Place	Date	Hour	Summary of Events and Information	Remarks and references to Appendices
FOUCAUCOURT AREA	1/10/18		Weather fair. Battalion leaving for MONTAUBAN AREA at 0815 hours by march route. Later Battalion arrived in MONTAUBAN AREA at 1500 hours. Billetted in Nissen huts.	See Appendix 'A'
MONTAUBAN AREA	2/10/18		Weather fair. Regiment bathing, by Companies, during the forenoon. Afternoon devoted to tactical training. Many visits being made by Officers and men to DELVILLE WOOD	
MONTAUBAN AREA.	3/10/18		Weather fine. Tactical training carried out from 0900 hrs to 1230 hours. Recreational training during the afternoon.	
MONTAUBAN AREA	4/10/18		Weather fine. Regiment left at 0845 hours for GUILLEMONT AREA. Arrived in GUILLEMONT AREA and billetted by 1100 hours. Training carried out during afternoon. Battalion left at 1930 hours for NURLU.	See Appendices 'B' and 'C'
NURLU	5/10/18		Arrived at NURLU and billetted by 0145 hours. Left NURLU at 0930 and arrived at Camp in vicinity of RONSSOY at 1245 hours. Battalion billetted in Trenches, Shacks and tents. Weather dull.	

74

Instructions regarding War Diaries and Intelligence Summaries are contained in F. S. Regs., Part II. and the Staff Manual respectively. Title pages will be prepared in manuscript.

WAR DIARY or INTELLIGENCE SUMMARY.

(Erase heading not required.)

Army Form C. 2118.

October, 1918

Place	Date	Hour	Summary of Events and Information	Remarks and references to Appendices
RONSSOY AREA.	6/10/18		Weather dull and showery. Men busy improving their shacks during the morning. No training carried out during the afternoon.	
RONSSOY AREA.	7/10/18		Weather dull and showery. Battalion moved at 1000 hours to HINDENBURG LINE and remained there until 2130 hours when it moved forward to assembly position in BEAUREVOIR, preparatory to attacking tomorrow morning. Casualties: 3 O/RS. wounded. Five Officers & 41 O/RS arrived from Base.	See Appendix D
BEAUREVOIR	8/10/18		Weather fair. Assembly complete at 0355 hours. Battalion suffered heavily during the assembly from an enemy barrage. Casualties prior to Zero hour were 17 other ranks killed and 43 other ranks wounded. ZERO hour was 0510. By 0530 hours LA SABLONNIERE was taken and mopped up and Battalion Headquarters moved forward to Cross roads at B.5.a.8.9. At 0740 hours enemy were reported to be massing for a counter-attack 800 yds. N.E. of LES FOLIES Farm. Attack did not materialise. At 0930 hours the first objective was taken and consolidated, strong points being established at HAMAGE and LES FOLIES Farms. At 1230 hours Battalion Headquarters moved forward to T.29.d.7.3. Casualties up to this time	See map attached showing operations from 7th to 14th Oct. 1918

(A9175) Wt W2358/P360 600,000 12/17 D. D. & L. Sch. 53a. Forms/C2118/15

75

Instructions regarding War Diaries and Intelligence Summaries are contained in F. S. Regs., Part II, and the Staff Manual respectively. Title pages will be prepared in manuscript.

WAR DIARY
or
INTELLIGENCE SUMMARY.
(*Erase heading not required.*)

Army Form C. 2118.

October, 1918

Place	Date	Hour	Summary of Events and Information	Remarks and references to Appendices
—	8/10/18		(Continued)	
			time were Killed: 28 O/Rs Wounded: 4 OFF. and 151 O/Rs Wounded but	
			remaining at duty: 2 OFF. and 2 O/Rs. At 1810 hours an order was received	
			from Brigade to occupy line held by the 198th Brigade on our left.	
			*Officers were issued with instructions to reconnoitre the new positions.	(* Company Commanders)
	9/10/18		Line taken over from the 198th Brigade by 0100 hours. Orders	
			received at 0245 hours to attack at 0520 hours in conjunction with 198th	
			Brigade. At Zero hour the Battalion moved forward through SERAIN	
			On the eastern outskirts of SERAIN the Battalion was held up from	
			0815 hours to 0850 hours, owing to the advance of the Battalion it was	
			following (Lanc. Fusiliers) being delayed. No opposition was met	
			with until the wood in P.19 and P.25 was reached. This was held	
			in some strength by enemy machine gun rearguards but its resistance	
			was overcome by a flanking movement round the northern edge	
			and the advance was continued. At 1212 hours the S.W. outskirts	
			of BERTRY were reached. The village of BERTRY, while not forming	76

(A9175) Wt W2353/P360 600,000 12/17 D. D. & L. Sch. 52a. Forms/C2118/15.

Instructions regarding War Diaries and Intelligence Summaries are contained in F. S. Regs., Part II. and the Staff Manual respectively. Title pages will be prepared in manuscript.

WAR DIARY
or
INTELLIGENCE SUMMARY.

(Erase heading not required.)

Army Form C. 2118.

October, 1918

Place	Date	Hour	Summary of Events and Information	Remarks and references to Appendices
	9/10/18		(Continued) forming a part of the Battalion's objective, had to be taken on account of its dominating position and because the Corps, whose objective it was, had not been seen on the Battalion's left at the time the Battalion assaulted BERTRY. It would not have been possible to have taken and held MAUROIS if the enemy had still been in possession of BERTRY. In view of the increased frontage, two Companies were asked for from the Battalion in Brigade Reserve, but they were not at that time available. The village was however captured at 1445 hours. At 1915 hours Battalion Headquarters was established at P.16.d.3.1. the Battalion being at this time dug in on its objective. Casualties for 9th Killed 1 OFF and 23 O/Rs. Wounded 1 OFF and 70 Wounded but remaining at duty 3 OFF and 1 O/R.	
	10/10/18	-	At 1235 hours instructions were received from Brigade to move to a position in P.6.d and P.12.b. At 1644 hours the Battalion was in position, Battalion Headquarters being established at P.12.b.7.8. Casualties: Wounded 10 O/Rs. Wounded but remaining at duty: 2 OFF and 1 O/R. Weather fine.	77

(A9175) Wt W2355/P360 600,000 12/17 D. D. & L. Sch. 52a. Forms/C2118/15.

Army Form C. 2118.

Instructions regarding War Diaries and Intelligence Summaries are contained in F. S. Regs., Part II. and the Staff Manual respectively. Title pages will be prepared in manuscript.

WAR DIARY
or
INTELLIGENCE SUMMARY.
(Erase heading not required.)

October, 1918

Place	Date	Hour	Summary of Events and Information	Remarks and references to Appendices
—	11/10/18.	—	Weather fine. At 1930 hours, in pursuance of a Brigade order, the Brigade moved forward to relieve the 198th and 199th Brigades in the line, 1st Regt. S.A. Infantry taking over the line, the 2nd Regiment South African Infantry and South African Scottish being in Support. The line taken over by the Battalion ran from K.26 b.8.8. (Divisional Boundary) to K.27 d.3.2., the Support Company being in position from K.27 a 5.0. to K.27. c.4.2. and reserve Company on the Railway from K.26 c.5.3. to K.35 a.0.3., posts being established on the high ground in K.27. Casualties: Wounded: 1 O/R.	
—	12/10/18		Weather fine. Relief of Royal Inniskilling Fusiliers complete by 0330 hours. Area occupied by Battalion was shelled intermittently during the day. Casualties: Wounded:- 25 O/Rs.	
—	13/10/18		Weather fine. Position held by Battalion runs from Divisional Boundary (K.26.b.8.8.) to the Cemetery K.27 d.3.2. Observation posts pushed forward on to the high ground. Casualties: Wounded: 1 Off. and 6 O/Rs.	

(A9175) Wt W2358/P360 600,000 12/17 D. D. & L. Sch. 52a. Forms/C2118/15.

78

Instructions regarding War Diaries and Intelligence Summaries are contained in F. S. Regs., Part II. and the Staff Manual respectively. Title pages will be prepared in manuscript.

WAR DIARY
or
INTELLIGENCE SUMMARY.
(Erase heading not required.)

Army Form C. 2118.

October, 1918.

Place	Date	Hour	Summary of Events and Information	Remarks and references to Appendices
–	14/10/18		Weather dull. No change in dispositions occurred before the evening when the Battalion withdrew to a shell hole position in Q.7.b, which was occupied by 2325 hours. Casualties – Wounded. 1 O/R. Wounded but remaining at duty: 3 O/RS.	
–	15/10/18		Weather Sulky. No change in the disposition of the Battalion. Casualties – Wounded: 4 O/RS.	
–	16/10/18		Weather fair. At 1830 hours, on receipt of orders for the Offensive operation to be undertaken the following day, the Battalion moved forward to the position occupied by it on the 14th inst. in K.27. At 1745 hours the 1st Regt. S.A. Infantry had cleared the line of the SELLE River to cover the construction of bridges by the Royal Engineers. Casualties: Wounded: 1 off. 6 O/RS	
–	17/10/18		Weather fair. Bridges across the SELLE River were in position at 0225 hours. Half an hour before that time the Battalion moved off to its assembly position on the eastern bank of the river, for the attack. Assembly of attacking and Support Companies was successfully carried out, but it was found impossible, because of the enemy	

(A9175) Wt W2358/P560 600,000 12/17 D. D. & L. Sch. 52a. Forms/C2118/15.

79

Instructions regarding War Diaries and Intelligence Summaries are contained in F. S. Regs., Part II. and the Staff Manual respectively. Title pages will be prepared in manuscript.

WAR DIARY
or
INTELLIGENCE SUMMARY.
(Erase heading not required.)

Army Form C. 2118.

October, 1918

Place	Date	Hour	Summary of Events and Information	Remarks and references to Appendices
	17/10/18		(Continued) enemy wire on the eastern bank of the river, to move the reserve Company across. This latter Company took a position on the western side of the river where it had good cover and from which it could readily be manoeuvred. Assembly complete by 0450 hours under cover of a heavy mist. At 0805 hours the Battalion advanced to the attack. 150 yards in front of the assembly position the first obstacle, the Sunken road running parallel with the line of the river, was met with. This road was defended generally by a kind of brushwood palisade which in places had been reinforced with wire entanglements, which held up the right company for a time. Left Company advanced without meeting with any great opposition, reaching Railway Cutting by 0830 hours. This Company was in touch throughout with the 2nd Regt. S.A.I. but lost touch with the Company on the right after crossing the Sunken road. The Sunken road was then cleared by the left Company from the left flank, thus enabling the right Company to advance.	80

(A9475) Wt W2355/P360 600,000 12/17 D. D. & L. Sch. 52a. Forms/C2118/15.

Army Form C. 2118.

Instructions regarding War Diaries and Intelligence Summaries are contained in F. S. Regs., Part II. and the Staff Manual respectively. Title pages will be prepared in manuscript.

WAR DIARY
or
INTELLIGENCE SUMMARY.
(Erase heading not required.)

October, 1918

Place	Date	Hour	Summary of Events and Information	Remarks and references to Appendices
—	17/10/18		(Continued) The Railway Cutting on the whole of the Battalion front; which had been held in some strength by machine guns and which was protected by six barbed wire fences which were also inter-wired, was finally occupied at 0925 hours. The advance on the left was made through a gap in the wire cut by Lewis Gun fire and through a shallow communication trench running under the wire. Various machine gun posts were bombed by individuals or driven out by Lewis Gun fire and the Cutting was cleared by troops of the left Company working S.E. towards LE CATEAU. The Section of the Cutting which was the Battalion's objective was continuously under enfilade machine gun fire from both the Station (K.35. C.8.4) on the right and the Signal Box (K.29. C.8.8) on the left. Trench mortar and artillery fire was brought to bear on both these points but without any success. During the day no attempt by the enemy was made to counter-attack on the Battalion front. Enemy snipers, machine guns and trench mortars were	81

(A9175) Wt W2358/P560 600,000 12/17 D. D. & L. Sch. 52a. Forms/C2118/15.

Instructions regarding War Diaries and Intelligence Summaries are contained in F. S. Regs., Part II. and the Staff Manual respectively. Title pages will be prepared in manuscript.

WAR DIARY
or
INTELLIGENCE SUMMARY.
(Erase heading not required.)

Army Form C. 2118.

October, 1918

Place	Date	Hour	Summary of Events and Information	Remarks and references to Appendices
—	17/10/18		(Continued) were very active throughout the day. On both flanks the enemy was trying hard to strengthen his hold on that portion of the railway not in our possession, as from time to time small parties of the enemy were seen to be making their way forward. After the railway cutting had been occupied, out posts pushed ahead to a distance of about 200 yards, but on meeting with machine gun opposition and having suffered a number of casualties had to be withdrawn. At night, however, these posts were again put out, returning at day light. Casualties: Killed 23 O/Rs Wounded: 4 OFF. 91 O/Rs Wounded but remaining at duty: 12 O/Rs	
—	18/10/18		Weather fair. At about 1800 hours instructions were received to push forward and occupy the line of the road from K.29 central to K.38 a.1.9 connecting up with the Lanc. Fusiliers on the right at the latter point. Patrols pushed out during the afternoon from the Battalion front and by the 2nd Regt. S.A.I. on the left, but met with considerable opposition immediately on	

(A9475) Wt W2358/P360 600,000 12/17 D. D. & L. Sch. 52a. Forms/C2118/15.

82

Instructions regarding War Diaries and Intelligence Summaries are contained in F. S. Regs., Part II. and the Staff Manual respectively. Title pages will be prepared in manuscript.

WAR DIARY
or
INTELLIGENCE SUMMARY.
(Erase heading not required.)

Army Form C. 2118.

October, 1918

Place	Date	Hour	Summary of Events and Information	Remarks and references to Appendices
–	18/10/18		(Continued) on leaving the line of the railway. Wst Considered, from personal reports of the Officers who were in Charge of the patrols, that the advance contemplated was practicable. A further patrol was sent out which this time made contact with the Lanc: Fusiliers whose position up till this had been obscure. Casualties Killed: 5 O/Rs Wounded 17 O/Rs Wounded but remaining at duty: 6 O/Rs	
–	19/10/18		Weather Dull and Showery. On receiving report from Officer i/c last patrol sent out on 18th inst. the Battalion was ordered to advance at 0130 hours. The Objective was secured without loss and consolidated by 0312. The enemy's posts, which had been holding the road, apparently withdrew under increasing pressure from the right. Three machine Guns captured on the Battalion front. Casualties Killed 1 O/R Wounded 3 O/Rs	
–	20/10/18	–	Weather fair. Battalion relieved at 0130 hours and proceeded by march route to ~~[illegible]~~ REUMONT, arriving at 0415 hours. Battalion left ~~[illegible]~~ REUMONT for SERAIN at 1330 hours arriving at 1530 hours.	

(A9175) Wt W2358/P360 600,000 12/17 D. D. & L. Sch. 52a. Forms/C2118/15.

83

Army Form C. 2118.

Instructions regarding War Diaries and Intelligence Summaries are contained in F. S. Regs., Part II. and the Staff Manual respectively. Title pages will be prepared in manuscript.

WAR DIARY
or
INTELLIGENCE SUMMARY.
(Erase heading not required.)

October, 1918

Place	Date	Hour	Summary of Events and Information	Remarks and references to Appendices
—	20/10/18		(Continued). Battalion comfortably billeted by 1630 hours	
SERAIN	21/10/18	–	Weather indifferent. Battalion devoting the day to cleaning up. No training.	
SERAIN	22/10/18		Weather Showery. Battalion reorganising during forenoon. Recreational training during afternoon. Captain R.D. GRIERSON arrived from Base and assumes command of 'D' Company.	
SERAIN	23/10/18		Weather fair. Training under Company arrangements during the morning. Recreational training during afternoon.	
SERAIN	24/10/18		Weather fine. Training under Company arrangements.	
SERAIN.	25/10/18		Weather fair. Training under Company arrangements. Lewis Gunners and Signallers parade under their respective Sergeants during the forenoon for instruction.	

(A9175) Wt W2358/P360 600,000 12/17 D. D. & L. Sch. 52a. Forms/C2118/15.

84

Army Form C. 2118.

WAR DIARY
or
INTELLIGENCE SUMMARY.
(Erase heading not required.)

October, 1918

Instructions regarding War Diaries and Intelligence Summaries are contained in F. S. Regs., Part II. and the Staff Manual respectively. Title pages will be prepared in manuscript.

Place	Date	Hour	Summary of Events and Information	Remarks and references to Appendices
SERAIN	26/10/18		Weather fine. Battalion paraded as strong as possible at 0830 hours and proceed on a ten mile route march. Dress Drill order. Recreational training during afternoon.	
SERAIN	27/10/18		Weather fine. Church parades during the forenoon.	
SERAIN	28/10/18		Weather fine. Battalion on ten mile route march in Battle order, leaving at 0830 hours. Recreational training during afternoon	
SERAIN	29/10/18		Weather fair. Training carried out under Company arrangements during forenoon. Recreational training during afternoon.	
SERAIN	30/10/18		Weather fine. Bathing by Companies from 0900 hours	85

(A9175) Wt W2358/P360 600,000 12/17 D. D. & L. Sch. 52a. Forms/C2118/15.

Instructions regarding War Diaries and Intelligence Summaries are contained in F. S. Regs., Part II. and the Staff Manual respectively. Title pages will be prepared in manuscript.

Army Form C. 2118.

WAR DIARY
or
INTELLIGENCE SUMMARY.
(Erase heading not required.)

October, 1918.

Place	Date	Hour	Summary of Events and Information	Remarks and references to Appendices
SERAIN	30/10/18		(Continued) to 1330 hours. Training carried out by Companies during forenoon, when not bathing. Signallers and Lewis Gunners parade during forenoon for instruction under their respective Sergeants, when not due for Baths. Foot-ball match during afternoon between 'A' team (picked from Officers and N.C.Os) and 'B' Team (picked from men in Battn.) 'B' team won.	
SERAIN.	31/10/18		Weather fine. Training instructional attack by 198th, 199th and S.A. Brigades. This Battalion in reserve.	

J. M. MacLeod Lieut Col
~~Major~~
Commanding
South African Scottish
(4th Regt. S.A.I.)

(A9175) Wt W2358/P360 600,000 12/17 D. D. & L. Sch. 52a. Forms/C2118/15.

86

87

SECRET.

COPY NO.....14.....

SOUTH AFRICAN SCOTTISH.

O R D E R NO. 7.

Reference Map.

57 C. 1/40,000.

Thursday, 3rd. OCTOBER, 1918.

1. The South African Scottish will move by march route to-morrow the 4th instant to the COMBLES AREA.

2. The Battalion will form up on the Battalion parade ground in mass ready to move off at 8.45 a.m.

Two markers per Company will report to the Regimental Sergeant-major on the parade ground at 8.30 a.m.

3. The route will be S.W. corner of BERNAFAY WOOD - GUILLEMONT.

4. Order of march for Companies will be as under.-

"D" Company.
"C" Company.
"B" Company.
"A" Company.
Headquarters.
Transport.

5. Distances of 100 yds. will be maintained between Companies and between the Battalion and its Transport.

Distances of 25 yds. will be maintained between every six vehicles.

6. Clock hour halts will be observed.

7. All men's blankets, Officers' kits, Officers' mess kits and stores requiring to be carried will be handed into the Regimental Quartermaster's Stores by 8 a.m.

SECRET.

COPY NO.......17.....

SOUTH AFRICAN SCOTTISH.

O R D E R NO. [illegible].

Reference Map.

AMIENS 17. 1/100000. Tuesday, 1st. OCTOBER, 1918.

1.. The Regiment will move to-day by march route to billets in [illegible] AREA.

2. The route followed will be via BRAY-SUR-SOMME - MARICOURT.

3. The Regiment will form up facing west in order of Companies as under ready to move off at 0915. -

"[illegible]" Company.
"[illegible]" Company.
"[illegible]" Company.
"[illegible]" Company.
Headquarters.
Transport.

4. Distances of 100 yds. between Companies and the Battalion and Transport will be maintained.

5. 1 lorry will report to the Quartermaster at 0800 and will do a second trip if necessary.

6. All Blankets, Officers' kits, mess kits and stores requiring to be carried must be handed into the Quartermaster's stores by 0715.

7. Company Commanders will hand to the Adjutant on forming up a marching out state.

8. Company Commanders will immediately on arrival at New Area render to the Regimental Orderly Room a marching in state.

Captain and Adjutant.

4th Regt. South African Infantry.
(South African Scottish)

IN THE FIELD.

Copies issued by runners at [illegible].
as under.-

1 - 4 All Coys.
[illegible]. Sec. in Command.
[illegible]. Quartermaster.
[illegible]. Transport Officer.
[illegible]. Signalling Officer.
[illegible]. Medical Officer.
[illegible]. [illegible]
11/12. War Diary.
13. File.

8. Company Commanders will, before marching out, render to the Battalion Orderly Room:

(a) Marching out State.
(b) Clean Billet Certificate.

The 2nd. in Command and the Medical Officer will inspect the Camp before the Battalion moves out.

Companies are responsible for the cleanliness of the area in the vicinity of the huts occupied by them.

9. The following personnel only, in addition to the Transport personnel, are allowed to march with the Transport.-

2 Cooks per Field Kitchen.

Company Lewis Gun Corporal with the Lewis Gun Limber.

1 Medical Orderly with the Maltese Cart.

Headquarter Mess Corporal with Mess Cart.

1 man per Water Cart.

1 Pioneer with limber containing Pioneer's tools.

Captain and Adjutant.

4th Regt. South African Infantry.
(South African Scottish)

IN THE FIELD.

Copies issued by runners at 1855
as under.-

1. South African Brigade.
2 - 5. All Coys.
6. 2nd. in Command.
7. Quartermaster.
8. Transport Officer.
9. Signalling Officer.
10. Medical Officer.
11. R.S.M.
12/13. War Diary.
14. File.

C

90

SECRET.

COPY NO..........

SOUTH AFRICAN SCOTTISH

O R D E R NO. 8.

Reference Map.

57 C. 1/40,000.

FRIDAY, 4th. OCTOBER, 1918.

1. The SOUTH AFRICAN SCOTTISH will move to-day by march route to NURLU

2. The route will be via MOISLAINS.

3. The order of march for Companies will be as under.-

Headquarters.
"A" Company.
"B" Company.
"C" Company.
"D" Company.
Transport.

4. Starting point will be pt on road where Companies led into camp this morning.

5. Head of column will pass starting point at 1930

6. 100 yds. distance will be maintained between Companies. 35 yds. between every six vehicles.

7. All KITS and stores requiring to be carried must be collected forthwith and dumped at respective Headquarters of Companies.

8. Company Commanders will render a Marching out state before moving out and a Marching in state immediately to Battalion Orderly Room.

Captain and Adjutant.

4th Regt. South African Infantry.
(South African Scottish)

IN THE FIELD.

Copies issued by runners at

D. 91

Secret. Copy No.

SOUTH AFRICAN SCOTTISH.

Reference:
Mont Brehain
1/20,000. 7th. October, 1918.

1.

(a) - With a view to increasing the breech in the enemys defences, Major Operations are about to be taken in a general North-Easterly direction by the 3rd. and 4th. Armies.

(b) - The 66th. Divn. will attack the RED LINE with the South African Infantry Brigade on the right and the 198th. Infantry Brigade on the left - each on a two battalion frontage. The 199th. Infantry Brigade will follow this attack, and after the capture of the RED LINE will pass through the South African and 198th. Brigades in order to seize the GREEN LINE (SERAIN and the high groung in U. 13. , U.14 and U.24.)

(c) The attack to the RED LINE will be made by the 66th. Division in conjunction with one Brigade from the 25th. Divn. on the Right of the SOUTH AFRICAN BRIGADE and one Brigade from the 50th. Divn. on the LEFT of the 198th. Brigade.

(d) The task of the Brigade of the 50th. Divn. will be to protect the LEFT flank of the CORPS and to Co-operate with the 38th. Divn. in the capture of VILLIERS OUTREAUX.

(e) The capture of SERAIN will be carried out in conjunction with the 2nd. American Army who will take PREMONT.

11. INTENTION.

The S. Afr. Inf. BDE. will attack in normal formation

with the 2nd. Regiment on the RIGHT, the 4th. on the LEFT and the 1st. Regiment in SUPPORT.

The SOUTH AFRICAN SCOTTISH will attack in normal formation. A Coy. on left, B Coy. on right, C Coy. in support and D Coy. in reserve.

Company Commanders will take particular care their flanks are interlocked with tropps on their flanks.

111. BOUNDARIES

The Brigade Boundaries are shewn in RED on the reference. The dividing lines between the attacking Battalions is shewn in BROWN.

IV. ASSEMBLY.

(a) The position of assembly for the two assaulting Battns. is that approximately shewn on the reference in BLACK. The SUPPORT Battn. will assemble immediately in rear of the assaulting Battalion alone the N.E. edge of BEAUREVOIR village.

1V. Continiued.

The BLACK LINE referred to abov e i s immediately in rear of our present front line, held by troops of the 25th. Divn.

(b) Battalion Commanders will arrange for the positions of assembly to be reconnoitred, as well as the necessary lines of approach tomorrow the 7th. inst.

(c) Each Battalion will detail a responsible officer to accompa-ny the Brigade Major tomorrow morning star ting at 6a.m. from Brigade Headquarters for the purpose of reconnoitring the posit ions of assembly. These officers will be prepared to tape the positi ons on the evening of "Y-Z" night.

(d) The two assaulting Battalions will each detail six reliable N.C.Os to reconnoitre routes between MU SHROOM QUARRY and their positions of assembly who will be prepared to guide the TAN KS allotted to the Brigade from their pos itions of readiness to the assembly positions "Y-Z" night.

These N.C.Os will be required to travel in the TANKS during t h e attack for the purpose of keeping touch between the tanks and the Infantry.

(e) On "Y-Z" night Battalions will be required to complete th e assembly by ZERO minus two hours.

V. ATTACK.

(a) The Battalions will attack in in normal formation precede d by the tanks and closely followed the c reeping barrage to the RED objective.

(b) In order to assist the rapid exploitation of the situation and the capture of the GREEN line, the O/C 2nd. Regiment will, assisted by the tanks, arrange the capture and hold LES FOLIES as soon as the protective barrage ceases.

(c) When the 199th. Brigade has pa ssed through the RED line the O/C 2nd. Regiment will arrabge for two Platoons to occupy an d hold the high ground in U. 26. a. and b .

(d) The Supporting Battalion will follow in support of the attacking battalion paying particu lar attention to the protec tion of their flanks, and on the arrival of the assaulting battalion s at their objectives will occupy a supporting position approximately along the line of the attack running th rough C. 1.a., U.25.c., T. 30. d. and T. 30. a. and thence to the left Brigade boundary about T. 23. d.7.5.

V1. ARTILLERY.

(a) The attack on the RED line wil l b e made under cover of a strong barrage. The barrage will c ome down and rest for three minutes two hundred yards in front of the Infantry forming-up tapes . It will then move forward by lifts of a hundred yards in three minutes for twelve hundred yards and then slow down to a hundred yards in four minutes until it reaches a line three hundred yards in front of th e RED line.

A protective barrage will dwell t hree hundred yards in advanc e of the RED line for thrity minutes whe n it will lift and th e second phase of the attack will commenc e.

(b) The attack on the RED line wil l be further supported b-y a mobile field battery which will mo ve f orward with the Battns. one section in support of each Battn. to give supporting fire over open sights.

Details of Field Artillery barrage and employment of Corps heavy artillery will be supp lied later.

The Section Commander of the supp- orti ng F .A. Sections wi ll be in close touch with the Battn. Comma nder concerned.

VII. TANKS.

(a) Twelve mark V tanks will accompany the South African Brigade in the attack on the RED line, and will be disposed under the order of TANK Squadron Commander on the Brigade front, six with each attacking battalion.
(b) The tanks will pay particular attention to probable opposition at LA SABLONNIERE, PETIT FOLIE FARM and HAMAGE FARM.
(c) After the protective barrage has ceased, two tanks will be prepared to assist the 2nd. Regiment in capture of Les Folies.

VIII. MACHINE GUNS.

85th Machine Gun Battalion (attached to the 66th. Divn) will be disposed as follows

(a) Four Guns will deal with USIGNY RAVINE(B.12.a.)
Four Guns will deal with SABLONNIERE(B.4.b.)
Four Guns will deal with Copse and Dug-outs N. of SABLONNIERE.
Four GUNS will deal with T. 28.d. and T. 29.a.
Four Guns will deal with PETIT VERGER Farm (T.22 d.)

These twenty guns will co-ordinate their barrage with artillery programme allowing necessary clearances. They will be in position by mid-night "Y-Z" night.

After ceasing fire on above targets they will concentrate in the valley b. 5. central, and be in Divisional reserve.

They will then be prepared to deal with any counter-attack from a northerly direction.

(b) Sixteen guns will concentrate at B. 13.b.3.0. by 1900 hours on "Y-Z" night, sending liaison officer to MUSHROOM QUARRY to keep in touch with assembly of Infantry.
After ZERO they will advance with the Infantry of S. A. and 198th. Brigades and will take up positions from which they will be able to deal with the following points of direct fire
4 guns on HAMAGE FARM (T.34.c.)
4 guns on PWTIT FOLIE FARM (U.19. a.0.3.))
4 guns on LES FOLIES (U.19.d.)
4 guns on redoubt about U.25.central.
On capture of RED line these guns will remain laid on above targets until further orders.
(c) Six guns each are allotted to 198th. and S.A.Brigades these guns will be given definite tasks before hand by B.G.Cs concerned which they will carry out under their own officers.

On capture of RED line these will take up suitable defensive positions to secure their line in case of counter attack.

IX. CONSOLIDATION.

(a) Each objective or line gained will be consolidated by the assaulting troops at once. The importance of continuing this work, even after other troops have passed through any particular line cannot be too strongly impressed on all concerned.
(b) Strong points will be constructed near the following positions:

1. Cross Roads U. 25. c.
2. PETIT FOLIE FARM U.19.c.
3. U. 26.b.) protecting right flank
4. U. 26.a.)
5. LES FOLIES.

(c) To assist in the construction of the above strong points, two sections of 430 Field Coy. R.E. will be attached to the right assaulting battalion,

Instructions regarding War Diaries and Intelligence Summaries are contained in F. S. Regs., Part II. and the Staff Manual respectively. Title pages will be prepared in manuscript.

WAR DIARY
or
INTELLIGENCE SUMMARY.
(Erase heading not required.)

4th SAI

Army Form C. 2118.

NOVEMBER – 1918 –

Place	Date	Hour	Summary of Events and Information	Remarks and references to Appendices
REF MAP 57 B 1.40.000				
SERAIN	1/11/18		Warning Order received for forward move to REUMONT. Preliminary Operation Order No 249 also received. Battalion completes reorganisation. Weather: showery.	
REUMONT	2/11/18		Battalion moved by march route to REUMONT. Billets fair. Weather dull. Intermittent shelling of outskirts of village by long range H.V. gun.	
[R]EUMONT	3/11/18		S.A. Brigade warning order received notifying that the Brigade will move forward to LE CATEAU to morrow the 4th inst. Weather dull.	
LE CATEAU	4/11/18		Battalion moved by march route to LE CATEAU, head of column passing starting point at junction of REUMONT-BERTRY & main LE CATEAU road at 10.05 & arriving at destination at 1.00. Billets good.	(APPENDIX "C")
POMMEREUIL	5/11/18		Regiment moved by march route to POMMEREUIL passing starting point at 09.25. "B" Teams were left at LE CATEAU. Weather: Wet. S.A. Brigade order No. 275 received, detailing general situation & giving general plan of attack, Divl plan of attack, objectives, communications &c.	APPENDIX "D"

94

Instructions regarding War Diaries and Intelligence Summaries are contained in F. S. Regs., Part II. and the Staff Manual respectively. Title pages will be prepared in manuscript.

WAR DIARY
or
INTELLIGENCE SUMMARY.
(Erase heading not required.)

NOVEMBER 1918.

Army Form C. 2118.

Place	Date	Hour	Summary of Events and Information	Remarks and references to Appendices
POMMEREUIL	6.11.18		Standing by to move all morning. Weather dull.	
LANDRECIES (REF MAP 57A 1/40 000)	6.11.18		The Regt eventually moved off by march route at 16.25 & arrived at LANDRECIES at 20.00 being billeted in the French Barracks which had held British prisoners of war during the German occupation. The building was burning & parties were told off to extinguish the fire which was confined to the top stories.	APPENDIX "E"
BASSE NOYELLES	7.11.18		The Scottish left LANDRECIES at 16.10 for BASSE NOYELLES arriving at 18.20. Billets fair. An order was received by wire at 23.50 for the Bn to move on to DOMPIERRE at 08.00 the following morning.	APPENDIX "F"
DOMPIERRE	8.11.18		Moved by march route to DOMPIERRE via TAISNIERES leaving BASSE NOYELLES at 08.00. Arrived in billets in DOMPIERRE at 09.55. The 66th Div took over the front on this date. A second echelon of H.T. for delivery of supplies has been formed at TAISNIERES. Billets fair. Weather good.	~~APPENDIX "G"~~
DOMPIERRE	9.11.18		Moved off by march route to SOLRE LE CHATEAU leaving DOMPIERRE	~~APPENDIX "H"~~

95

Instructions regarding War Diaries and Intelligence Summaries are contained in F. S. Regs., Part II. and the Staff Manual respectively. Title pages will be prepared in manuscript.

Army Form C. 2118.

WAR DIARY
or
INTELLIGENCE SUMMARY.
(*Erase heading not required.*)

NOVEMBER - 1918.

Place	Date	Hour	Summary of Events and Information	Remarks and references to Appendices
			(continued)	
DOMPIERRE	9/11/18		at 13.17. the S.A. Brigade having from this point taken up the pursuit. A long march ensued, the S.A. Scottish carrying on far beyond the outpost line and arriving in	
SOLRE LE CHATEAU (REF MAP: NAMUR 1,100.000)	9.11.18		SOLRE LE CHATEAU at 19.30. The enemy only evacuated the town in the morning and left a large dumps + three train loads of ammunition at the Railway siding. The progress of the transport was slightly hindered by the mine craters along the main roads and some of the G.S. wagons are unable to get through until a route has been made. The Regt is in very dirty billets lately occupied by the enemy. Weather: fine with bright moonlight and the usual precautions are taken to prevent location by enemy aircraft.	
SOLRE LE CHATEAU	10.11.18		The Transport unable to get through yesterday arrived this morning. Enemy reported to be retiring rapidly and our mounted troops hold the	~~APPENDIX "I"~~

96

Instructions regarding War Diaries and Intelligence Summaries are contained in F. S. Regs., Part II. and the Staff Manual respectively. Title pages will be prepared in manuscript.

WAR DIARY
or
INTELLIGENCE SUMMARY.
(*Erase heading not required.*)

NOVEMBER. - 1918.

Army Form C. 2118.

Place	Date	Hour	Summary of Events and Information	Remarks and references to Appendices
			10.11.18 (continued).	
SOLRE LE CHATEAU	10.11.18		frontier from a point E of HESTRUD to the E of CLAIRPAYTS and from thence due South. The Scottish have been ordered to remain at SOLRE LE CHATEAU under Divisional Orders while the 1st & 2nd Regts move on to BEAUMONT. The enemy commenced shelling the outskirts of the town about 16.00 apparently ranging on his abandoned ammunition and at 20.00 he succeeded in getting a hit. The whole village was badly shaken by the resulting explosion but after this the shelling ceased. The dump continued burning throughout the night with intermittent explosions but no material damage was done.	
SOLRE LE CHATEAU	11.11.18		Active operations ceased from 11.00 at which time the Armistice came into force & this Regiment returned to S.A. Brigade command from its period in Divisional Reserve. Pipe band played on Church Square in afternoon.	

97

D. D. & L., London, E.C.

Instructions regarding War Diaries and Intelligence Summaries are contained in F. S. Regs., Part II. and the Staff Manual respectively. Title pages will be prepared in manuscript.

WAR DIARY
or
INTELLIGENCE SUMMARY.
(Erase heading not required.)

NOVEMBER – 1918.

Army Form C. 2118.

Place	Date	Hour	Summary of Events and Information	Remarks and references to Appendices
			11. 11. 18 (continued).	
SOLRE LE CHATEAU	11.11.18		At 15·00 a draft of reinforcements arrived from Base consisting of 3 officers and 185 O.R. The officers were 2nd Lt. J. McGUIRE, M.M., 2nd Lt W. W. SHEARER and 2nd Lt W. T. WOOLMORE. Order received to move tomorrow to BEAURIEUX the Regt to be clear of SOLRE LE CHATEAU by 0900. Weather good. Slight frost.	
BEAURIEUX	12.11.18		Left SOLRE LE CHATEAU at 08·45 by march route & arrived at BEAURIEUX at 01 00. One platoon on working party at mine crater near L'ECREVISSE. Billets good. Weather: Showery.	(APPENDIX "J")
GRANDRIEU	13.11.18		The Regiment (less 3 Companies on 6 hrs task on roads with R.E) moved from BEAURIEUX to GRANDRIEU at 10.00 & arrived at the latter village at 11.37. Billets good. Weather good but roads in very muddy condition for marching.	(~~APPENDIX "K"~~)

98

Instructions regarding War Diaries and Intelligence Summaries are contained in F. S. Regs., Part II. and the Staff Manual respectively. Title pages will be prepared in manuscript.

WAR DIARY
or
INTELLIGENCE SUMMARY.
(Erase heading not required.)

NOVEMBER - 1918.

Army Form C. 2118.

Place	Date	Hour	Summary of Events and Information	Remarks and references to Appendices
GRANDRIEU	14.11.18		Special order issued by Lt. GEN SIR T.L.N. MORLAND, K.C.B. K.C.M.G., D.S.O., Commanding XIII Corps, to 66th DIVISION on their leaving XIII Corps. This read as follows:- "I wish to express to the G.O.C. and all ranks of 66th Divn my appreciation of their gallant & distinguished service during the recent operations, which have resulted in complete victory. To each individual of the British, Irish & S.A. Troops comprising the Division, I express my hearty thanks for his splendid efforts." A congratulatory message was also received from Divisional H.Q. complimenting the Regt on the guard which had been doing duty at D.H.Q.	APPENDIX "I"
GRANDRIEU	15/11/18		Companies were at the disposal of Company Commanders during the day. Weather: frosty.	
BEAURIEUX	16/11/18		Battalion moved from GRANDRIEU to BEAURIEUX by march route at 12.30 less unfits & named men who	APPENDIX [illegible]

D. D. & L., London, E.C. (A8003) Wt W3771/M1031 750,000 5/17 Sch. 52 Forms/C2118/14

Instructions regarding War Diaries and Intelligence Summaries are contained in F. S. Regs., Part II. and the Staff Manual respectively. Title pages will be prepared in manuscript.

WAR DIARY
or
INTELLIGENCE SUMMARY.
(*Erase heading not required.*)

Army Form C. 2118.

NOVEMBER - 1918.

Place	Date	Hour	Summary of Events and Information	Remarks and references to Appendices
			16.11.18 (continued)	
BEAURIEUX	16/11/18		were sent to the Divisional Reception Camp at VAUX ANDIGNY. This march to-day is the preliminary one to the commencement of the advance to the RHINE and the evacuation of unfits is in accordance with the order to take only men able to stand the sustained effort.	
			LT COL MACLEOD D.S.O., M.C., D.C.M., the Commanding Officer was evacuated to C.C.S. this day with neuritis in his wounded arm. & MAJOR BROWNE, M.C., took over Command of the Battalion with CAPT TOMLINSON, D.S.O., as Second-in-Command.	
			On arrival of the Regiment at BEAURIEUX ~~the~~ a draft of one Officer (2nd LT H.H. BAXTER) & 47 O.R. were found waiting & were taken on Strength.	
BEAURIEUX	17.11.18		Order No 22 issued giving details of organisation for the march to the RHINE.	see Appendix "N"
			Church Parades for R.C's & C of E. in the morning.	

D. D. & L., London, E.C. (A8004) Wt W2771/M2031 750,000 5/17 Sch. 52 Forms/C2118/14

100

Army Form C. 2118.

Instructions regarding War Diaries and Intelligence Summaries are contained in F. S. Regs., Part II. and the Staff Manual respectively. Title pages will be prepared in manuscript.

WAR DIARY
or
INTELLIGENCE SUMMARY.
(*Erase heading not required.*)

NOVEMBER – 1918.

Place	Date	Hour	Summary of Events and Information	Remarks and references to Appendices
SIVRY	18/11/18		Marched from BEAURIEUX at 13.30 for SIVRY via MOULARD. 25 Officers and 696 O.R. Arrived in SIVRY at 15.15 + occupied fairly good billets. Weather frosty + roads hard and good.	APPENDIX "O"
SIVRY – SENZEILLE	19.11.18		Second day of the advance to the RHINE. Left SIVRY by march route at 10.00 and passing thro RANCE, FROID CHAPELLE and CERFONTEIN reached SENZEILLE at 18.00 no one falling out en route. The roads were bad and deep with mud + marching conditions were not good. Billets: good. Weather: Cold + frosty at night.	APPENDIX "P"
SENZEILLE	20.11.18		One officer and 50 O.R. at work on roads. G.O.C's Parade at 1100 every available man being present. Pipe band played on Square in afternoon.	~~APPENDIX "Q"~~
SENZEILLE	21.11.18		Companies at disposal of Company Commanders. Football match in afternoon (Rugby) between teams representing	

D. D. & L., London, E.C. (A8001) Wt W1771/M2931 750,000 5/17 Sch. 52 Forms/C2118/14

101

Instructions regarding War Diaries and Intelligence Summaries are contained in F. S. Regs., Part II. and the Staff Manual respectively. Title pages will be prepared in manuscript.

WAR DIARY
or
INTELLIGENCE SUMMARY.
(Erase heading not required.)

Army Form C. 2118.

NOVEMBER 1918

Place	Date	Hour	Summary of Events and Information	Remarks and references to Appendices
			(CONTINUED)	
SENZEILLE	21.11.18		the SOUTH AFRICAN SCOTTISH and the SOUTH AFRICAN MEDICAL CORPS. resulting in a win for the latter. Reading room opened for the Regiment. Pipe band played on Square in afternoon.	
SENZEILLE	22.11.18		Battalion Parade at 10.00 after which Companies were at the disposal of Company Commanders. Pipe Band played on Square in the afternoon & billeting parties left for VILLERS LE GAMBON to which place it was intended to continue the advance. The destination of the Regiment for tomorrow night was, however, fixed for ROSEE some distance further on & cyclist runner notified billeting party of the change.	
ROSEE	23.11.18		The Regiment continued the advance to-day leaving SENZEILLE by march route for ROSEE at 08.45. The morning was sharp & frosty but marching conditions were excellent, and, passing thro PHILLIPVILLE the	

102

D. D. & L., London, E.C. (A8004) Wt W1771/M2031 750,000 5/17 Sch. 52—Forms/C2118/14

Army Form C. 2118.

WAR DIARY
or
INTELLIGENCE SUMMARY.
(Erase heading not required.)

NOVEMBER - 1918.

Instructions regarding War Diaries and Intelligence Summaries are contained in F. S. Regs., Part II. and the Staff Manual respectively. Title pages will be prepared in manuscript.

Place	Date	Hour	Summary of Events and Information	Remarks and references to Appendices
			23.11.18 (continued)	
ROSEE	23.11.18		Regiment arrived in ROSEE at 13.00 hrs. The villages passed through during the day were decorated with the different allied flags but their populations were not enthusiastic. Billets were good and weather continued fine.	
HERMETON	24.11.18		The Regiment continued the march to-day, pushing right to the MEUSE RIVER at HERMETON in good marching time. The route laid down to be followed was via AGIMONT and BAC DE PRINCE but a considerable saving of distance was effected by cutting straight thro the hills to the MEUSE VALLEY. The Regiment left ROSEE at 08.15 hrs and arrived in HERMETON at 12.05 hrs. The roads were in excellent condition for marching, but their frozen surface made the gradients stiff for the Horse Transport which, however, had all	APPENDIX "R"

D. D. & L., London, E.C. (A5004) Wt W1771/M2031 750,000 5/17 Sch. 52 Forms/C2118/14

103

Instructions regarding War Diaries and Intelligence Summaries are contained in F. S. Regs., Part II. and the Staff Manual respectively. Title pages will be prepared in manuscript.

WAR DIARY
or
INTELLIGENCE SUMMARY.
(Erase heading not required.)

NOVEMBER. 1918

Army Form C. 2118.

Place	Date	Hour	Summary of Events and Information	Remarks and references to Appendices
			24.11.18 cont'd	
HERMETON	24.11.18		arrived by 18.00 hrs. The Divisional Commander watched the Regiment march into the town. The retreating enemy has left a very large dump of miscellaneous war material at the Railway Station here including many new machine guns, search light apparatii + some rolling stock. There seems to be no great shortage of food here + quite a number of the smaller luxuries of life are apparently available. Weather continues good but hard frost at night.	
HERMETON	25.11.18		The Regt did not continue the advance to-day + in the morning Companies were at the disposal of Company Commanders. A Commanding Officers parade was held in the afternoon + the Regiment was informed that there was a possibility of HIS MAJESTY THE KING reviewing the Brigade within a few days.	

D. D. & L., London, E.C.
(A8004) Wt W1771/M2051 750,000 5/17 Sch. 52 Forms/C2118/14

Army Form C. 2118.

Instructions regarding War Diaries and Intelligence Summaries are contained in F. S. Regs., Part II. and the Staff Manual respectively. Title pages will be prepared in manuscript.

WAR DIARY
or
INTELLIGENCE SUMMARY. NOVEMBER 1918

(Erase heading not required.)

Place	Date	Hour	Summary of Events and Information	Remarks and references to Appendices
HERMETON	26.11.18		All Companies carried out training according to Training programme, less One officer and 25 O.R. on road fatigue. Weather wet.	
HERMETON	27.11.18		Training carried out for 4 hours daily - working party as for the previous day. Pipe band played in afternoon outside officers MESS.	
HERMETON	28.11.18		Training carried out as for yesterday. The Regtl MASCOT the Springbok NANCY died to-day. Weather: drizzly.	
HERMETON	29.11.18		Training for all Companies as per training programme for 4 hrs daily.	
HERMETON	30.11.18		St ANDREWS DAY - The C.O & officers of the Regt entertained guests in the MESS in the evening. Training as usual - weather continues wet.	

[signature] Major
T/Commanding
South African Scottish
4th Regt S.A.I.

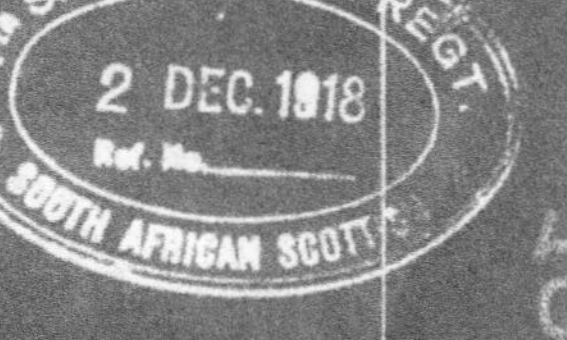

105

D. D. & L., London, E.C.
(A8004) Wt W1771/M2051 750,000 5/17 Sch. 52 Forms/C2118/14

106

Copy No..........

SOUTH AFRICAN SCOTTISH.

O R D E R NO. 12.

Ref. Map.
57 B. 1/40.000.

Monday, 4th November, 1918.

---

1. The South African Scottish will move by march route to-day to LE CATEAU.

2. Order of Companies will be as under.-

Headquarters.
"A" Company.
"B" Company.
"C" Company.
"D" Company.
Transport.

3. Usual distances will be maintained.

4. Starting point will be junction of REUMONT -BERTRY and main LE CATEAU road.

5. Head of column will pass starting point at 10.05.

6. Clock hour halts will be observed.

7. Blankets will be carried on the man. Company Commanders will ensure that there is uniformity in the packs of their Company.

8. Mess, kits, Officers' kits and stores requiring to be carried will be dumped at R.Q.M. Stores by 8 a.m.

9. Companies will notify location of Headquarters on arrival at LE CATEAU.

[signature]
Captain and Adjutant.
South African Scottish.

IN THE FIELD.

Issued by runners at 1730
as under.-

1 - 4 All Coys.
5. 2nd. in Command.
6. Quartermaster.
7. Transport Officer.
8. Medical Officer.
9. Signal Officer.
10. R.S.M.
11/12 War Diary.
14. File.

Copy No.........18

107

SOUTH AFRICAN SCOTTISH.

ORDER NO. 13.

Ref. Map. 57 B.
1/40,000.

Tuesday, 5th November, 1918.

---

1. The South African Scottish will move by march route to-day to POMMEREUIL.

2. The route will be via X roads K. 35. c. 2.5. - X raods K 35. c. 9.3. - Y road K 35 d. 6.0. - Y road K. 36 c. 8.4.

3. Order of Companies will be as under.-
"D" Company.
Headquarters.
"C" Company.
"B" Company.
"A" Company.
Transport.

4. Usual distances will be maintained.

5. Starting point will be R.Q.M. Stores.

6. Head of column will pass starting point at 0925.

7. Blankets and great-coats will be rolled in bundles of 10 and will be dumped at R.Q.M. Stores by 8 a.m.

8. Mess kits, Officers' kits and stores requiring to be carried will be dumped at R.Q.M. Stores by 8 a.m.

9. B Teams will be left at LE CATEAU, billets being notified later.

Captain and Adjutant.

IN THE FIELD.

South African Scottish.

Issued bu runners at 0630
as under.-
1 - 4 All Coys.
5. 2nd. in Command.
6. Quartermaster.
7. Transport Officer.
8. Medical Officer.
9. Signal Officer.
10. R.S.M.
11/12 War Diary.
13. File.

108

E/

South African Scottish. Copy No 12

Order No 14.

Ref Map 57A} 1/40,000. Wed. Nov. 6 1918
& 57B}

1. The South African Scottish will move by march route to-day to LAUNDRECIES.
2. Battalion will form up on the Pommereuil – Landrecies road ready to move off at 4.25 pm
3. Order of companies will be:-
A, B, C, D, H.Q. Transport.
4. Blankets & greatcoats, mess kits, officers kits & stores requiring to be carried will be loaded into Omni Bus on receipt of this order.
5. Usual distances will be maintained.
6. Clock hour halts will be observed.

T.G. Mayne

109

Copy no. [illegible]

F

South African Scottish
Order No. 15.

Ref maps
57A }
57B }

Thurs. 7th Nov. 1918

1. South African Scottish will move by march route to-day to BASSENOYELLES.
2. Route will be via Marcilles to MARCILLES, thence via X road H.16.c.9.8, X road H.11.c.3.5, X road H.6.a.8.2.
3. Battalion will form up immediately ready to move off in the following order of Company:

D, C, B, A, HeadQrs.

Company Commanders will report when ready to move off.
4. Blankets will be carried on the man.
5. Usual distances will be maintained.
6. Clock hour halts will be observed.
7. Companies on arrival will notify to O.Room location of their Headquarters.

Issued to all
Coys at 1400

T.G. Mc[illegible]
Capt.
[illegible]

E/

South African Scottish Copy No [illegible]
Order NO 14

Ref map
5 7 / A) 1/40,000 Wed. Nov 6th 1918
& 5 7 / B)

1. The South African Scottish will move by march route to-day to LANDRECIES
2. Battalion will form up on the Pommereuil - Landrecies road ready to move off at 4.25 pm
3 Order of Companies will be -
'A' 'B' C, D, Hdqrs. Transport.
4 Blankets & greatcoats, mess kits, Officers Kits & stores requiring to be carried will be handed into QM Stores on receipt of this order.
5 Usual distances will be maintained
6. Clock hour halts will be observed.

T G Marfie

J

[illegible] No. [illegible] 111

[illegible] Orders No. 17.

NAMUR [illegible] 12th Nov. [illegible]

1. [illegible] BEAURIEU [illegible] 12th inst.
2. [illegible] A B C D [illegible]
3. [illegible]
4. [illegible] at 0845.
5. [illegible]
[illegible] by 7.15 am.
6. [illegible] N.C.O. per Company will [illegible] of the Battalion [illegible]
[illegible]

[illegible]
[illegible]

J

112

South African Scottish. Copy No. [illegible]

Order No. 19.

Ref map.
NAMUR 1/100,000.

Tuesday 12th Nov. 1918.

1. The South African Scottish will move to BEAURIEUX to-day, 12th instant.
2. Order of march will be as follows:- Headquarters, A, B, C & D Coys, Transport.
3. Starting point will be road junction at which billets are situated.
4. Head of Column to pass starting point at 08.45
5. Blankets to be carried on man. Officers kits, mess kits & stores requiring to be carried will be handed into Quartermasters Stores by 8-15 am
6. 2 Sergt. of Police and one N.C.O. per Company will proceed in advance of the Battalion at 7-30 am to arrange billets in BEAURIEUX.
7. Clock hour halts will be observed.

[illegible]
Capt. & Adjutant
South African Scottish.

Issued to all concerned
at 01.00.

113

SOUTH AFRICAN SCOTTISH.

Copy No.....13.

ORDER NO. 22.

Ref. Map.
NAMUR 1/100,000.

17th NOVEMBER, 1918.

MARCH TO THE RHINE.

1. In accordance with the terms of the armistice, occupied portions of FRANCE, BELGIUM, and LUXEMBURG, are to be evacuated by the enemy by Novr. 26th.
A further withdrawal to east of the RHINE will take place at a later date.

2. The advance of the Allied forces will commence on Novr. 17th.

3. 66th Divn. will lead the advance on the Right of the British Army. 169th French Div. will be on its right, and 1st (British) Divn. on its left.
66th Divn. will be preceded by the 2nd. Cav. Divn., which will cover the front of the Fourth Army.
32nd. Divn. will follow 66th Divn. 1 day's march in its rear.

4. Divl. Boundary to the MEUSE will be as follows.-
(a) Northern boundary.- L'ECREVISSE (excl.) - FRASIES (excl.) - SIVRY Station (incl.) - RENLIES - SILLERIEUX - FONTAINE - FLORENNES - JUSIANES -(all excl.) ROSSE (incl.) - ROSE-DINANT road (excl.)...
(b) Southern boundary.- EPPE SAUVAGE (incl.) - through 'DN' of FORET DE RANCE - railway crossing a quarter of an inch S. of 'C' of CARFONTAINE - SAMART (excl.) - VILLERS-le-GANBON (incl.) - SURICE (incl.) - road junction three quarters of an inch W. of 'H' in HEER.

5. Preliminary Moves.-
(a) On Novr. 16th., 1st. Divn. will take over the portion of front from FRAISIES (incl.) to E. Army boundary. Relief to be completed by 12.00. Dividing line between 66 and 1 Divns.- FRAISIES - BOIS de BEAURIEUX - l'SOREVISSE all incl. to 1st Divn.
(b) On Novr. 17th. 2nd. Cav. Div. will pass through our present out-post line. The Cavalry will be followed by billeting parties to be detailed by 66th Divn. 'Q' and by working parties to be detailed by the leading Bde. Group; reconnaissance will be carried out to ascertain whether state of roads will permit a full day's march on the 18th.

6. On Novr. 18th. the Divn. will advance in Bde. Groups with 199 Bde. Group leading along the road RANCE - FROIDCHAPELLE - CERFONTAINE - PHILIPPEVILLE - ROSSE. Should the road be sufficiently good it is intended that the march on 18th should be to the line of L'EAU D'HEURE.

7. Militray precautions will be observed during the march as follows.-
(a) Leading Inf. Bde. Group will detail an escort and covering party of 2 Coys. to accompany the billeting and working parties which will be moving a day in advance of the main body of the Div.
Working parties will consist of.- 1 Fld. Co. R.E.
1 Sec. Tunnelling Co. R.E.
Proportion of Pioneer BN. 1.
and additional working parties will be held in readiness at the head of the Bde. Group in case they should be required.
(b) Leading Bde. Group will march with an advance Guard including 1 Battery, R.F.A.

(c) In billets the leading Bde. will picquet the roads leading from front and flanks to their billets.
(d) Troops will be distributed in sufficient depth to facilitate supply, but arrangements will be made to ensure that a sufficient force can be available at 48 hours notice to overcome the resistance of the enemy should any attempt be made to oppose out advance.

8. TransportnOfficer must reconnoitre route beforehand.

9. (a) Subject to above, the comfort of the troops will be the principal object in the conduct of the march, Bands will be, and colours may be, taken on the march.
(b) Bde. Group Commanders will be responsible that the strictest march discipline is maintained by all Units in their respective groups.
(c) DRESS. Full marching order: 1 blanket in lieu of greatcoat; 70 rounds SAA. to be carried by each man in lieu of 120 rounds. 1 day's hard ration to be carried by each man in addition to emergency ration and unexpended portion of day's ration.

10. The following stores will be carried.-
On the Transport.-
Great coats.
1 blanket per man (second blanket)
100 prs. boots (if available)
1 pr. socks per man
Cleaning material
Officers' kits.
Officers' messes.
On the Man.-
1 Blanket
2 prs. socks (not including pair worn).
1 set clean clothing
1 iron ration.
1 emergency ration (hard)
Unconsumed portion of day's ration.
Cleaning material etc.

11. The Brigadier-General Commanding wishes particular attention to be paid to men's packs in order to see that they are not overloaded.

12. Officers should endeavour to cut their valises down to within reasonable limits.

TH Marse

Captain and Adjutant.

South African Scottish.

In the FIELD.

Issued by runners as under.

1-4 All Coys.
5. Quartermaster.
6. 2nd. in Command.
7. Transport Officer.
8. Medical Officer.
9. Signalling Officer
10. R.S.M.
11./12 War Diary
13. File.

SOUTH AFRICAN SCOTTISH.

Copy No. 13 115

ORDER NO. 23

Ref. Map.
NAMUR 1/100,000.

SUNDAY, 17th NOVEMBER, 1918.

---

1. On November 18th the 66th Division will continue the march to the RHINE by Brigade Groups.
The 199 Inf. Bde. Group will lead, followed by the 198 Inf. Bde. Group and the Division Headquarters Group.

2. The South African Infantry Brigade Group will concentrate in the SIVRY area.

3. South African Scottish will move to SIVRY by march route to-morrow.

4. The route will be via MOULARD - SIVRY.

5. The Battalion will parade at 13.30.
One marker per Company will report to the Regimental Sergeant-major at 13.15.

6. The following distances will be maintained on the march until further orders.-

In rear of Infantry Company	10 yards.
In rear of Infantry BN.	50 yards.
Bewteen Battalion and its Transport ...	20 yards.

7. Clock hour halts will be observed.

8. Billeting N.C.Os. will report to Battalion Orderly Room at 8.30 a.m. to-morrow.
2nd. Lieut. J. Peters will take charge of this party reporting to the Staff Captain at Brigade HQS. in SIVRY at 9.30 a.m.

9. One baggage wagon will report to each Company at 12 noon to-morrow.
Company Commanders will be responsible that the baggage wagon assigned to their Company reports back to the Transport Officer before the Battalion moves off.
Headquarter Officers' kits will be dumped at Regimental Quartermaster's Stores by 12 noon.

10. Companies will render by 13.00
(1) Marching -out state.
(2) Clean billet certificate.
2nd. in Command and the Medical Officer will inspect all billets occupied by the Battalion after they have been evacuated and before the Battalion moves out.

11. Companies will on arrival in new area report immediately location of their Company Headquarters and will render a marching-in state.

T G Macfie
Captain and Adjutant.
South African Scottish.

IN THE FIELD.
ISSUED TO ALL CONCERNED
by runners at 23.00.

P/

13. File

116

SOUTH AFRICAN SCOTTISH.

Copy No.......

O R D E R NO. 24.

Monday 18th November, 1918.

The following standing orders are issued for the march to the RHINE and will not be incorporated in any operation order issued hereafter.

I. The usual distances will be maintained on the line of march.

II. Clock hour halts will be observed after the starting point has been passed.

III. The Transport Officer will arrange to have Company G.S. wagons at the disposal of Company Commanders in sufficient time to allow of their being loaded and ready to move one hour before the Company is due to move.

IV. Latrines will be dug immediately on reaching every new area and will be filled in and marked with notices before leaving.

V. The location of Company H.Q. will be notified to Battalion Headquarters immediately on arrival in new area.

VI. (a) The following will be required on marching out
(i) Marching out state.
(ii) Clean Billet certificate.

(b) The following will be required immediately on arrival
(i) Roll of men falling out

VII. The 2nd. in Command and Medical Officer will inspect the billets of the Battalion before the Battalion quits each billeting area.

VIII. Daily Routine, unless specially notified from Battalion Orderly Room, will be Company Commanders' discretion.

IX. The Commanding Officer wishes to see all Company Commanders at Headquarters Mess one hour after arrival in a new area.

T G Macfie

Captain and Adjutant.

South African Scottish.

IN THE FIELD.

Issued by runners as under.-

1-4 All Coys.
5. 2nd. in Command.
6. Quartermaster.
7. Transport Officer.
8. Medical Officer.
9. Signalling Officer.
10. R.S.M.
11/12 War Diary.
13. File.

File

Copy No. 13

117

SOUTH AFRICAN SCOTTISH.

ORDER NO. 25.

Ref Map.
NAMUR 1/100,000.

Monday, NOVEMBER, 18th 1918.

---

1. The South African Scottish will march by march route to-morrow November 19th. 1918, to SENZEILLE.

2. The route will be via TRIEU BOUCHAUX - RANCE CERFONTAINE

3. The order of Companies on the march will be as under.-

"A" Company.
"B" Company.
"C" Company.
"D" Company
Headquarters
Transport

4. The starting point will be Regimental Orderly Room.

5. The head of column will pass the starting point at ~~0955~~ 0945 hours.

6. 1 Guide per Company will report on arrival at Battalion Orderly Room to guide Company G.S. wagon to its destination.

7. Midday halt will be from 1150 hrs. until 1300.

8. Baggage wagons join 542 Coy. A.S.C. at 0900 hrs.

T.H. Mackie

Captain and Adjutant.

South African Scottish.

Issued by Runners at 2350 hrs.
as under.-

1-4 All Coys.
5. 2nd. in Command.
6. Quartermaster.
7. Transport Officer.
8. Medical Officer.
9. Signalling Officer
10. R.S.M.
11/12 War Diary
13. File.

Instructions regarding War Diaries and Intelligence Summaries are contained in F. S. Regs., Part II. and the Staff Manual respectively. Title pages will be prepared in manuscript.

WAR DIARY
or
INTELLIGENCE SUMMARY.
(Erase heading not required.)

4 S A Infy Regt

DECEMBER - 1918.

Army Form C. 2118.

Place	Date	Hour	Summary of Events and Information	Remarks and references to Appendices
HERMETON	1/12/18		Church Parades were held in the morning for the various denominations with voluntary services for C of E's & R. C's in the evening. Sports & general recreational Committees formed for the promotion of Rugby & Association Football, Boxing &c &c. Weather: wet. Pipe Band played outside Officers Mess at Retreat. Inter Company Competition continued & the total points awarded to date are as follows:- "A" Coy: 630 points; "B" Coy: 624 "C" Coy 577; "D" Coy: 600.	
HERMETON	2/12/18		Training was carried out by Companies as per programme issued. The Brigadier General also inspected the Regimental Transport. Weather continues wet.	
HERMETON	3/12/18		Parades were held as per Training Programme issued men being passed out as they satisfied the C.O as to their general efficiency. — Capt T. ~~[illegible]~~ McFIE M.C.	

118

D. D. & L., London, E.C.
(A8004) Wt W1771/M2031 750,000 5/17 Sch. 52 Forms/C2118/14

Army Form C. 2118.

Instructions regarding War Diaries and Intelligence Summaries are contained in F. S. Regs., Part II. and the Staff Manual respectively. Title pages will be prepared in manuscript.

WAR DIARY or INTELLIGENCE SUMMARY.

(Erase heading not required.)

DECEMBER — 1918

Place	Date	Hour	Summary of Events and Information	Remarks and references to Appendices
			(continued)	
—	3.12.18		evacuated to C.C.S. & 2nd Lt. J. D. COWAN took over the duties of Adjutant to the Battn. Weather continues dull & showery. The Grand Totals in the Inter Company Competition to date, are as follows: "A" Coy: 916; "B" Coy: 928; "C" Coy: 897; "D" Coy: 939.	
—	4.12.18		Parades & routine as for yesterday. Baths were available & bathing commenced by Companies. Grand Totals in Inter Company Competition are: "A" Coy: 1112; "B" Coy: 1082; "C" Coy: 1058; "D" Coy: 1097.	
—	5.12.18		Routine & training as usual. Rugby Football Match took place in the afternoon between teams representing S. A. Brigade Officers & the 198th Brigade resulting in a win for the S. A. Brigade Officers by 24 points to nil. A meeting of the Rugby Football Committee was held in the evening an Inter. Regimental Rugby League was formed. Pipe Band played at Retreat.	

119

D. D. & L., London, E.C. (A8004) Wt W1771/M2031 750,000 5/17 Sch. 52 Forms/C2118/14

Instructions regarding War Diaries and Intelligence Summaries are contained in F. S. Regs., Part II. and the Staff Manual respectively. Title pages will be prepared in manuscript.

WAR DIARY
or
INTELLIGENCE SUMMARY.
(*Erase heading not required.*)

Army Form C. 2118.

DECEMBER – 1918 –

Place	Date	Hour	Summary of Events and Information	Remarks and references to Appendices
HERMETON	6.12.18		Parades were as per training programme issued. CAPT. T. McFIE. M.C., returned from C.C.S. The Inter Company Competition was continued & points to date totalled: "A" Coy: 1430. "B" Coy: 1450; "C" Co 1420. "D" Coy. 1420. Pipe Band played at Retreat.	
HERMETON	7.12.18		Parades & Training as usual. Capt T.S. McFIE M.C., proceeded on Leave & 2nd Lt J. COWAN carried on with the duties of Adjutant. An Association Football Match was played in the afternoon between teams representing "A" & "C" Coys, the latter winning by 7 goals to their opponents 2. The Grand Totals in the Company Competition are: "A" Coy: 1589; "B" Coy: 1615. "C": 1586; "D": 1631. Weather - dull.	
HERMETON	8.12.18		Church Parades for all denominations were held in the morning. An inter Company Rugby Match was played in the afternoon between "D" & "B" Coy the ~~former~~ winning by 16 points to 8. Boxing classes are being held every [the Grand] evening under the direction of LT BOUSTEAD, M.C.	

D. D. & L., London, E.C. (A8004) Wt W1771/M2031 750,000 5/17 Sch. 52 Forms/C2118/14

Army Form C. 2118.

Instructions regarding War Diaries and Intelligence Summaries are contained in F. S. Regs., Part II. and the Staff Manual respectively. Title pages will be prepared in manuscript.

WAR DIARY
or
INTELLIGENCE SUMMARY.
(Erase heading not required.)

Place	Date	Hour	Summary of Events and Information	Remarks and references to Appendices
			(Continued)	
HERMETON.	8.12.18		Totals in Inter Company Competition remained as for yesterday no points being given for to-day.	
HERMETON	9.12.18		Parades were as usual during the forenoon & recreational training took place in the afternoon under Company arrangements. The Grand Totals of points in the Inter Company Competition were increased to-day to the following: "A" Co: 1716; "B" Co: 1748; "C" Coy: 1681; D Co. 1726. Pipe Band played at Retreat.	
HERMETON	10.12.18		Routine for to-day was the same as for yesterday with recreational Training & a Rugby Football Match in the afternoon between teams representing the S.A. Scottish & the 2nd Regt S.A.I. The latter won by 18 points to 3. A Board of Audit also sat to pass the Regimental Canteen a/c's. Points in Competition to-day stood as follows: "A" Co: 1814 "B" Co: 1846 "C" Co: 1819; "D" Co: 1824. Pipe Band played at Officers Mess. after Retreat.	

D. D. & L., London, E.C.
(A5004) Wt W1771/M2031 750,000 5/17 Sch. 52 Forms/C2118/14

121

Instructions regarding War Diaries and Intelligence Summaries are contained in F. S. Regs., Part II. and the Staff Manual respectively. Title pages will be prepared in manuscript.

Army Form C. 2118.

WAR DIARY
or
INTELLIGENCE SUMMARY.
(Erase heading not required.)

DECEMBER. 1918.

Place	Date	Hour	Summary of Events and Information	Remarks and references to Appendices
HERMETON	11.12.18		Parades were held in the morning as per training programme with musketry application practice at the short ranges. The C.O. also inspected the transport at the transport lines. – The "advance party" left for HOUYET preparatory to the Battalion move to the MARCHE area on the 14th – 16th inst. Points scored by the Companies to date are respectively :- "A" Coy : 1913 ; "B" Coy 1944 ; "C" Coy : 1917 ; "D" Coy : 1962. Weather : wet.	
HERMETON	12.12.18		Training was carried out as per the usual training programme with educational training in the afternoon.	
HERMETON	13.12.18		Training in the forenoon as usual. An Association Football match was played in the afternoon between teams representing this Regiment & the ROYAL DUBLIN FUSILIERS resulting in a win for the latter by 1 goal to nil. Order No. 28 was issued giving instructions for to-morrow's forward move.	App. A
				122

Instructions regarding War Diaries and Intelligence Summaries are contained in F. S. Regs., Part II. and the Staff Manual respectively. Title pages will be prepared in manuscript.

WAR DIARY
or
INTELLIGENCE SUMMARY.
(Erase heading not required.)

DECEMBER. 1918.

Army Form C. 2118.

Place	Date	Hour	Summary of Events and Information	Remarks and references to Appendices
HOUYET	14.12.18		The Regiment left HERMETON-SUR-MUESE by march route at 08·30 hrs & after observing the usual clock hour halts & halting for one hour at midday for a meal, arrived in HOUYET appro 15 hrs. Billets were good. Though the weather was indifferent & roads muddy, not one man fell out during this march of over 20 kilos.	REF MAP MARCHE 1/100,000
JEMELLE	15.12.18		The forward move to the MARCHE area was continued to-day, the Battalion leaving HOUYET at 08·30 hrs & after the usual roadside halts, arrived in JEMELLE at 16 hrs. The distance covered was approx. 24 kilos & no one fell out. Billets were good & the people of the town were apparently pleased at our arrival. Weather: indifferent & showery.	{APP: B}
AYE	16.12.18		The S.A. SCOTTISH continued the march to-day leaving JEMELLE at 09.00 hrs & arriving in AYE at 12.50 having covered the whole of the distance from HERMETON to	

D. D. & L., London, E.C. (A8004) Wt W1771/M2031 750,000 5/17 Sch. 52 Forms/C2118/14

Instructions regarding War Diaries and Intelligence Summaries are contained in F. S. Regs., Part II. and the Staff Manual respectively. Title pages will be prepared in manuscript.

WAR DIARY
or
INTELLIGENCE SUMMARY.
(*Erase heading not required.*)

DECEMBER — 1918

Army Form C. 2118.

Place	Date	Hour	Summary of Events and Information (Continued)	Remarks and references to Appendices
~~AYE~~	16.12.18		AYE without a single man falling out. Billets are good on the whole but very scattered.	
AYE	17.12.18		A draft of reinforcements consisting of 375 O.R with 2 Officers joined the Battalion to day from BOHAIN. The Officers were Lt. F. A. JACKSON & 2nd Lt. F. E. HOPKINS. It was notified in orders that the rate of Exchange for the German Mark has been fixed as follows ~~=~~ viz:- 5 marks = 2/8 English & 3 fr 50 French. The Regiment rested during the day. Weather frosty.	
AYE	18.12.18		The Regt followed the usual routine & reinforcements were paraded for shortages &c. preparatory to C. O's inspection.	
AYE	19.12.18		Routine for the day as usual. Pipe band played in afternoon. Weather changed to rain in the evening.	
AYE	20.12.18		Routine as usual for the Regt & Commanding Officer inspected the reinforcements	
AYE	21.12.18		Training was carried out during the day under Company arrangement with Commanding Officers inspection of the best platoons.	124

D. D. & L., London, E.C.
(A8004) Wt W1771/M2031 750,000 5/17 Sch. 52 Forms/C2118/14

Instructions regarding War Diaries and Intelligence Summaries are contained in F. S. Regs., Part II. and the Staff Manual respectively. Title pages will be prepared in manuscript.

WAR DIARY
or
INTELLIGENCE SUMMARY.
(Erase heading not required.)

Army Form C. 2118.

DECEMBER. 18

Place	Date	Hour	Summary of Events and Information	Remarks and references to Appendices
		21.12.18	continued	
AYE	21.12.18		A Concert was given by "A" Coy in the evening in the Company barracks. The Inter-Company competition which had been discontinued for some days was recommenced to day & the respective totals to date now stand as follows: viz:- "A" Coy 2209; "B" Coy: 2228; "C" Coy: 2142; "D" Coy: 2220.	
AYE	22.12.18		Church Parades were held for the various denominations in the forenoon with voluntary services in MARCHE in the evening for Wesleyans, Baptists & Congregationalists. Weather: wet.	
AYE	23.12.18		Training carried out as per Training programme in the forenoon with recreational exercises & games in the afternoon. Lt A.E. SHARP reposted to S A SCOTTISH from the 3rd S.A.I from date. Weather continues showery & dull.	
AYE	24.12.18		The Eve of Christmas & the Battalion not "keeping up the festival" supplied the guards in MARCHE for both the 1st & 2nd REGTS. S.A.I over the holiday. 2nd Lt. G.W. GORDON was taken on strength this day as from the 1st Novr & posted to "A" Company.	

Army Form C. 2118.

Instructions regarding War Diaries and Intelligence Summaries are contained in F. S. Regs., Part II. and the Staff Manual respectively. Title pages will be prepared in manuscript.

WAR DIARY or INTELLIGENCE SUMMARY.

(Erase heading not required.)

DECEMBER - 18 -

Place	Date	Hour	Summary of Events and Information	Remarks and references to Appendices
			Cont^d	
AYE	24.12.18		A telegram from the High Commissioner for South Africa conveying XMAS & NEW YEAR Greetings was received during the day & published in orders. The Inter-Company Competition was closed to-day leaving "D" Coy the winners. The final Totals of points were: "A" Coy. 2450; "B" Coy. 2420; "C" Coy: 2278 "D" Coy: 2460. Weather: wet.	
AYE	25.12.18		Christmas day though not celebrated in the Battalion was observed as a holiday. Weather continued wet.	
AYE	26.12.18		The Regiment this day, was inspected by H.R.H. THE PRINCE OF WALES in the Gun Park adjoining the Railway Station. After inspecting the Battalion H.R.H. briefly addressed the Regt in the following terms: "I am very pleased to have the privilege of inspecting the SOUTH AFRICAN SCOTTISH & to note their smart appearance & soldierlike bearing. I wish you all a Happy New Year & a speedy return to SOUTH AFRICA". After the inspection the Regt marched past H.R. HIGHNESS & the the ceremony concluded. The Commanding	126

WAR DIARY
or
INTELLIGENCE SUMMARY.
(Erase heading not required.)

Army Form C. 2118.

Instructions regarding War Diaries and Intelligence Summaries are contained in F. S. Regs., Part II. and the Staff Manual respectively. Title pages will be prepared in manuscript.

DECEMBER - 18

Place	Date	Hour	Summary of Events and Information	Remarks and references to Appendices
			Contd	
AYE	26.12.18		Commanding Officer lunched at Brigade H.Q with the C.O's of the other Regts of the Brigade, H.R. HIGHNESS being present.	
AYE	27.12.18		Routine for the day was as for the Tuesday preceding the Christmas holiday & parades were as per training programmes. Weather still continues wet & cold.	
AYE.	28.12.18		Routine as usual & parades in forenoon as per training programme. The following appointments & commissions were made this day: Temp Capt. L.W. TOMLINSON D.S.O. to be acting Major from 1st Dec. 18. & Temp Lieut E. MIDDLETON M.C to be acting Captain from 1st Dec 1918. Temp 2nd Lt J. PETERS was this day the recipient of the MILITARY CROSS. The following notice was also issued thro Regl Orders: "VISIT OF H.R.H. the PRINCE of WALES :- The Brigadier Genl Commanding wishes all ranks to know that he was extremely gratified by the success of the Parade (Dec 26th) in honour of H.R.H. the PRINCE of WALES. The distinguished visitor expressed himself as highly delighted with the appearance	

127

D. D. & L., London, E.C. (A8001) Wt. W2771/M2031 750,000 5/17 Sch. 52 Forms/C2118/14

Instructions regarding War Diaries and Intelligence Summaries are contained in F. S. Regs., Part II. and the Staff Manual respectively. Title pages will be prepared in manuscript.

WAR DIARY
or
INTELLIGENCE SUMMARY.
(Erase heading not required.)

Army Form C. 2118.

DECEMBER - 18

Place	Date	Hour	Summary of Events and Information	Remarks and references to Appendices
AYE	28.12.18	–	Contd appearance & soldierly bearing of all units both when being inspected & during the March Past. The CORPS & DIVISIONAL Commanders were also most complimentary about the parade. The BRIGADIER - GENERAL Commanding wishes to make special mention of the Guard of Honour which exhibited a high standard of excellence both in turnout & handling of arms."	
AYE	29.12.18		Church Parades were held in the forenoon for the various denominations. In the afternoon a Rugby Football match was played between teams from "B" & "D" Companies, "B" Company team winning by 3 points to Nil. —	
AYE	30.12.18	–	Routine for to-day was as for Saturday the 28th inst. In the afternoon a Rugby MATCH was played between teams from "A" & "C" Companies "C" Company winning by 6 points to Nil. Weather still showery. Lieut.	
~~AYE~~ H.Q.	[illegible]		J. B. M. WILLIAMS was struck off the strength of the Regt on evacuation to England.	

D. D. & L., London, E.C.
(A8504) Wt W1771/M2031 750,000 5/17 Sch. 52 Forms/C2118/14

128

Instructions regarding War Diaries and Intelligence Summaries are contained in F. S. Regs., Part II. and the Staff Manual respectively. Title pages will be prepared in manuscript.

WAR DIARY
or
INTELLIGENCE SUMMARY.
(Erase heading not required.)

Army Form C. 2118.

DECEMBER — 18.

Place	Date	Hour	Summary of Events and Information	Remarks and references to Appendices
AYE	31.12.18	—	Routine for the day was as usual with a Commanding Officers parade in the forenoon. The year 1918 was played out by the Pipe Band + preparations were well ahead for the celebratory New Year dinner of the following ~~[illegible]~~ day. The following message was received from the GOVERNOR GENERAL PRETORIA :- "I desire, as Governor General + HIGH COMMISSIONER, and, I am sure, on behalf of citizens of the UNION of S. AFRICA generally to send you our greetings for New Year, a year of Peace. A.A.A The armistice emphasises to us all here the debt of heartfelt gratitude we owe + feel to you + to officers + men of all overseas forces for the magnificent work which has been done during the war sacrifices which have been made, + for the lustre which has been added to name of this great dominion"	

[signature]

129

SOUTH AFRICAN SCOTTISH.

ORDER NO.30.

Ref.Map., MARCHE, 1.100,000. 15th December 1918.

---

1. The South African Scottish will move by march route tomorrow, 16th December 1918, to AYE.

2. The route will be via HARGIMONT.

3. The order of Companies on the March will be as under.-

   "A" Company,
   "B" Company,
   "C" Company
   "D" Company,
   Headquarters Company,
   Transport.

4. The Battalion will be formed up in column of route along the Avenue des Marchandises ready to move off at 0900 hours. Head of column to rest at the corner of Route Grand Rue and Avenue des Marchandises.

5. Blankets will be rolled in bundles of ten and handed to the Q.M.Stores by 0745 hours. Officers' kits and usual boxes to be handed to Q.M. Stores by 0800 hours.

6. Reveille will be at 0700 hours.

7. First line transport and baggage wagons will move with the unit.

J D Cowan
2nd.Lieut., Actg.Adjutant,
SOUTH AFRICAN SCOTTISH.
(4th. S. A. INFANTRY).

IN THE FIELD.

Issued by runners as under at 1900 hours.-

1-4. All Coys.
5. Commanding Officer.
6. 2nd in Command.
7. Quartermaster.
8. Transport Officer.
9. Medical Officer.
10. [illegible]
11. Headquarters.
12-13. War Diary.
14. File.

SOUTH AFRICAN SCOTTISH.

File 131

ORDER NO. 28.

Ref.Map. NAMUR, 1.100,000.
MARCHE, 1.100,000.

13th December 1918.

---

1. The South AfricanScottish will move by march route tomorrow, 14th December 1918, to HOUYET.

2. The route will be via HASTIERE - MESNIL ST.BLAISE.

3. The order of Companies will be as under.

   "D" Company.
   Headquarters Company.
   "A" Company.
   "B" Company.
   "C" Company.
   Transport.

4. The Battalion will be formed up in column of route on road between Railway crossing and Bridge near "D" Company billets by 0830 hours.

5. Great coats will be carried in packs, and leather jerkins rolled on top of pack. The second blankets will be rolled in bundles of 10 and handed to the Q.M.Stores by 0630 hours. Officers' kits and usual boxes will be handed to Q.M.Stores by 0700 hours.

6. First line transport and baggage wagons will move with the unit.

7. Reveille will be at 0545 hours.

IN THE FIELD.

J.D. Cowan
2nd.Lieut. Actg. Adjutant,
SOUTH AFRICAN SCOTTISH.
(4th. S. A. INFANTRY).

Issued by runners as under, at 1930 hours.

1-4 All Coys.
5. Quartermaster.
6. Commanding Officer.
7. Transport Officer.
8. Medical Officer.
9. Signalling Officer.
10. R.S.M.
11-12. War Diary.
13. 2nd. in Command.
14. File.

13

1132

SOUTH AFRICAN SCOTTISH.

ORDER NO. 29

Ref.Map.; MARCHE, 1.100,000.   14th December 1918.

---

1. The South African Scottish will move by march rou te tomorrow 15th December 1918, to JEMELLE.

2. The route will be via CIERGNON.

3. The order of Companies on the march will be as under.-

   Headquarters Company.
   "A" Company.
   "B" Company.
   "C" Company.
   "D" Company.
   Transport.

4. The Battalion will be formed up in column of route ready to move off by 0815 hours. Head of column to rest at corner of Rue St.Roch and Rue de la Station.

5. Blankets will be rolled TIGHT LY in bundles of ten and handed to the Q.M. Stores, by 0 45. Officers' kits and usual boxes to be handed to Q.M. Stores by 0700 hours.

6. First line transport and baggage wagons will move with the unit.

7. Reveillé will be at 0600.

[signature]

IN THE FIELD.

2nd.Lieut., Actg.Adjutant,
SOUTH AFRICAN SCOTTISH,
(4th. S. A. INFANTRY).

Issu ed by runners as under at 2000 hours.-

1-4. All Coys.
5. Commanding Officer.
6. 2nd. in Command.
7. Quartermaster.
8. Transport Officer.
9. Medical Officer.
10. R.S.M.
11. Headquarters.
12-13. War Diary.
14. File.

133

(c) continued.

one section to the left assaulting battalion and one in reserve in rear of the supporting battalion.

X. COMMUNICATIONS.

(a) The Divisional axial line of communication will be the road - BONY- A.17. c. 5.. 5 . - LORNISSET -BELLVUE FM. - LA SABLONNIERE- LA FOLIE FM .

(b) Runner posts will be established at suitable intervals alon this line.

(c) Details of visual signalling will be communicated later.

XI. LIAISON.

Battalion Commanders will exercise the usual care in keeping up liaison with troops on their flanks by means of interlocking posts.

XII. HEADQUARTERS.

Brigade HQ. will be established on " Y" day at A.17.a. 7. and at ZERO at MUSHROOM QUARRY.

Captain and Adjutant

4th.Regt. S. A . Infty.
SOUTH AFRICAN SCOTTISH.

In the Field.

Instructions regarding War Diaries and Intelligence Summaries are contained in F. S. Regs., Part II. and the Staff Manual respectively. Title pages will be prepared in manuscript.

WAR DIARY
or
INTELLIGENCE SUMMARY.
(Erase heading not required.)

Army Form C. 2118.

4th Reg. S.A. Infantry.

Place	Date	Hour	Summary of Events and Information	Remarks and references to Appendices
AYE	1/1/19		Day observed as a Holiday. Companies dining separately in various Billets and doing justice to the liberal an excellent fare specially provided; a Regimental Dinner was held by the Officers in the evening, concluding with a rugger match in the Dining Hall – Guests versus Regt. 'B' and 'D' Companies organised a Dance in the village Schoolroom to while away the evening, same being voted a huge success by the village fair sex. A great day for all. The cooks deserve special mention for the excellency of the catering served up by them. Weather fairly good	
	2/1/19		Routine as usual. Route march under Coy. arrangements in the morning. Wire received from Governor General Pretoria sending greetings for the New Year. Weather showery. F.G.C.M. held in lines of 2nd S.A.I. for trial of Pte A.H. Boss, Pte. C.B. Tel, Pte C. Wiles of this Battalion. Court to sit at 10.00 hours.	
	3/1/19		Kit inspection, Company Drill, Commanding Officer's inspection and Best Platoon Competition – winner being 'D' Company who won easily; the other Companies in order of merit as follows:— 'C' 'B' 'A'. Publication in Routine Orders of authority granting Major C.M. Browne, M.C. to wear badge of rank of Lieut. Colonel. Lt. L.M. Baxter, Lt. W. Patterson, M.M., 2/Lt. J.J. Young, M.M., 2/Lt. D.A.R. Leathem, 2/Lt. W. Mollison joined Battalion from U.K.	134

A5834 Wt. W4973/M687 750,000 8/16 D. D. & L. Ltd. Forms/C.2118/13.

Instructions regarding War Diaries and Intelligence Summaries are contained in F. S. Regs., Part II. and the Staff Manual respectively. Title pages will be prepared in manuscript.

WAR DIARY
or
INTELLIGENCE SUMMARY.
(Erase heading not required.)

Army Form C. 2118.

Place	Date	Hour	Summary of Events and Information	Remarks and references to Appendices
AYE	4/1/19		Regimental Censorship of letters discontinued from this date. Training under Coy. arrangements. Weather fair	
	5/1/19		Church Parades for all denominations. Rugby Football Match in Marche SA. Scottish versus S.A.M.B. resulting in win for the Scottish by 6 points to NIL	
	6/1/19		Company Inspection and Route March under Coy. arrangements. Court of Enquiry sat in the afternoon to investigate into illegal absence of 16898 Pte W.J. Lancaster, 'A' Coy. Weather wet.	
	7/1/19		Usual Parades also Physical Training run under Coy arrangements. An Association Football Match in the afternoon at MARCHE — SA. Scottish versus 2nd Regt. SAI. resulting in a draw each side scoring two goals. Sports Officers appointed with a view to organizing the sporting element of the Battalion to the best advantage in readiness for the forthcoming Brigade and Divisional Competition as follows: Sports + Amusements — Lt. L.R. Johnston, Rugby — 2/Lt. R.J. Johnson, Association — 2/Lt L.A.R.	135

Instructions regarding War Diaries and Intelligence Summaries are contained in F. S. Regs., Part II. and the Staff Manual respectively. Title pages will be prepared in manuscript.

Army Form C. 2118.

WAR DIARY
or
INTELLIGENCE SUMMARY.
(Erase heading not required.)

Place	Date	Hour	Summary of Events and Information	Remarks and references to Appendices
AYE	7/1/19		Leathem, Boxing — Lt H Bustead, Cross Country Running — 2/Lt H.H. Baxter, Wrestling — Lieut L.A. Stevenson, Tug of War — 2/Lt C. Ross. F.G.C.M. Case of 2nd SAI. Trial of Pte W. Bell, Pte A.D. Grotten [illegible] Battalion at 1000 hours	
	8/1/19		Company Inspection. Battalion March to MARCHE to witness Rugby Football Match S.A. Brigade versus 13th Australian Infantry Brigade at 11 am. which resulted in a win for the S.A. Brigade by 14 points to Nil. Battalion acted as guests to a party of N.C.O's and men of the Kings Liverpool Regt. who were invited as spectators to the match. Battalion represented by Lieut. Basset, 2/Lt. Hopkins, 2/Lt. and Pte McLean in Brigade team. Fine Day. 4 prisoners escaped from Guard Room at 9 pm.	
	9/1/19		Usual Morning Training. In the afternoon Soccer match at Marche on 2nd SAI. Ground S.A. Scottish versus 542 Train Coy. A.S.C. resulting in a good win for the Scottish by 5 goals to 3. Statement published in Routine Orders referring to the Brigade's fine stand at Marrieres, 1918, forwarded by G. Pierson (16th Division) see appendix A. herewith	Appendix 'A'
	10/1/19		Company Inspection. Route March. Range Firing by men of 'A' and 'B' Companies. Performance by "Clickerty Clicks" Pantomime Coy in "Cinderella", for benefit of Scottish, given in Cinema Hall, MARCHE, during the evening.	

136

A5834 Wt. W4973/M687 750,000 8/16 D. D. & L. Ltd. Forms/C.2118/13.

Instructions regarding War Diaries and Intelligence Summaries are contained in F. S. Regs., Part II. and the Staff Manual respectively. Title pages will be prepared in manuscript.

WAR DIARY
or
INTELLIGENCE SUMMARY.
(Erase heading not required.)

Army Form C. 2118.

Place	Date	Hour	Summary of Events and Information	Remarks and references to Appendices
AYE	11/1/19		Kit Inspection, Company Drill, Commanding Officers inspection of Billets, Best Platoon Competition. 'D' Company again proved winners of Platoon Competition, remaining Coys in order of merit being 'C' 'B' 'A'. A repeat performance of "Cinderella," given by the "Clickety Clicks" Party for the Battalion's benefit, during the evening. Promulgation of finding of F.G.C.M: in the case of Pte Van der Walt – 90 days F.P. No 2; in the case of Pte Gratton – 14 days F.P. No 2.	
	12/1/19		Church Parades for all Denominations. Publication in Routine Orders of following gazettals – to be T/LIEUTS: T/2nd Lt V.H. POUGNET, M.C, T/2nd Lt E.A. GOODWIN; To be T/2nd Lts. Sgt. H.G. Goddard, Cpl J.L. Dinsdale, Cpl. E.G. Blaze, Sgt. H.R. Brown, Cpl G.F. Hale, D.C.M, Cpl. S.P. Rundle, M.M, Cpl F.G. Hall. Notification authorising the wearing of 1914-1915 Star Ribband to members of the Battalion entitled to same, received and published in Routine Orders. 21 ORS (S.A. RAILWAYS MECHANICAL STAFF) left unit to proceed to England for Demobilization. 'C' Coy held a Dance in their Chateau, same being immensely enjoyed by members of the Company and their village friends of the fair sex.	
	13/1/19		Brigade ceremonial parade held on Football ground MARCHE, being a rehearsal in view of the probable inspection shortly by the Premier of S.A. and presentation of colours to the S.A. Brigade. Court of Enquiry held into illegal absence of 11463 Pte G.J. Herbst, 'A' Coy. The following Officers joined unit from U.K. 2/Lt K.J. McClintock, 2/Lt G.W. Walters, 2/Lt D.J. Hyde.	137

A5834 Wt. W4973/ 750,000 8/16 D. D. & L. Ltd. Forms/C.2118/13.

Army Form C. 2118.

Instructions regarding War Diaries and Intelligence Summaries are contained in F. S. Regs., Part II. and the Staff Manual respectively. Title pages will be prepared in manuscript.

WAR DIARY
or
INTELLIGENCE SUMMARY.
(Erase heading not required.)

Place	Date	Hour	Summary of Events and Information	Remarks and references to Appendices
AYE	14/1/19		Route March in the morning. The following Honours and Awards published in Routine Orders – Capt. J. Farrell "mentioned in despatches" 14916 C.S.M. Mc. W. Feell "Mentioned in despatches" being New Year Honours. Permission granted to send Officers and Men on 48 hours leave to Namur. Pte Van der Walt sent to F.P. Compound Namur to undergo sentence of 90 days F.P. No 2, awarded by F.G.C.M.	
	15/1/19		Training Programme for the morning took the form of a Cross Country Run over 4 Kilos, prizes being awarded for the first and second Platoons home; No 14 Platoon took 1st Prize (100 francs) and No 1 Platoon the 2nd Prize (50 francs). An ideal day for the nature of training done.	
	16/1/19		Companies at the disposal of Coy Commanders for specializing in Guard Mounting Drill, Platoon Drill and Handling of Arms. The Model Platoon being placed at the disposal of Coy Commanders for demonstration purposes in Guard Mounting Drill. A successful Dance was held by 'A' Coy. in the Cinema Hall, MARCHE; a most enjoyable evening was also spent by members of that particular Company. During the afternoon, First Round Bouts of the Regimental Boxing Competition were fought, some rare hearty tussles resulting, which afforded great sport to the onlookers; see appendix 'B' for results. Inter-Company Competition commenced; points awarded being – (MAX 150) A 95, B 92, C 75, D 97	Appendix 'B'

138

A5834 Wt. W4973/M… 750,000 8/16 D. D. & L. Ltd. Forms/C.2118/13.

Army Form C. 2118.

Instructions regarding War Diaries and Intelligence Summaries are contained in F. S. Regs., Part II. and the Staff Manual respectively. Title pages will be prepared in manuscript.

WAR DIARY
or
INTELLIGENCE SUMMARY.
(Erase heading not required.)

Place	Date	Hour	Summary of Events and Information	Remarks and references to Appendices
AYE	17/1/19		Morning devoted to a thorough Kit Inspection of every man. Afternoon devoted to Second Round Bouts of Boxing Competition; some fine fighting being witnessed; see appendix 'B' for results. Company Competition points for the day awarded as follows (MAX 150) A 115 B 91 C 90 D 92 result to date (MAX 300) A 210 B 173 C 175 D 189. A very bleak day	appendix 'B'
	18/1/19		Training took the form of a Route March under Company arrangements. Court of Enquiry held into illegal absence of 15141 L/Cpl Lt H. Lowe, 'D' Coy. The finals of Boxing Competition were fought in the Cinema Hall, MARCHE, some splendid bouts resulting, especially so in the 'B' Class Feather weight, this providing the tit-bit of the evening; see appendix 'B' for results. Company Competition points for the day awarded as follows (MAX 150) A 99 B 107 C 84 D 97 result to date (MAX 450) A 309 B 280 C 259 D 286. Inter-Company Platoon Competition held, resulting as follows 'D' 'B' 'A' 'C'	appendix 'B'
	19/1/19		Church Parades for all Denominations. Company Competition — Points only awarded for Quarter Guard bringing result to date (MAX 500) A 309 B 280 C 279 D 286. Weather showery. Warning Order received from Brigade reference probable move to HUY commencing 31st January.	

A5834 Wt. W4973/M687 750,000 8/16 D. D. & L. Ltd. Forms/C.2118/13.

Army Form C. 2118.

Instructions regarding War Diaries and Intelligence Summaries are contained in F. S. Regs., Part II. and the Staff Manual respectively. Title pages will be prepared in manuscript.

WAR DIARY
or
INTELLIGENCE SUMMARY.
(Erase heading not required.)

Place	Date	Hour	Summary of Events and Information	Remarks and references to Appendices
AYE	20/1/19		The following Training was carried out – Company Inspection, Physical Training, Range Firing, and Companies at disposal of Company Commanders for two hours in Guard Mounting Drill, Platoon and Squad Drill and the handling of arms. "A" Coys Model Platoon being placed at disposal of Company Commanders for demonstration purposes. Paragraph inserted in Routine Orders to the effect that no circulars issued by the War Office on Demobilization are applicable to the S.A. Contingent. Company Competition – Points only awarded for Quarter Guard; result to date now standing at (MAX 550) A 309 B 280 C 279 D 321.	
	21/1/19		Training comprised Coy. Inspection, Squad Drill, Handling of Arms, Physical Training, Platoon Drill, Coy. Drill and Coy. March Past. Company Competition points awarded as follows – (MAX 150) A 128 B 98 C 94 D 97 Grand Total (MAX 700) A 437 B 378 C 373 D 418. Weather frosty. S.A.H.A. Rugby Team arrived in readiness for match on following day	
	22/1/19		Route March under Coy. arrangements to MARCHE to witness Rugby Match – S.A. Brigade versus S.A. Heavy Artillery. After an exceptionally fine game the Infantry claimed	

A5834 Wt. W4973/M687 750,000 8/16 D. D. & L. Ltd. Forms/C.2118/13.

Instructions regarding War Diaries and Intelligence Summaries are contained in F. S. Regs., Part II. and the Staff Manual respectively. Title pages will be prepared in manuscript.

WAR DIARY
or
INTELLIGENCE SUMMARY.
(Erase heading not required.)

Army Form C. 2118.

Place	Date	Hour	Summary of Events and Information	Remarks and references to Appendices
AYE	22/1/19		a superiority of 3 points, the final score reading S.A. Brigade 6 points S.A. Heavy Artillery 3 points — a pretty accurate margin on the run of the game. Company Competition points awarded as follows — (MAX 150) A 100 B 129 C 96 D 98 Grand Total (MAX 950) A 537 B 507 C 469 D 576. A fine frosty day. The Battalion were represented in the Brigade Team by 2/Lt Hopkins, Lieut Basset, Lt Paterson, L/Cpl Boase and Pte McLean.	
	23/1/19		Training suspended owing to fall of snow during the morning; weather bitterly cold. F.G.C.M. held in lines of 2ND S.A.I. (MARCHE) for trial of Cpl W.A. Hughes and Pte W.A. Olliveria of this Battalion. Summary of Evidence taken in case of Pte H.H. Lowes. Inspection of Billets, Transport, and Quarter Stores by Major General H.K. Bethell, C.M.G., D.S.O. Commanding 66th Division, commencing 14.00 hours. Company Competition points awarded as follows (MAX 150) A 96 B 94 C 131 D 99 Grand Total (MAX 1000) A 633 B 601 C 600 D 615. 9 off. 20 o/rs of 9th Manchesters arrived in readiness for match against Battalion on the 24th.	
	24/1/19		Route March under Company arrangements. Rugby Match versus 9th Manchester's cancelled owing to frosty nature of ground. The following officers joined unit from U.K. — Lt. W.C. Forbes, 2/Lt. E.G. Chase, 2/Lt. F.G. Hall, 2/Lt H.J. Goddard (the latter three on appointment to Commissioned rank). 2/Lt W.J. Woolmore returned from Animal Husbandry Course at Rouen. Soccer Team journeyed to HAVELANGE to play 331ST BRIGADE R.F.A.	

141

A5834 Wt. W4973/M687 750,000 8/16 D. D. & L. Ltd. Forms/C.2118/13.

Army Form C. 2118.

Instructions regarding War Diaries and Intelligence Summaries are contained in F. S. Regs., Part II. and the Staff Manual respectively. Title pages will be prepared in manuscript.

WAR DIARY
or
INTELLIGENCE SUMMARY.
(Erase heading not required.)

Place	Date	Hour	Summary of Events and Information	Remarks and references to Appendices
AYE.	24/1/19		in FIRST ROUND DIVISIONAL CUP, the game resulting in a draw each side scoring 2 goals. Two of the prisoners who escaped from Guard Room on the 8th inst. — Pte Wiles and Pte Welding — were brought back under escort, having surrendered to Military Police, CALAIS. Company Competition points awarded as follows:— (MAX 150) A 98 B 96 C 94 D 128 Grand Total (MAX 1150) A 731 B 697 C 694 D 743	
	25/1/19		Capt. Macfie (The Adjt) detailed for duty at 'Q' Office. Training for the morning was carried out on the following lines — Kit Inspection, Company Drill, Commanding Officer's Inspection of Billets and Best Platoon Competition. The Best Platoon Competition was judged by Major Leask (Brig-Major) the winners being 'C' Coy, others in order of merit 'A' 'D' 'B'. In the evening the Warrant Officers and Sergeants celebrated Burns Night in the form of a Dinner and Dance held in the Cinema Hall, MARCHE invitations sent to all units of the Brigade, also to the C.O., Adjt. and Coy. Commanders; a most enjoyable evening resulting, all voting a most excellent time. Coy Competitions points awarded as follows (MAX 150) A 128 B 91 C 90 D 96 Grand Total (MAX 1300) A 859 B 788 C 784 D 939. Bitterly cold day.	

142

A5834 Wt. W4973/M687 750,000 8/16 D. D. & L. Ltd. Forms/C.2118/13.

Instructions regarding War Diaries and Intelligence Summaries are contained in F. S. Regs., Part II. and the Staff Manual respectively. Title pages will be prepared in manuscript.

WAR DIARY
or
INTELLIGENCE SUMMARY.
(Erase heading not required.)

Army Form C. 2118.

Place	Date	Hour	Summary of Events and Information	Remarks and references to Appendices
AYE	26/1/19		Church Parades for all denominations. Capt. Macfie left for Division H.Q. for attachment in Staff Duties. Quite a decent fall of snow commencing shortly after dinner and continuing well on to late evening. Coy. Competition points only awarded for Quarter Guard (MAX 1350) A 959 B 928 C 784 D 839.	
	27/1/19		Route March under Coy arrangements. Promulgation of F.G.C.M. in respect of Pte. G. Wiles – 6 months I.H.L. and Pte. G.B. Hill – 28 days F.P. No 2. Operation Order received from Brigade in respect of move to HUY on 30/1/19. Company Competition points awarded as follows (MAX 150) A 100 B 88 C 131 D 98 Grand Total (MAX 1500) A 959 B 916 C 915 D 937. A Fine Day	
	28/1/19		Training as per programme – Companies at disposal of Coy Commanders, special attention being given to guard mounting drill, platoon and squad drill, and handling of arms. Court of Enquiry held at 1000 hours to enquire into illegal absence of 8148 Pte D.J. Richards (Lt. F.A. Jackson, President; 2/Lt D.A.G. Leathem + 2/Lt J.J. McGuire, Members). Promulgation of F.G.C.M. in respect of Pte W.A. Olivera; sentenced to 18 months I.H.L. Major to	143

Instructions regarding War Diaries and Intelligence Summaries are contained in F. S. Regs., Part II. and the Staff Manual respectively. Title pages will be prepared in manuscript.

WAR DIARY
or
INTELLIGENCE SUMMARY.
(Erase heading not required.)

Army Form C. 2118.

Place	Date	Hour	Summary of Events and Information	Remarks and references to Appendices
AYE	28/1/19		New area cancelled. Boxing Tournament at MARCHE arranged by 2nd SAI — Pte Hayes and Pte Walker representing unit, both winning their bouts. Company Competition points awarded as follows (MAX 150) A 98 B 98 C 97 D 133 Grand total (MAX 1650) A 1057 B 1014 C 1012 D 1070. A cold but fine day.	
	29/1/19		Route March under Company arrangements. Under the Battalion Educational Scheme Lectures in Motor Mechanics and Law were given in the village Schoolroom in the morning, the lecturers being Sgt. E.J. Hearnden and Sgt. D.G. Iverach respectively, both of whom are serving with the unit. Company Competition points awarded (MAX 150) A 140 B 99 C 99 D 100 Grand Total (MAX 1800) A 1197 B 1113 C 1111 D 1170. A fine day.	
	30/1/19		The following training was done during morning — Squad Drill, Handling of Arms, Physical, Platoon + Company Drill, and Company March past. Boxing Party consisting of 3 trainers, 2 heavy weight, 2 welter weight, 3 light weight, 2 Bantam weight, boxers, under supervision of Boxing Officer (Lt. H Boustead, MC) and the Commanding Officer proceeded to SPA to participate	

A5834 Wt. W4973/M687 750,000 8/16 D. D. & L. Ltd. Forms/C.2118/13.

Army Form C. 2118.

Instructions regarding War Diaries and Intelligence Summaries are contained in F. S. Regs., Part II. and the Staff Manual respectively. Title pages will be prepared in manuscript.

WAR DIARY
or
INTELLIGENCE SUMMARY.
(Erase heading not required.)

Place	Date	Hour	Summary of Events and Information	Remarks and references to Appendices
AYE	30/1/19		in Boxing Tournament organised by the R.A. Cavalry Corps. Points for Quarter Guard only given in Coy Competition making Grand Total to date as follows — (MAX 1850) A 1197 B 1151 C 1111 D 1172. A bitterly cold day.	
	31/1/19		Companies went for Route March after customary Inspection. All officers and 50 other ranks per Coy paraded and proceeded to MARCHE to hear Lecture by Genl. Montgomery (H.Q. IVth Army), the subject being "The Battle of Waterloo", commencing at 11.00 hours, and held under Brigade arrangements. Company Competition points awarded for the day (MAX 150) A 98 B 99 C 140 D 98 Grand Total (MAX 2000) A 1295 B 1250 C 1251 D 1269 — thus 'A' Coy has the proud distinction of leading at the end of the month.	
In the Field			L W Tomlinson Major ~~Lieut-Colonel~~ Commanding South African Scottish	145

A5834 Wt. W4973/M687 750,000 8/16 D. D. & L. Ltd. Forms/C.2118/13.

STATEMENT BY CAPT. G. PEIRSON, WHO WAS CAPTURED BY THE ENEMY IN MARCH 1918 WHILE HOLDING THE APPOINTMENT OF BRIGADE MAJOR IN THE 16th (IRISH) DIVN.

After being captured at LA MOTTE near CORBIE I was taken to the German Battalion H.Q. for examination by an intelligence officer. In the course of his examination the officer asked me if I knew the 9th. Division, he said that the fight it put up was considered one of the best on the whole front and particularly the last stand of the South African Brigade at (I think) MOISLAINS which he said was magnificent. Both men and officers fought to the last against overwhelming odds, the Brigadier himself being taken firing a machine gun whilst his Brigade Major was killed beside him.

After this conversation I was sent to LECATEAU and on the way many German officers spoke to me and all mentioned the splendid fight put up by the South Africans.

On reaching LE CATEAU I met two officers (British) who said that whilst their party was being marched to this place they were stopped by the Kaiser who asked if anyone present belonged to the 9th. Division. The Kaiser then said that had all Divisions fought as well as the 9th. Division he would have had no more troops to carry on his attack with.

The truth of this statement I cannot vouch for and unfortunately I have forgotten the names of the officers but Brig. Gen. Bellingham and Lt. Col. Gell were both at LE CATEAU at the time and heard the story.

On my way to LE CATEAU I met 30 or 40 men of the South Afr. Bde. working as prisoners of war close to EPEHY. They were in a very bad condition as no rations were allowed them and they had to exist on what the individual German soldiers chose to give them and what they could find in the old trenches, consequently nearly all of them were suffering from Dysentry.

(sgd). G. Peirson, Capt.
Gen. List.

APPENDIX 'A'

The following is a list of todays results of the fights finished in the first round and semi-finals of the Regimental Boxing Competition.

The Finals will be fought in the CINEMA HALL at MARCHE, commencing at 6. P.M. SATURDAY the 18th inst.

"B" Class. BANTAM. WEIGHT. 53 Kilos and Under.

A. Coy. JOHNSTONE. Finals.

"C" Class BANTAM WEIGHT.

B. Coy HAVERLEY. C.C. } Finals. HAVERLEY
C. " THOMPSON. J }

"A" Class FEATHER. WEIGHT 57 Kilos and Under.

D Coy WALKER C.L. } WALKER C.L. } Finals. WALKER
B " KERSHAW A.W. }
C " LINDE. H. } THOMAS A.J. }
A " THOMAS. A.J. }

B Class FEATHER WEIGHT

B Coy HARRIS V.C. } HARRIS V.C. } Finals. CHENEY
C " McMORRAY. }
D " CHENEY. H.G. Bye. CHENEY H.G. }

C. Class. FEATHER WEIGHT.

D Coy. De Late C.G. Finals.

A Class. LIGHT WEIGHT 61 Kilos and Under.

C Coy HAGAR C } Finals. HAGAR
C " ROSS H. }

B. Class.
A Coy VAUGHAN-SCOTT. C. } VAUGHAN-SCOTT. } ERASME } FINALS.
D " PICKEN J. }
A " L.CPL. BOTHA. } ERASME
A " ERASME }
B " MOIR J.J. } NETHERTON }
B " NETHERTON. W. }

ERASME

APPENDIX 'B'

C. Class. LIGHT WEIGHT.

A Coy STEEL J.E. } STEEL } FINALS. GOODALL
C " ROBINSON. J. }

D " GOODALL GOODALL

A. Class WELTER WEIGHT 67 Kilos & under.

D Coy WHYTE J.J.R. FINALS.

B Class.

A Coy LESLIE T } RICHARDSON. } FINALS. RICHARDSON
C " RICHARDSON J. }

C " KEENAN J } HEPBURN
D " HEPBURN D. }

C. Class.

A Coy CPL LEAK } CPL LEAK } WARE. } FINALS. WARE
D " WEBSTER C.A. }

B " WARE J.J } WARE
D " FREEMAN. L. }

C " TAYLOR A.C. TAYLOR } WHYTE

C " URRY. R.S. } WHYTE.
D " WHYTE. J. }

B Class MIDDLE WEIGHT 73 Kilos and Under.

A Coy PEARSON V.G. } TAYLOR. } FINALS. HUNTER
D " TAYLOR J.B. }

C " HUNTER BYE HUNTER

C CLASS. MIDDLEWEIGHT

B Coy LCPL ESTMENT	TAYLOR.	TAYLOR.	FINALS.	TAYLOR
D " TAYLOR C J				
D " SWARTS B H	WOODLEY			
D " WOODLEY C.				
B " SALMON H		GERHARDY		
D " GERHARDY A F				

A CLASS. HEAVY WEIGHT. CATCH.

D Coy CELETANA H.	Finals.	CELETANO
C " WOOLVEN D C.		

B CLASS

B " McLEAN H A	Finals.	LIDDLE
D " LIDDLE J		

C Class.

D Coy. L/CPL LOGAN. Finals.

Army Form C. 2118.

4 SA Infy Bn

Vol 5

WAR DIARY
or
INTELLIGENCE SUMMARY.

(Erase heading not required.)

Instructions regarding War Diaries and Intelligence Summaries are contained in F. S. Regs., Part II. and the Staff Manual respectively. Title pages will be prepared in manuscript.

Place	Date	Hour	Summary of Events and Information	Remarks and references to Appendices
HYE	1/2/19		Major L.W. Tomlinson DSO. returned from Leave. Training for the morning was carried out which included, Kit Inspection, Company Drill, Inspection of Billets by Company Commanders and Best Platoon Competition. The best Platoon Competition was won by "B" Company followed by "D" "C" and "A" Companies. The HeadQuarter Company gave a very successful Dance in the Maison Liberale Hall, Marche, in the evening, which was thoroughly enjoyed by every one present. Inter-Company Competition points awarded as follows. (MAX 150) A. 100 B. 98 C. 97 D. 137. GRAND TOTAL (MAX 2150) A. 1395. B. 1348 C. 1348 D. 1405. Weather - very cold, a little snow falling towards evening.	
	2/2/19.		Church Parades for all Denominations. Result of Inspection of Transport by Divisional Commander ending in this Battalion being 28 on the list in order of merit. The Brigade Rugby Football Team which visited COLOGNE returned, having played one match against the New Zealanders Resulted in a win for the latter by 21 points to nil. The following of this Unit played in the Brigade Team, Lt. C.C. McN. Russel Lt. W. Patterson M.M. 2/Lt. D E Hopkins,	

A5834 Wt. W4973/M687 750,000 8/16 D. D. & L. Ltd. Forms/C.2118/13.

Instructions regarding War Diaries and Intelligence Summaries are contained in F. S. Regs., Part II. and the Staff Manual respectively. Title pages will be prepared in manuscript.

WAR DIARY
or
INTELLIGENCE SUMMARY.
(Erase heading not required.)

Army Form C. 2118.

Place	Date	Hour	Summary of Events and Information	Remarks and references to Appendices
			4/Cpl. Boase & Pte. McLean. 2/Lt. N. J. Johnson was in reserve. The match took place on 29/1/19. The Band attended a Patriotic Manifestation arranged by the Belgian Civil Authorities at Marche in the afternoon. Points were awarded as follows - MAX 150: A 40, B -, C -, D -. GRAND TOTAL (MAX 2300): A 1435. B 1348. C 1348. D 1405. The day was cold.	
	3/2/19		The following training was carried out Company Inspection, Squad Drill, Handling of Arms, Physical Training, Platoon Drill, Company Drill and March Past. At 2.30pm in the afternoon a Lecture was given, in the Maison Liberale, Marche, by Lt. Comdr. EVARARD RN. the subject being "The Navy's work - The Submarine". Court of Enquiry held on the illegal absence of 11463 Pte HERBST. C.N. "A" Coy. President Lieut P.C NEILLE MC Members 2/Lt. N.J. JOHNSON and 2/Lt. D.J. KYLE. - declared a Deserter. Boxing Tournament at Spa resulted in this Battalion winning 3 Cups. The Winners were. 4/Cpl. LOGAN. Pte WALKER and Pte. HANAFEY. No points were awarded today only for quarter Guard result to date. A. 1435 B. 1381. C. 1348 D. 1405. Very cold day. A concert was held in the YMCA in the evening.	

151

A5834 Wt. W4973/M687 750,000 8/16 D. D. & L. Ltd. Forms/C.2118/13.

Army Form C. 2118.

WAR DIARY
or
INTELLIGENCE SUMMARY.
(*Erase heading not required.*)

Instructions regarding War Diaries and Intelligence Summaries are contained in F. S. Regs., Part II. and the Staff Manual respectively. Title pages will be prepared in manuscript.

Place	Date	Hour	Summary of Events and Information	Remarks and references to Appendices
HYE	4/2/19.		Company Inspection and a Route March was the training for today. Inter-Company competition points were not awarded only for Quarter Guard GRAND TOTAL TO DATE A. 1435 B. 1381. C 1388 D 1405. Cold.	
	5/2/19		Training for today was:- Company Inspection, Physical Training, Company Drill and handling of arms. Capt T.G. Macfie MC (Adjutant) returned to Unit today from Division. The weather was very cold and snow falling towards evening. Inter-Company Competition points were awarded viz:- MAX 150. A 100 B 100 C 100 D 100 GRAND TOTAL (MAX 2450) A 1535 B 1481 C 1488 D 1545.	
	6/2/19.		Company Inspection and a Route March was carried out [illegible]. A F.G.C.M. was held in the 2nd Regt. lines for the trial of:- 15141 Pte LOWIES H.H. and 7658 L/Cpl McKAY J.W. Major L.W. TOMLINSON. DSO. President. Snow fell during the day. No Inter-Company Competition points were awarded ~~(MAX 150) A B C~~ Grand TOTAL A 1535 B 1481 C 1488 D 1545.	
	7/2/19.		Training today included:- Company Inspection Squad Drill, Arms Drill	152

A5834 Wt. W4973/M687 750,000 8/16 D. D. & L. Ltd. Forms/C.2118/13.

Army Form C. 2118.

Instructions regarding War Diaries and Intelligence Summaries are contained in F. S. Regs., Part II. and the Staff Manual respectively. Title pages will be prepared in manuscript.

WAR DIARY
or
INTELLIGENCE SUMMARY.
(Erase heading not required.)

Place	Date	Hour	Summary of Events and Information	Remarks and references to Appendices
HYE.	16/2/19.		C. D and H.Q. Companies moved by Lorry to HUY arriving at 1 pm. in the new area. No training was carried out, the afternoon was spent in getting settled in the new billets, which the Commanding Officer visited, billets occupied by "A" Coy. were found to be in a very filthy condition.	
HUY.	17/2/19		No training was carried out. The Commanding Officer inspected Billets and Companies, nothing further was carried out, and the day was occupied with cleaning up generally. Lt. Hopkins proceeded to England to take part in the International Rugby Football matches.	
	18/2/19.		Training for today was as follows. Company Inspection, Military Training, Recreational Training + Educational Training. A Battalion Sports Meeting was held to decide on various branches of Sport for the week. Weather mild, the sun shining for a few hours during the day.	
	19/2/19.		Training for to-day was as for yesterday. The day was very dull.	

A5834 Wt. W4973/M687 750,000 8/16 D. D. & L. Ltd. Forms/C.2118/13.

Instructions regarding War Diaries and Intelligence Summaries are contained in F. S. Regs., Part II. and the Staff Manual respectively. Title pages will be prepared in manuscript.

WAR DIARY
or
INTELLIGENCE SUMMARY.
(Erase heading not required.)

Army Form C. 2118.

Place	Date	Hour	Summary of Events and Information	Remarks and references to Appendices
HOY	20/2/19		The following training was carried out during the day, Company Inspection Military training, Recreational and Educational training, a muster parade was held at which G.R.O. 6312 was read out. A concert was given in the Theatre de Huy, by the 13th Battalion Canadians, 250 seats being reserved for this Battalion.	
	21/2/19		Kit Inspection, Recreational & Educational training was carried out. Baths were also allotted for the day. A Rugby Football Match was played against the Canadians, our team winning by 14 points to Nil. A Soccer Match was also played in the afternoon against the Canadians. Result 5 A Scottish 7 goals Canadians Nil. Concert in the evening by the "RED HECKIES" Fine weather.	
	22/2/19		Battalion Parade, Recreational + Educational training was the training programme for today. Showers of rain falling consequently	154

Instructions regarding War Diaries and Intelligence Summaries are contained in F. S. Regs., Part II. and the Staff Manual respectively. Title pages will be prepared in manuscript.

WAR DIARY
or
INTELLIGENCE SUMMARY.
(Erase heading not required.)

Army Form C. 2118.

Place	Date	Hour	Summary of Events and Information	Remarks and references to Appendices
HUY	22/7/19.		All parades were cancelled, training being carried out in Billets. Rain continued to fall during the whole day. A Soccer Football Match was played between Head Quarters and Transport which ended in draw each 4 goals.	
	23/7/19		Church parades for all denominations were held. The "Red Herrings" gave a concert in the evening, this Unit being especially invited. Fatigue party of 1 off 10 ORs for grave digging.	
	24/7/19.		Training for today was as follows Company Inspection, Military exercises, Recreational & Educational Training. A lecture was given in the Theatre for all Subaltern Officers. Wire received today Brigade will be camped at Shoreham by Sea in England.	
	25/7/19.		Training for today was as for yesterday. All places of entertainment placed out of bounds for Military owing to outbreak of Influenza. Rugby v SAMC. Result SA Scottish 6. SAMC 0	155

A5834 Wt. W4973/M687 750,000 8/16 D. D. & L. Ltd. Forms/C.2118/13.

Army Form C. 2118.

Instructions regarding War Diaries and Intelligence Summaries are contained in F. S. Regs., Part II. and the Staff Manual respectively. Title pages will be prepared in manuscript.

WAR DIARY
or
INTELLIGENCE SUMMARY.
(*Erase heading not required.*)

Place	Date	Hour	Summary of Events and Information	Remarks and references to Appendices
Aye.	7/2/19.		Physical Training, Platoon Drill and Company Drill and March past. A Brigade Concert was given in the Cinema Hall, Marché. Soccer Football Match took place at CINEY against 31st Brigade R.F.A. ended in a win for this Unit by 3 Goals to 2 Goals.	
	8/2/19.		Training for this morning was – Company Inspection, Kit Inspection, Company Drill, Commanding Officer's Inspection of Billets, and a best Platoon Competition. The best Platoon was won by "C" Company followed by "B" "D" and "A" Companies. Court of Enquiry was held to investigate illegal absence of - 16303 Pte STEVENS D. 12069 Pte BASS A.H. 1660 Pte WEBSTER W. 16418 Pte ORR F.F. and 8486 Pte DARLING W. President Lt. W. Wallace. 2/Lt. J. Peters, and 2/Lt. E. G. Chase. A return Football Match was played at Marché against the New Zealanders, which ended in a win for the S.A. Brigade Team by 8 points to 3. 2/Lt. N. J. Johnson. 2/Lt. J. E. Hopkins and 4/C Boase represented this Unit in the team. Inter Company Competition points were not awarded only for Quarter Guard. Total A 1615. B 1621. C 1628. D 1645.	

156

A5834 Wt. W4973/M687 750,000 8/16 D. D. & L. Ltd. Forms/C.2118/13.

Instructions regarding War Diaries and Intelligence Summaries are contained in F. S. Regs., Part II. and the Staff Manual respectively. Title pages will be prepared in manuscript.

WAR DIARY
or
INTELLIGENCE SUMMARY.
(Erase heading not required.)

Army Form C. 2118.

Place	Date	Hour	Summary of Events and Information	Remarks and references to Appendices
AYE.	9/2/19.		Church Parades for the following took place - Church of England & Roman Catholics. Weather very cold. Inter Company Competition points to date are A 1675. B 1621. C 1628. D 1645.	
	10/2/19.		Training for today was Company Inspection and a Route March. Nothing of interest happened during the day.	
	11/2/19.		Training for today was ordered as usual. A Board of Officers sat today, Capt R.D. GRIERSON. President Lt S.G. THOMPSON and 2/Lt D.A.R. Leathern, members. The Court was adjourned. Inter Company Competition result A 1675 B 1656 C 1628 D 1675. The weather was cold.	
	12/2/19.		2/Lt S.P. Rundell joined for Duty. No parades were carried out. Lt Col E.D. Thackeray CMG DSO addressed a meeting in the evening of Company Commanders & a Representative from Transport, on Demobilization. Company points A 1710 B 1656 C 1663 D 1675. This ended this Competition "A" Coy winning.	

D. D. & L., London, E.C.
(A8004) Wt W1771/M2051 750,000 5/17 Sch. 52 Forms/C2118/14

157

Instructions regarding War Diaries and Intelligence Summaries are contained in F. S. Regs., Part II. and the Staff Manual respectively. Title pages will be prepared in manuscript.

WAR DIARY
or
INTELLIGENCE SUMMARY.
(Erase heading not required.)

Army Form C. 2118.

Place	Date	Hour	Summary of Events and Information	Remarks and references to Appendices
AYE.	13/2/19.		Lt Colonel L. F. Thackeray CMG. DSO assumed Command of the Battalion pending the arrival of Lt Col. D.M. MacLeod. DSO.MC.DCM, Major C.M. Browne MC proceeding on Leave. General Rt. Hon. Louis Botha visited the Brigade Group. In the evening the Company Commanders and 2 Representatives from each Company attended a meeting at which Gen. the Rt. Hon. Louis Botha presided.	
	14/2/19.		There was no training programme for today. Weather very cold. Transport left for Huy.	Order No 45 issued
	15/2/19.		Operation Order issued for move to Huy area. Lorries arrived at 2.30 which conveyed A and B Companies to the new area, C.D and H.Q. remained in Aye for the night.	O.O. attached.

D. D. & L., London, E.C.
(A8004) Wt W1771/M2031 750,000 5/17 Sch. 52 Forms/C2118/14

Instructions regarding War Diaries and Intelligence Summaries are contained in F. S. Regs., Part II. and the Staff Manual respectively. Title pages will be prepared in manuscript.

WAR DIARY
or
INTELLIGENCE SUMMARY.
(Erase heading not required.)

Army Form C. 2118.

Place	Date	Hour	Summary of Events and Information	Remarks and references to Appendices
HUY	26/2/19.		Training for today was:- Company Inspection, Military exercises Recreational & Educational Training. A Soccer Match was played in the afternoon against 15th Canadians, ending in a win for this Unit by 2 goals to 1. Weather very cold.	
	27/2/19.		Battalion parade was held, followed by Recreational & Education training. Inter-Company Tug-of-War "D" beat "C" 2 pulls nil. "A" beat "B" 2 pulls 1. "A" beat "D" (Final). 2291 Cpl. Sommerville W. awarded M.M.	
	28/2/19.		Training for today was as for 26/2/19. Mess meeting was held by Officers in the morning. The Finance Committee also met. A party of 33 ORs left for Purham [?] Down for Demobilization this being the first weekly quota to leave. F.G.C.M. held for trial of 18916 Pte REED W.M. 2181 Pte MATTHEWS R.G. 1922 Sgt. RHODES C.C. 15141 Pte LOWES H. all cases being postponed for 3 days.	159

E. Thackeray
Lieut. Colonel
Commanding [illegible] [illegible] South African Scottish [?]

A5834 Wt. W4973/M687 750,000 8/16 D. D. & L. Ltd. Forms/C.2118/13.

SOUTH AFRICAN SCOTTISH, 160

Order No. 36.

15th February 1919.

---

1. Reference Order No.35 dated 14th instant, "A" and "B" Companies will prepare to move immediately to HUY. Lieut.W.WALLACE will be in charge of this party.

2. "A" and "B" Companies will take with them all Company stores and cooking utensils.

3. H.Q., "C" and "D" Companies will stand fast prepared to move to-day if necessary.

4. In connection with the above move, 8 lorries will report to "A" Coy., 8 to "B" Coy., and 2 to R.Q.M.Stores.

5. Lorry parties will rendezvous, after loading, at junction of MARCHE - AYE and MARCHE - HOGNE roads.

Captain and Adjutant,
SOUTH AFRICAN SCOTTISH.

15/2/19.
1315 hours.

161

SOUTH AFRICAN SCOTTISH,

Order No. 37.

15th February 1919.

---

1. H.Q., "C" and "D" Companies will NOT move to-day.

   Further instructions will be issued later.

Captain and Adjutant,
SOUTH AFRICAN SCOTTISH.

162

SOUTH AFRICAN SCOTTISH.

Order No. 35.

Reference Map
MARCHE - LIEGE 1/100,000.

14th February 1919.

---

1. The South African Scottish, less Transport, will move by lorry to-morrow 15th instant, to HUY.

2. The Battalion Transport (2nd.Lieut.W.T.WOOLMORE in command) will move to-morrow independently by march route to HUY, staying at NAFFE on the night 15/16th February.
Head of Transport column will pass 2nd.Regiment South African Infantry Stables in MARCHE at 1000 hours.
Company Lewis Gun Corporals will accompany their respective Lewis Gun Limbers.
1 Pioneer will accompany Pioneers' limber.
1 cook per kitchen will travel with Transport.

3. Lorries have been allotted as under.-

H.Q.Company.	4.
"A" Company.	8.
"B" Company.	8.
"C" Company.	9.
"D" Company.	8.
R.Q.M.Stores.	5(including 1 for cooks).
Officers Mess and Canteen.	1.
Sporting kit and Orderly Room boxes.	1.
Officers' kits.	1.

Departments of Companies to whom lorries have been allotted will detail 1 other rank to report at the Railway Bridge, AYE, at 0900 hours to guide lorries to their respective loading points.

4. All Company stores, including small box respirators and iron rations, will be carried on lorries allotted to Companies. Men's blankets will be baled and carried on the lorries carrying the men to whom they belong.

5. 1 lorry has been set aside for the transport of cooks, cooking utensils and soyer stoves. The loading of this lorry will be under the supervision of the Sergt. Cook.

6. Rations for 15th instant will be carried on the man. Rations for 16th will be issued on arrival in new area.

7. All area stores, i.e., latrine buckets and washbasins, will be dumped at ~~Battalion~~ D Coy. Orderly Room by 0830 hours.

8. All officers' kits will be dumped by 0830 hours
(a) For those officers living above the Railway at Battalion Orderly Room.
(b) For those officers living below Railway at H.Q.Mess.

9. Companies will make every effort to take with them all available coal, and any tables constructed regimentally. Tables should have legs cut off to facilitate packing.

10. A rear party consisting of 3 other ranks including 1 sanitary man, per Company will be left behind under the command of Major L.W.TOMLINSON,D.S.O. Corpl.Durler, "D" Company, will be the N.C.O. in charge of this party.

11. Company Commanders will forward clean billet certificates to reach Battalion Orderly Room by 0845 hours. The Medical Officer will inspect billets of the Battalion before the Battalion moves out.

12. <u>DRESS</u>. Full marching order. Greatcoats will be worn under equipments.

Captain and Adjutant,
SOUTH AFRICAN SCOTTISH.

<u>IN THE FIELD</u>.

SOUTH AFRICAN SCOTTISH.

ORDER No. 38.

Reference Map
MARCHE - LIEGE 1/100,000.

15th February 1919.

---

1. The South African Scottish, less Transport, "A" and "B" Companies will move by lorry to-morrow, 16th instant, to HUY.

2. Lorries have been allotted as under.-

H.Q.Company,	4.
"C" Company,	9.
"D" Company,	8.
R.Q.M.Stores,	3 (including 1 for cooks).
Officers' Mess & Canteen.	1.
Sporting kit and Orderly Room boxes.	1.
Officers kits.	1.

Departments or Companies to whom lorries have been allotted will detail one other rank to report to the Railway Bridge, AYE, at 0745 hours to guide lorries to their respective loading points. (0745)

3. All Company stores including small box respirators and iron rations will be carried on lorries allotted to Companies. Men's blankets will be baled and carried on the lorries carrying the men to whom they belong.

4. 1 lorry has been set aside for the transport of cooks, cooking utensils, and soyer stoves. The loading of this lorry will be under the supervision of the Sergt.Cook.

5. All area stores, i.e., latrine buckets and washbasins will be dumped at "D" Company by 0715 hours.

6. All officers' kits will be dumped by 0715 hours.
   (a) For those officers living above the Railway, at Battalion Orderly Room.
   (b) For those officers living below the Railway, at H.Q.Mess.

7. Companies will make every effort to take with them all available coal, and any tables constructed regimentally. Tables should have legs cut off to facilitate packing.

8. A rear party consisting of 2 other ranks, including one sanitary man, per Company will be left behind under the command of Major L.W.TOMLINSON, D.S.O. Corpl.Durler, "D" Company, will be the N.C.O. in charge of this party.

9. Company Commanders will forward clean billet certificates to reach Battalion Orderly Room by 0730 hours. The Medical Officer will inspect billets of the Battalion before the Battalion move out.

DRESS. Full marching order. Greatcoats will be worn under equipments.

Captain and Adjutant,
SOUTH AFRICAN SCOTTISH.

IN THE FIELD.

ROUTINE ORDER No. 45.

by

LIEUT. COLONEL. E. F. THACKERAY. C.M.G. D.S.O.

Commanding

SOUTH AFRICAN SCOTTISH.

Friday 14th. February, 1919.

The following points have been brought to notice and will be dealt with as indicated under each heading. -

1. DEMOBILIZATION.
a) All outlying detachments are to rejoin the Unit by the 15th. Feb. 1919.
b) Quota groups i.e. Thirty three and one third ~~XXXX~~ per cent for Brigade (compassionate cases) will leave as soon as possible.
c) Cases of married men with their wives in South Africa will be represented to a higher authority.

Every endeavour is being made to procure additional transport to expedite demobilization. It is pointed out to all Ranks that loyal co - operation and a strict maintenance of discipline will expedite matters and help to keep time tables and will be conducive to general comfort.

2. DELOUSING.
Foden Disinfectors and Russian pits will be utilised as far as possible.

3. BATHS.
By an interchange of Company baths and the use of the Brigade Baths facilities will be given for regular bathing.

4. CLEAN CLOTHING.
Clean clothing will be effected by the exchange of dirty clothing for clean at the Baths. Company Commanders will render a state and requisition shewing the numbers changed and required weekly. Particular attention must be paid to men returning from detachment and hospital etc.

5. DRESS.
Steel helmets will be worn on guard, Ceremonian Parades and Fighting ~~Order~~ Marching Order. Balmorals will be worn on all other occasions. It is pointed out that the reputation of the Regiment is largely gauged by other Units and by foreign armies by their smartness and soldierly appearance.

6. HOURS OF PARADE. Parades etc. will be held as under.

Parade.	Time.	Dress.
Platoon Inspection	0800 - hours	Skeleton Order.
Military Exercises	0906 - 0100 hours	do
Recreational Training	1000 - 1100 hours	Clean Fatigue.
Educational "	1100 - 1200 hours	do

Interchange of these hours may be made when required. When necessary great coats will be worn.
Standing fatigues will be carried out as far as possible in the mornings.

7. MEDICAL INSPECTION.
At Medical Inspection Room, by Companies at quarter of an hour intervals commencing 0900 hours. Medical Officer to arrange waiting Room where possible. Companies will parade in the following order "C" "B" "D" "A".

8. MILITARY COMPETITIONS.
These will be held in obeyance pending the reorganisation of conditions etc.

9. COMPLAINTS. Army Act. Sect. 43 is published for information.
If any soldier thinks himself wronged in any matter by any officer other than his Captain or by any soldier, he may complain thereof to his Cptain and if he thinks himself wronged bu his Captian, either in respect of any other matter he may complain thereof to his Commanding Officer and if he thinks himself wronged by his Commanding Officer either in respect of his complaint not being addressed or in respect of any other matter he may complain thereof to the prescribed general Officer or in case of a soldier serving in India to such Officer as the Commander -in-Chief of the forces in India with the approval of the Govenor - General of India in Council may appoint and every Officer to whom a complaint is made in pursuance of this section shall cause such complaint to be enquired into and shall, if on inquiry he is satisfied of the justice of the complaint so made take steps as may be necessary for giving full redress to the complainant in respect of the matter

www.ingramcontent.com/pod-product-compliance
Lightning Source LLC
Chambersburg PA
CBHW080902230426
43663CB00013B/2601

* 9 7 8 1 4 7 4 5 3 4 5 9 8 *